Victim

Book 2
Crocodile Dreaming Series

Novel by

Graham Wilson

VICTIM   GRAHAM WILSON

CONTENTS

VICTIM   GRAHAM WILSON

Acknowledgements

Thanks to the various people who have reviewed and commented on the book since the initial version, Crocodile Man was published. These comments have been valuable in making it better. It is gratifying to hear of the enjoyment people gain from reading this book and the prior book in the series Visitor.

Particular thanks to Candra Hodge, a reader from the United States who volunteered to assist with editing this edition. She diligently revised it over many months, particularly focusing on readability in the US market. Also my great thanks to my Australian editor, Kathryn Moore. Her skill along with her English and Australian backgrounds have been invaluable in improving this story.

And many thanks to all those readers whose comments have also contributed to this new version's improvement.

VICTIM   GRAHAM WILSON

Background to Story

This is a story set in two places, England and Australia. The Northern Territory of Australia is the key location in which the main events unfold. An important feature of this part of Australia is its thriving aboriginal population. These first Australians have a culture which has continued and evolved over an enormous span of time, believed to be upwards of 50,000 years.

These people adapted to this place and shaped it with their occupation. Rock art, dotted over many of the rock faces and caves, tells their stories which are handed down from generation to generation, ever since the coming of the first people, a time often called the Dreamtime or Dreaming.

In these stories animals of the land sit alongside its first people, with their spirits too forming and shaping the people and the land. Many tribal clans and language groups have their own stories and totems which feature a range of animals living in this place.

One of the most well-known totems is the salt-water crocodile, a huge ferocious predator. Large adult crocodiles reach over seven metres, weigh well over a ton and attain ages measured in decades or even centuries. These ancient creatures, whose ancestral stories have been passed down from stories of the Dreamtime, form a central part of this story.

Aboriginal people continue to be a vibrant part of the NT community, making up more than a quarter of all its population. During the last 200 years they have also mixed with and shared influences with many other migrant communities. These aboriginal people not only trace their aboriginal history but also that of European, Chinese, Afghan or other ancestral ethnic groups.

I have had many aboriginal friends in the NT over decades. Countless hours spent in their company, hearing stories, ideas and words of their language, have contributed substantially to this story.

VICTIM   GRAHAM WILSON

Synopsis of Story so Far

Book 1 -Visitor

The first book of the Crocodile Dreaming Series, *Visitor*, follows an English backpacker, Susan, who comes to Australia on a holiday and meets an Australian man, Mark, while diving on the Barrier Reef. He works in the Outback and has a wild, reckless charm.

They have a passionate affair and she is captivated by him. But she soon notices some odd behaviours which seem asocial. Despite her reservations she accepts his invitation to meet and go travelling together through the outback of the Northern Territory. However she decides not to tell anyone else about this.

At first the trip goes well. But chance discoveries lead her to believe he is not who he says he is, and that he may have harmed other backpackers. He also has an obsessive love of crocodiles. Notwithstanding her growing suspicions, the relationship grows ever more intense.

Then he discovers her suspicions. Her love turns to terror. She believes he will kill her and feed her body to crocodiles to hide her existence. She seeks to escape through use of her sexual attraction. She distracts and knocks him unconscious. Then she drags his body to the edge of the waterhole where the crocodiles take him. Alone, she is filled with shame and remorse. As no one knows she is here she decides to hide the evidence, remove the signs of her presence from around the waterhole and destroy all evidence of his identity, to pretend it never happened. She catches her flight back to England, determined to block out the whole experience and ensure nobody ever finds out what took place. *She was just a visitor and now the trip is past*, she says to herself, over and over.

VICTIM   GRAHAM WILSON

Chapter 1 – Darwin – Catfish Man's Catch

Charlie was getting old. He could feel it in his bones. The weather was moving from the Gurrulwa, big wind time, into the Dalirrgang, the build-up time. The hot, sweaty weather was steadily building each day now. In the way white fellas counted time it was the end of September. The mornings were still starting out cool but, by morning smoko time, he could feel his shirt stick to his back from sweat. By lunchtime a lie-down under a shady tree was clearly the best place to be.

Once upon a time, way back when he was a young and fiery buck, he could go all day. Ten hours or twelve hours working in the stinking October heat was nothing to him. Then he could hit the town at night-time with his mates for a party and still be up at the crack of dawn for another just as long day of work.

He had lived a full, good life. Sure, at times he had lived rough, sometimes the grub was poor. But, as a boy who'd come from the Retta Dixon Children's Home, in Darwin, one whose mother was a proud Larrakia woman and whose father was a stockman from the buffalo lands east of Darwin, out in Point Stuart Country where the Mary and Wildman Rivers ran, he had done okay.

His father had not been much good really, a white fella, with a bit of Chinese. He mostly shot buffalo for their skins. At odd times he shot a few crocs and broke in horses. He only visited his mum now and then, mostly when he wanted a bit, but she'd stuck to him while he fathered three kids, two with mostly dark skin like his mother's. He was the third and had a lot more of his father's white-fella skin and even a dash of the Chinese look about him; some people had called him a yella fella when he was young. So, when the cops and field officers spotted him in a camp near Darwin, they'd grabbed him, quick smart, and had taken him to the Retta Dixon Home for half castes, where he'd lived for ten years.

They had thought of it as trying to civilise the black fella out of him and turn him into a proper white fella. He thought they had it a bit arse about. More civilisation was in his mother's Larrakia tribe than in many of the scum whites that hung about the town. His father was really one of them scum whites, if the truth was told.

Anyway, his mum was determined not to give him up easily, but also not to leave her other two children with the tribe's aunties and uncles and get cut off from her culture. So, while she was given a house on the Retta Dixon grounds for when she wanted to visit, and it was a place where Charlie could stay when she came, mostly he'd stayed in a dormitory with other boys around his age.

But she kept coming to see him at least every week, bringing his brother and sister, and she kept making sure his uncles, aunts and the clan's old people came to see him too. She also found ways to bring him out of the home a lot. That way he kept getting tribal learning and knowledge about the bush.

Then, one day, when he was almost old enough to leave Retta Dixon and get a job working on a station, a beautiful girl named Elsie had come to stay at Retta Dixon. She'd lived for most of her childhood on Goulburn Island, and her family had come from the Alligator Rivers, somewhere around Jim Jim Falls. She was a half-caste, like him. She'd been taken from her parents at a camp near the South Alligator when she was only little. However, her family could not visit her at Goulburn Island so she'd lost track of them.

Then, when she was thirteen and just turning into a woman, they'd sent her to Retta Dixon so that she could learn more; they said she was too smart for the Goulburn Island mob. She was really the clever one in the family and had done real good with her school lessons. So they'd thought that, maybe, she should go to school in Darwin, where they could educate her better.

She had come to Retta Dixon. From the first time he'd seen Elsie, Charlie had thought her the most beautiful thing in the world. She had lovely honey-coloured skin and eyes like glowing coals, dark and deep. He was fourteen to her thirteen. Before then he could not wait to get away and go bush. Suddenly, he didn't want to leave Retta Dixon anymore. He took every chance to be close to her. It was like puppy love. At first she'd been shy but he could tell she liked him; she gave him a sort of secret, special smile.

When the year was gone, he had to leave and work on a station as he was not so good with books. But he kept coming back to visit Elsie whenever he could and, early on, he'd told his mum about her and made sure she still kept visiting too. Gradually he had brought Elsie into his family and she'd learnt their customs.

Then, when he was eighteen and she was seventeen, he had wooed her and, when she turned eighteen, he had married her. To this day she was just as beautiful to him as the day her first saw her, back when she was thirteen. Sure her hair had gone grey and she was rounder and plumper than the slip of a girl he'd married. But that was how grown-up women were supposed to look.

His mum had been like that, plump and shiny, almost until the day she died ten years ago, and now his wife had taken over her tribal role, as tribe grandmother, even though her true country was somewhere out at the edge of the stone country, the place where Jim Jim Creek came over the cliffs in those big waterfalls.

Elsie had lost her own tribal knowledge as a child and only lately got a bit back through tracing cousins. So, now she was mostly Larrakia but with a bit of the Gagadju culture as well.

One thing that Elsie had got from his own mum was a recipe for the best catfish curry he had ever tasted. His mum told him she'd learned it from her own mum who'd told her she'd first learned it from a Chink in Chinatown, and then improved it.

So now, each year, just at the start of the build-up when the catfish were big and fat, it was his job to go out and get one or two really big catfish for Elsie's catfish curry. This year she'd said she wanted at least two, maybe even three, because she wanted to do an extra-big curry to celebrate the engagement of their youngest daughter, Becky, to a lad from the Roper, a boy named Jack.

He was a wild one that boy, not real big but a good horseman with great reflexes and a handy pair of fists. He had gone a few rounds in the ring with some fancied names and was pretty to watch, so light-footed and quick. Somehow he'd taken a shine to Becky and Becky to him. So now Elsie wanted to have a big family feast this weekend when Jack would be in town along with a gang from his family. It was a sort of engagement party.

Charlie liked the lad too. Perhaps Jack reminded him a bit of himself when he too was a wild one in his young days; he could scrap a bit as well. Then it was Elsie, like his Becky now, who was doing the calming down.

The one useful thing his own father had done for him, when he was but a lad, was taking him fishing and teaching him the ways of fish. He supposed his dad had also given him a way with horses, even if he more learned that from doing station work. But his father, when not shooting or poaching crocs, was a seriously good fisherman. It was like he thought with a fish brain. So, he'd taken young Charlie to his favourite fishing spots, way out along the Mary and Wildman Rivers, and taught him the many ways and places to jag a big fish.

So here he was now, at one of those special places his father had shown him, long, long ago, on the Mary River. Here the biggest catfish could be found, along with a barra and other fish. Today it was a catfish day and he, Charlie, was far and away the best catfish fisher that he knew.

He had come here last night, leaving home in the dark after dinner. He had driven through the closed gate that stopped most tourists and Darwin weekend warriors. Then he'd put up his mosquito net, not right alongside the billabong but well back.

This billabong had some of the biggest bloody lizards he'd ever seen, what others called crocs. He thought they were overgrown lizards, with not much more brain. But, even though he did not think they were real smart, he knew they were plenty dangerous. So, he kept away from the edge when he was sleeping, better than sharing his swag with one in the middle of the night, when those crocodile spirits came out and searched the land for food. They might only be spirit crocodiles but they could eat you just the same.

Now he'd just woken up and put a billy on the fire in the pre-dawn light. The early-morning coldness made his old bones ache. He shivered. He wanted to start early and be away before smoko when the real heat started. That way he'd be back in Darwin in time for a siesta. He looked forward to the smile when he presented his catch to his dear Elsie. He could, even now, imagine her cackle.

"Well, Charlie, we'se both bin gittin bit ole, but you just as good a fisher as in dem ole days. Ye still catch a fine fish or two and I can still make a fine fish stoo."

He sipped his tea. Time to get down to the fishing business.

He took two hand lines and baited each with his own special catfish bait. When he came close to the water's edge he sat down, real still, waiting for a good five minutes, looking for any sign that a big lizard was lurking.

There was a strange murky mist over the water further out. It gave him the creeps, it raised the hairs on his arms and gave him goosebumps along his neck. It felt like there was an ancient spirit of some ancestor creature lurking out there in the mist, seeking something to devour. Unbidden, an image of an incredibly ancient dreamtime crocodile spirit rose in his mind, as if warning him to be gone from this place which was claimed by another. But he pushed the image away, determined not to let his blackfella side get drawn into this superstitious magic stuff.

Instead he concentrated on the nearby water, eyes and ears alert to seek out any danger lurking there. He watched and waited some more, still nothing moved; the fear was only his imagination. Satisfied it was safe he came to the water's edge, dropped his two bait lines into what looked like the best places and waited.

Five minutes of nothing happening passed, then first one line began to twitch, then the other; two different fish, two different water places, well apart. He hoped to Christ they both did not hook on at the same time. He waited until he got the definite bait pick-up feel on the right line and gave that line a good jerk. Now he knew he had that sucker, he could feel the weight and the real tug.

He wound the loose line onto the reel so he had a proper grip. This felt like one real big mother of a fish. He could feel the other line still twitching. He thought he'd better pull it in for a minute lest he end up with a fish on each line together. He gave this line a tug to jerk it away from its inquisitive visitor.

Bloody hell, now he had another big bloody fish on this line too; just as much weight as the first one. Good in one way; if he could land them both his fishing was as good as done. But jeez, they were both big, heavy fish. It would be a fair handful to get both in together.

Then he thought, *I must be turning into a pussy in my old age. I'm sure I can land two together, got two hands and arms haven't I?*

Rather than trying to haul them in with his arms, he used his two arms like shock absorbers, each hand holding a reel and his elbows flexing to ease the jerking on the fishes' mouths. Foot by foot he eased both fish towards the shore, walking backwards to pull in the lines, making quick movements to wind the loose line onto the reels, so as to keep himself close to the bank.

Finally he had both fish on less than six feet of line. He could see each of them sitting in the water beyond the bank. It was time to get them out, before a hungry gator tried to grab an easy feed.

Grasping the two reels firmly, one in each hand, he walked back steadily, hauling both fish to the edge with even pressure, accelerating as he went. They pulled against him like two big logs. Two glistening bodies popped free of the water. A quick slide and he had both over the lip of the bank. They lay flapping, side by side, on dry sand. They were seriously big mothers. He reckoned each fish weighed between twelve and fifteen pounds.

He knew these fish alone were enough to feed all comers. But hell, catching them had been a buzz. The sun had barely broken the horizon. Too early to give up for the day. So, while he could fix some tucker or lie back in the swag for another kip, he was too pumped for that. He thought, *I won't be greedy, I'll just try for one more.*

This time he decided to have a crack at the open water straight out from the bank. There was a nice clear patch between some water lilies maybe ten metres out. He baited a line to cast it into this space. As the line swung he was seized by powerful dread, feeling a huge crocodile creature resist his cast, forcing itself into his mind. But he was buggered if he would stop now. He let the line go and watched as it flew free and landed far out, past where he meant to cast. The ripples faded away and his baited hook sank out of sight.

It was a beautiful morning, the temperature now perfect with the early dawn colours fading into a perfect sunlight day. Charlie felt good to be alive, old bones and all. *One more fish and I'll be away,* he thought again.

His reverie continued for five minutes. Nothing was happening this time, not even a little fish nibble. He mind said, *Better haul in, check the bait' still on, then try a different spot.*

His hook snagged something big. *Too far out for a tree root, maybe a water lily bulb.* He gave a firm pull. It came free. He was dragging something heavy in on the line. It felt the weight of a good-sized fish but there was no fish-sized tugging. There was just a sort of bumping, like it was half bouncing along the bottom as it came in.

Charlie wound the excess line on his reel as it came in. At last he could see something, white-grey, at the end of the line in the water, sort of round and football-sized but way too heavy for that.

As it cleared the water he realised, with a mix of surprise and shock, that he had caught a human head.

In that last second before he pulled it to the bank there was an image of the huge crocodile spirit fighting to keep its own, fighting both with him and other large crocodiles not to surrender a part of its being. Charlie felt an assault on his senses and a great urge to cast away the line and let this object return to its crocodile home in the watery deep. He put his hand to his head to clear the tumult and the vision receded.

In the process, as if of its own volition, this object came out of the water and half rolled across the land, stopping next to his feet. His mind sensed two spirits struggling for mastery over the destiny of this person object; a human spirit which sought release from this place of crocodile destiny, as if to return to the lands of people; and a crocodile spirit which sought to hold fast to one of its own.

In the end the human spirit won but the crocodile spirit stayed beside it, calling out, "Return to the water." Charlie broke the mind connection with the spirits and, as he did, his own world returned.

Chapter 2 – Who Owns This

Charlie looked at the ugly object lying next to his feet. Clearly part of a person though both the eyes were gone. Odd skin and hair remnants clung to one side of the skull, he guessed small fish had nibbled off all they could get to and the bits that remained were lying in the mud.

He decided he'd better pull it further away from the edge, lest its scaly owner decided to try to come and retrieve it. He could not bear to touch it, but the hook seemed well attached. He half lifted and half dragged it across the ground. As he did so he felt a second tug of war going on between a crocodile spirit and human spirit. It was pulling hard at him too, making it real difficult to move. He sensed he'd messed up the balance of forces in this place. He no longer trusted his ability to keep out of harm's way. It seemed to take an age until this thing was ten metres back from the edge. The struggle abated. He let the skull rest on the ground, reel and line alongside. His body was weary with the effort.

He forced the spirits to leave his mind. He looked away, scanning the trees and earth around himself. He could feel the crocodile spirit sliding back to its watery place. It was still proper angry but had left for now. He felt safer himself at once too.

He looked again at this part of a person. *Poor bugger, this once was someone who should've taken more care to hide away from crocodile spirits,* he thought. The head shape suggested a man not a woman, name unknown. He wondered who? *Clearly a white man, and more than crocodile food the way the crocodile spirit had tried to hold him in the water.*

He felt a huge urge to cast this thing back to its watery grave but knew he could not.

He did not really believe in accidents. It was part of his destiny to find this. Now he must fulfil what the white man's law, and maybe what the spirit law of the land, required. Then, when it was all done, he would try to find a way to placate the crocodile spirits which lurked in this watery place. Without their blessing he dared not return here to fish.

He walked back to his Toyota. He needed to think, so he rolled up his swag. He sat on it while he rolled a smoke. A few blowflies were already drawn to this new prize. He did not want to handle it but could not leave it lying out there for the birds and flies. He must cover it. Then he would drive back to the nearest bit of civilisation, the Bark Hut Inn, and ring the police, he decided.

He had a big bucket with a rope which he used it to gather water from billabongs, when it was not safe to come close to the edge. There were good-sized rocks in an old fireplace at the far side of the open area where he'd camped. He placed the upended bucket over the head, carried the heaviest rock over and put it on top of the bucket.

That would stop hungry birds and flies, not much good for a big dog or pig, but it should do for an hour or two while he went to call the police.

He cleaned up his two fish and put them in his esky, on ice. He put the esky on the back of his truck, covered it with a tarp and some other things so it was not obvious.

He flung the fish guts into the water and noticed, with satisfaction, a big swirl as they vanished. At least he had returned some part of his catch to the river spirits.

He was determined to fulfil his mission to Elsie and keep these fish. So, he would not tell the police about this part. He thought, if he did tell, the cops would confiscate the fish for evidence. Instead, they could have the man's head and he would have his fish. So long as they did not know he had kept his share all would be happy.

At the Bark Hut Inn he asked to use the phone and got put through to the Darwin Police Station. A peculiar conversation followed, one where someone wanted to know lots more than he knew about how the head came to be there and who it belonged to. At last he got on to a senior policeman. This man told Charlie he understood what he was saying, a big relief after the other stupid questions. However, he asked Charlie to remain where he was until a police vehicle came to meet him.

It was two hours later before three policemen, in two cars, arrived. It was another half hour before they got back to the billabong. Charlie insisted on driving his own car, with the two police cars following, even though the cops asked him to come in one of their cars.

He was determined to leave as soon as he could. He would show them what he'd found and then get away somehow. It was close to lunchtime when he left the cool shade of the Bark Hut Inn and was stinking hot by the time they got back at the billabong.

Everything was as he'd left it, his line lying alongside the bucket which looked undisturbed. Charlie pointed to the bucket, saying. "Dis morning, real early, I try to catch him big catfish. I threw out bait, longa there," he said, pointing to a spot in the water. "Den, after a while, no fish bite and me think, *Maybe little fish eat bait.* So I pull in and instead I catch this thing, man head. I pull it to here, cover with bucket and rock, so bird or goanna not eat more."

The boss policeman lifted off the bucket, but it was smelly and he soon covered it again.

He turned to Charlie saying, "Show me where you cast your line when you caught that thing."

Charlie pointed to a spot, a bit over ten yards out where he had cast and picked up a pebble and threw it to hit the water nearby.

"Where were you were standing when you caught it?

Charlie led him to a gap in the trees, next to the water. He pointed to some scuff marks on the ground about two metres back from the edge. "I was standing right dere, not too close cause big gators in dere. Den, when I pull out it stop dere," he said pointed to a damp patch a metre away from the footmarks. "But den I pull up in air and carry it away from water, cos frightened dat same big gator might try and eat me too, like for dat man," he said, pointing to the bucket.

The policeman walked back to the bucket. He looked at the line and reel closely before saying, "Well it looks like you hooked him good. We will have to keep that fishing gear for evidence."

Charlie shivered and nodded. "I not want that line anymore, not want to touch it. You keep it. I got plenty spare one."

The policeman nodded and walked away to talk to his colleagues. Charlie shivered again and turned away from the water. He still felt that bad thing out there and really wanted to be gone.

The policeman came back and said, "When did you last come here before today?"

Charlie said, "Last year, bout same time, I come. Try to catch catfish, same as today."

They asked him a few more questions but it all seemed clear.

One policeman wrote in his diary a record of what he had told them and read it back to Charlie. He agreed it was correct and initialled the page. Then this man wrote down his contact details and checked them against his driver's licence.

Now he could see they were no longer interested in him. So he made an excuse about needing to get back to Darwin to meet his wife and some people who were visiting.

The cops nodded. It was like they had forgotten about him now; one cop, the boss man, got on the radio back to Darwin, organising a boat and a team to help search the nearby area and the billabong. A second was taping out the scene, and the third one was taking photographs.

Finally he got the boss man's attention, to confirm his departure. The man half nodded, so Charlie walked over to his Toyota and drove away. As he was leaving he could see one of them waving at him. He did not know if he was waving goodbye or telling him to come back. He ignored it and kept driving.

No one followed him. As he left he thought, *Bad spirit place, I not want to come back here anymore.*

Sergeant Alan McKinnon, the senior officer, watched Charlie leave and wondered if he should call him back. In the end he just waved to him. He knew the man was in a big hurry to leave and probably had not told them everything he knew. *But hell, if I fished out something like that I would want to get far away too,* he thought. This guy was clearly spooked, but who could blame him.

Truth was he felt a bit spooked himself when he first saw it, like it was somehow connected to a big crocodile which lived here. He could almost imagine a huge crocodile hiding deep in the shadowy water and eyeing him off, angry to have lost its prize. *Just superstitious nonsense*, his mind said, but still he shuddered.

Then he thought, *This man, Charlie, has done his job. We don't need him anymore. Investigating here will keep us busy for the next couple days and it's better to not have him or anyone else in our way. Plus, we have his details to interview him again later if we need to. And it's far too bloody hot to keep the poor old bugger standing around in the blazing afternoon sun, with nothing to do but watch.*

With that Charlie passed out of his mind.

Now it was an afternoon for organising. He thought he had seen some tooth punctures to the head, which made him think crocodile. The pathologist was an hour away, so nothing would be disturbed until then. If it was a croc attack it was funny nothing had been reported. No one he'd heard of was missing around here. But people, particularly tourists, came and went everywhere so how could you really know.

He didn't like the idea of trying to search this billabong for a body; it was a big and it was bound to be full of huge crocodiles. No divers would be going in here until they worked out how to do it safely. And there was little point trying to drag the bottom with all the other crap that would be down there, the innumerable logs and debris that washed along these rivers each wet season.

What was needed was a steel cage, a thing that a diver could work inside. This would allow the diver to search the area around where the head was found, to see if any other bits remained. But, before they got too serious about searching the water, they should do a careful search of the dry land and also get pathology done on the head to see if there was anything suggesting it was other than an unfortunate crocodile victim.

Now his radio crackled back to life. The pathologist, Sandy Bowen, had passed through the Bark Hut and asked for someone to meet them on the main road, to not to get lost on the last bit. It was a confusing place to find with roads running every which way.

He told his men to continue inspecting the site. He would go and meet the pathologist, back on the main road. The pathologist's name was new. He hoped Sandy had a strong stomach; this smelly, half-decomposed head was not a thing for the faint-hearted.

Sandy turned out to be a lady in her mid-twenties, one of those keen new grads who got sent to Darwin to learn their craft before getting a comfy big-city job.

She seemed very young and fresh-faced for something like this. Perhaps she'd need her hand held. He wouldn't mind doing that though he had his doubts about the level of her experience. He had spent ten years in the police force getting to where he was now and it was a steep learning curve. But he loved the bush and it was a pretty good job, truth be told.

He did not say this, but it must have been written over his face; a disdain for newcomers. He could feel in her a mix of antagonism to his manner and a desire to prove herself.

Back on site it was clear that she was sharper and tougher than he credited. First, she asked him to lift off the bucket so that she could look at the head from various angles but not touch anything.

She looked very carefully and said, "It looks like teeth marks, but looks like the upper left side of the skull has been fractured as well, perhaps from the force of a bite. You can see it's out of shape, compared to the right side."

She continued, "I'd guess this happened at least a fortnight past and no more than six weeks ago, though the laboratory tests will tell more. It looks like a man of young to middle age."

She did a careful walk around, noting the slight drag mark where the head had come out of the water and been pulled across the dirt. Then she tracked a mix of scuff marks and damp spots to the final destination. Then she pointed to two other drag marks nearby, but to one side of the one that led to the head. They were two feet apart and came in from the bank for about two metres, each ending in a flattened area in the dirt with a damp patch.

She said, "It looks like something else has been pulled out here, probably this morning too," pointing to the damp patches of mud.

"Pity that the man who hooked this head is not still here. I'd have liked to ask him about this. It looks like he caught a couple of fish first. If so, it'd be nice to know what sort they were and if they had been feeding on this. Not that I suppose it matters, it's just that I like to get a complete picture," she said, shrugging her shoulders.

Then she carefully scrutinised the rest of the site, looking from where she was standing, next to the bucket.

She said, "Before I look in detail at this head we should look around the site, just in case there's any dried blood or other information from the time when the victim went into the water."

She walked directly towards the water's edge, as if to begin her search there.

At first Alan just looked on. He was feeling a bit silly for letting old Charlie leave without a closer check. Maybe he should radio the Darwin office. They could arrange for someone to be there to meet Charlie and check his car for fish when he returned.

But, like she said, it was really of little importance. They could ask him later. Plus he did not really want any fish Charlie had caught, just in case they had a bit of a person in their stomachs. Not to mention that, if he read the signs in the damp earth right, Charlie had already gutted them and tossed the guts in the water. So it would be a total waste of time, not to mention seriously annoying this good-hearted old fellow.

Looking up he realised Sandy was walking right to the edge of the water. Well, she might be good at pathology but out here she needed to learn a few basic bush survival skills. He did not want her to become another statistic on his watch.

He called out, "Just wait a minute."

She stopped a metre back.

He came over to her and, as he walked towards her, he unclipped and removed his service revolver. He made a signal to her to step back. Now they both stood side by side, two metres from the edge.

He said, "You were right about catching the fish and questioning the old timer who found this. You're obviously good at your business. But you need to be careful in a place like this. If it was a crocodile that did this to him, it could be sitting below here, just a metre down and the same back. You'd never know. In less than a second, before you had a chance to move, it could come out of the water and drag you in.

If you really need to get that close to the water, I need to be standing right alongside you, with a gun in my hand. If possible, you should keep at least a couple of steps back and never turn your back to the edge when you're close."

She looked at him and laughed. Her face was kind of nice when she laughed. She said, "That makes us equal, one all. How about from now we both work together? I'll trust you for the bush sense and you'll trust me for the pathology bit."

He laughed back. "Deal."

They worked side by side, following a grid pattern, using a long stick to carefully push aside the leaves, twigs and debris without marking the ground. It was amazing how two sets of eyes from different levels and angles could together spot details that one alone might have missed.

He pointed to some regular scrape marks in the dirt which had been partly covered by leaves. "Unless I'm mistaken someone used a spade to scrape dirt away from this place, like they wanted to take off the top half inch of soil. I don't know how long ago it was done, not too recent with the leaves and dirt, but it's definitely since the rain last wet season. Last rain around here was a heavy burst at the start of May."

She nodded. They followed what looked to be the line of the spade marks away from the water. Sandy pointed to a new place a few metres back. "It might just be a stain, but I'm ninety percent sure that's dried blood. Looks like someone scraped away most of it but missed that bit. Can you keep your eye on the place and we'll photograph it and then I'll collect some in a sample jar?"

Alan called over his constable, who carried a camera, and had him take several photographs. Then Sandy returned with a jar and scalpel. She dug out a small piece of rust-coloured soil, placed it in the jar and labelled it. By the end of an hour of careful searching together they were almost sure they had worked out where the body originally lay and had also found a scraped-away drag route to the edge of the water. They'd also found two more small patches of soil with the same blood like staining that they'd sampled.

There was also something that looked like an old fireplace, to one side, further away from the water. The soil was blackened with sprinkles of ash and charcoal, but not the old fire debris one would expect to find. The centre was hollowed out for almost a metre. It looked like it had been dug out with a spade not so long ago.

Alan said, "It looks like there was a big fire here, maybe to burn stuff. Then, when it was finished, someone got a spade and dug out the ash and took it away. They may have dumped it somewhere else, but my guess is it went into the water. In fact, if you look hard, I think you can see a few bits that have dropped off near the water. It'll be a thing to look for when we go diving, a pile of ash sitting on top of the mud."

Sandy raised her eyebrows and grinned at him. "Quite the bush detective, aren't you? I could leave now and go away as I think you could've figured this all out without my help."

Then she screwed up her nose in mock disgust. "Well, I've been avoiding that smelly head for an hour now, but I can't really leave it cooking in the hot sun any longer. What do you think, time for me to take a proper look?"

He grinned back. "I suppose you must. I'll just have to hold my nose while I look on. Glad I don't have to touch it."

It was a blasting hot, sweaty afternoon as the sun streamed down, and lunch had been forgotten, they were both totally absorbed in their investigation and barely noticed anything else. Alan could feel that buzz of excitement as the shape of something that was not just a crocodile attack began to emerge.

Sandy gave her attention to the head. First she carefully palpated it through her gloves, saying that the left side of the skull was definitely fractured. Then she transferred it to a plastic specimen bag and placed it in an esky full of ice to preserve it until it was at the laboratory for a post-mortem later that afternoon.

With this done she announced that she must be on her way if she was to examine this today. Alan escorted her back to where the track met the main road. He arranged to call to the lab to see her and get initial results in the morning. It was mid-afternoon before their work was done, and Alan and his team were ready to leave.

A new team had arrived to continue the site investigation over the next two days, to search the billabong nearby for any more body parts or other things which may relate to the victim, and to finish searching the rest of the site. Alan briefed them on what he had found and what he thought they should look for. He knew this part would be in good hands. It was led by an old techy, Ron. He'd been doing this work since before Alan was born and was the best.

Alan waved goodbye to his two constables, saying, "No need to go back to the office, head straight home once you get to town. I'll follow behind soon in the other car."

The driver leaned out of his window saying, "Thanks boss, but my throat is like a leather glove from all the hours we spent in the hot sun. First stop is a beer and a feed at the Bark Hutt to make up for the lunch we never got. You owe us one, you were in such a hurry to get here. How about you join us on your way home?

"Maybe I will, just for one, I certainly need a drink."

Alan watched them drive out of sight then walked towards the water, stopping in the shade just back from the edge of the billabong. He relaxed his mind and soaked in the feel of the place for a few more minutes. He had always found this last look was really valuable because it grounded him in the scene and helped get a complete perspective.

He reviewed what he knew in his mind. *Male adult victim, high likelihood of crocodile involvement, but getting a murder-scene feel. Another person was here with the victim who had gone to considerable lengths to hide the evidence of the death. Maybe it was deliberate, maybe accidental; but if so why so much effort to cover up the signs?*

Plenty of questions to be answered: who owned this head, how did he get here, who else was here, how did this person leave, and most of all why, why the death, why the cover-up?

As he stood there contemplating, he saw two eyes watching him. They would have been easy to miss, over in the tree shade at the far side of the billabong. He had seen plenty of crocs in his years and was a fair judge of size.

This one was a long way away, and the eyes were all that showed. But he knew this was big, bigger than anything he'd seen before. It was watching him with intent, maybe as a food item, but the intent seemed personal and focused; almost sadness, as if it had lost something it cherished. Not just a meal but a companion.

He shuddered as if the devil was walking over his grave. A picture came, unbidden, into his mind. *A huge malevolent but grieving spirit, half man and half crocodile that belonged in this place and yet had a part taken from it and felt loss. It was claiming an ownership to what was taken.* He shook his head to break the spell, then walked to his car and drove away.

He caught up with his constables at the Bark Hut Inn for five-o'clock lunch, washed down with an icy VB, the best cold beer. It tasted extra good after the hot sun. He would have loved a couple more but one was his limit on the job. So, instead he had a couple of pint glasses of lemon squash to replace the lost fluids.

As they were finishing drinks, Fred, senior constable, turned to them both and said. "Don't know about you two, but I would be happy if I never went near that place again, there was something about it that spooked me, maybe that man Charlie was part. He really was freaked out. There was something bloody eerie about it, the idea of a huge big crocodile hiding away, sitting just under the water, having already had one of us for dinner, now maybe waiting again for his next meal. It was like I could feel it watching and waiting. I'm not the superstitious kind but it gave me the creeps."

Alan pushed aside his own memories, "Turning into a wimp, Fred, I would not have picked it." As he said it he knew it was as much to hide his own freaked out feeling.

He drove back to Darwin, towards the red ball of a setting sun, falling towards a smoky horizon, feeling strangely sombre when he knew he should be upbeat about the day's success.

He was heading back to the office to finish writing up his day's notes when a thought crossed his mind. Rather than turning down McMillans Road, heading for the station, he went on towards the town and turned right towards Parap, where Charlie's address was. Sure enough, Charlie was sitting on his verandah, beer in hand.

Charlie waved to him, then covered his face with mock chagrin when he saw the serious look on Alan's face. Alan walked over and sat in the chair next to Charlie, accepted the proffered beer and took a deep draught. "OK, Charlie, I think you'd better tell me the story about those real fish you caught," he said. He could have sworn Charlie was laughing behind his twinkling eyes.

"Better still I show you," said Charlie. He got up and went to the kitchen. He returned carrying a plate covered with rice and steaming curry.

He handed it to Alan. "More better to taste than talk. Maybe you'll kill me little bit for not giving you the fish. But if I'd let you take the fish and not bring them back, my Elsie, she'd kill me big time. So I had to decide, which trouble is biggest, and I know it's better to go to jail than make trouble with my Elsie."

They sat side by side, each eating a plate of fish curry in the dusk. Both agreed it was the best they had ever tasted. As they sipped their beers the story of the morning was told.

A second beer was brought by a beautiful girl with honey-coloured skin, aged in her early twenties. She was introduced to Alan as Charlie's daughter, Becky, who was having her engagement party tomorrow night. The fish curry would cement the bond between the two families. "Once we share this together we'll be friends for life," said Charlie.

Alan knew the matter of two catfish was something that would stay out of his and the pathologist's reports. But he collected a little plastic box of catfish curry to give to Sandy tomorrow. He was sure she'd enjoy both the story and its end result just as much as he had.

As he was getting up to leave Charlie asked him, dead serious amongst the banter, "Did you feel that bad crocodile spirit? It not want to let that body go. You tell youse men be real, real, real careful in that place. Very dangerous crocodile spirit that one. Maybe tis crocodile spirit body, body belong to crocodile and crocodile belong to body."

VICTIM   GRAHAM WILSON

Chapter 3 – England – The Consequence

Susan looks at the pregnancy test kit with dismay. She'd known in her heart what the result would be. As she stares at the double line, the second line as clear as the first control line -its meaning is clear.

She really is pregnant! She knows with certainty it is real. This is it- no clinging to a false hope that it might be her imagination. She knows the test kits are over 99 percent accurate. And that does not even account for the other signs in her body which all indicate the same thing. *She has THAT man's offspring growing inside her.*

She sits down on her bed with her mind reeling. Why did she feel this could not happen? She had been lax with precautions over the two weeks in which the sex was almost non-stop. This included her fertile period. Why does she feel both surprised and shocked?

For more than a month now, she has tried to pretend that Mark was just a figment of her imagination and her time in Australia was an imagined fantasy she had dreamt about.

However, this is no divine conception and it certainly has not happened since her return to England. There have been no men even remotely close to her since then, if you don't count those recurring awful dreams. The shocking truth her mind now must confront is the man, whose face evokes a shuddering horror in her mind, is the father of her child.

Suddenly, her mind shifts to her time in Sydney and David's forlorn face as she'd said goodbye. Is it at all possible the child is his? It is not likely, her period was barely finished the first night they slept together and the second was only a day later. Still- there is a slight chance it is David's child. She has heard of rare cases where it happened from sex almost right after a period. Somehow the idea that David could be the father of her child seems infinitely preferable to it being Mark's child.

One is a normal healthy man who is kind and decent with no significant flaws, at least none she is aware of. Her cousin, Ruth, knows him well and she said he was really lovely. And her own experience had confirmed this fact. The other man was … she tries to think of an appropriate term to describe Mark. Unsurprisingly, all she can come up with is the term she's been trying to avoid: a psychopath. Mark was a psychopath who had murdered numerous other people and she had almost been the next victim. Even though she knows she is probably clinging to a false hope, she is not prepared to totally discount a slight chance the father of her child is the good man, not the crazy evil one.

She looks around her bedroom. It really is time to get a place of her own again. Since splitting from former boyfriend, Edward, six months ago, she's been staying at her parents' house. However, this is not a long-term option when you're in your mid-twenties. She needs her own place located somewhere within the city of London. Here is forty miles away: comfortable and convenient though it is.

Her eyes fall on an envelope on the mantel- the letter from David she'd carelessly cast aside over three weeks ago when it arrived. She'd been unwilling to allow any memories of her Australian trip to find their way into her life back here. When this letter arrived, it had seemed an unwelcome intrusion from another place. Now she knows this other place cannot be so easily exorcised- at least not unless she's gets a termination of the parasite now growing inside her. Termination somehow seems more acceptable than 'abortion'.

Her mind seizes on this new idea- she's sure it's the best solution. In the same way she's physically excised Mark from her life, dispatching him to an obscure watery grave, inside the bellies of those hideous creatures: she'll excise this new unwelcome entity from her body.

She is on the point of making a doctor's appointment with thoughts of, *I will start the required arrangements; I'm still very early and it should only take a day or two to resolve.* However, before she can make herself do this, she finds her hand has picked up David's letter.

35

She feels very fickle for doing this. She'd not wanted to know him anymore before this situation arose. Yet she is contemplating whether he'd be a suitable father to her child- despite the possibility of him being the father is very unlikely. Why does she even let her mind go to this place?

But it's like an external force is controlling her hand. She feels an overriding need to bring certainty to this mess before acting to end it. She partially wishes it will just be a polite letter wishing her well and saying he has met someone else.

She rips open David's letter: it has only a single folded sheet inside. She removes the letter and examines it. The paper is three quarters covered with neat and precise writing.

She sits down on her bed again and consciously clears her mind of all extraneous things before she allows herself to read. She needs to think clearly and this letter deserves her full attention. *Focus on the here and now. Don't try to work out the future yet*, she tells herself. She starts reading, half saying the words aloud to give them more reality.

Dearest Susan,

I missed you more than I can say after you left. I'm not sure whether I was anything more to you than a passing fling, but to me you were someone wonderful and special. I would really love to stay in touch, or better still have a continuing relationship, should the chance arise.

You may be interested to know that I'm flying to London for ten days in a month's time, arriving the week that runs from the end of September to the start of October. The first two days are for business meetings related to my work, for which London is a key business node. However, I've set aside a further week for a holiday while I'm there. I fly in very early on the Monday morning and leave on the Wednesday evening of the following week, and my work is only the first Monday and Tuesday, with Tuesday clear after five pm.

Should you have some time to catch up while I'm there, I'd really love to see you. I've booked a sports car for a week, a car just like my one in Sydney.

Perhaps you could come with me on a drive through the beautiful English countryside to see some of those numerous grand old houses and castles, not to mention some of your cute village pubs.

Anyway I hope we can work something out that suits you. Seeing you, even at the weekend, would be great. My time is free all week and a week spent with you would be wonderful.

I don't want to intrude on your other relationships or commitments, but I'm hoping you're able to come away with me. Please let me know if you don't want to see me.

I won't try to contact you again if I don't hear from you. I'll treat it as you not wanting to keep in touch and respect that.

Love from David

It was signed with a cursive flourish and a couple of little gilt hearts were stuck on.

Susan cannot help smiling. Despite her situation, there is something so warm and engaging in the letter and his manner. Both are factual and to the point yet also like a breath of summer breeze.

She looks at her calendar. The month since he posted it has passed. He is arriving in two days. It is Saturday morning which means he must be flying out tomorrow at the latest. It's awfully late to make a reply.

She was very unkind to David when she last saw him. Sure, she gave him her address: but it was done under sufferance. However, sh0e does not want it to end that way. Her decision is made by the time she finishes reading. Yes, she will see him again. Perhaps she'll even go travelling with him. Her work is not so all-consuming that she can't find a few days to be away. Even though she really needs to ask first, she already knows she will be able to take off at least from Wednesday to Friday of next week.

Unbidden, panic rises into her mind – *another place in which she will be travelling alone with another man.* She winces and shudders. It won't be the same because he is not like Mark. David is a good and honourable- not like the other memory she is determined not to let surface. And English countryside is nothing like where she was.

She focuses her attention on locking away the awful experience in a basement part of her mind, where it cannot hurt her ever again. Gradually, her calm and self-control returns.

Despite this pimple of fear, she decides she will let nothing of her past intrude into her new life. She wants to take this heaven-sent opportunity to put time and distance between herself and having to make a decision on whether or not to have an abortion.

She realises she's just using this as a distraction to avoid having to face her real problem- but what a welcome escape it is to not have to think about this baby thing for a few days. After this trip, her mind should be much clearer. Then, there will be more than enough time for her to decide what to do about it.

She decides she will not tell David- at least not during their trip away. She feels she at least owes it to both of them to see whether there is any real substance to this relationship. After spending five days together, she hopes she will have a better idea about this. At the end of their trip, if things go well between them, she will tell him about the pregnancy to see how he responds. She'll do it before she makes any definite decision to terminate. Her mind rationalises this as a sensible and reasonable way forward.

Now, though, she has her own job to do. She must contact him to let him know she has not totally forgotten or ignored him. She looks at the address line on the letter. As she suspects, there is a phone number and email address along with the mail address. With the difference of time to Australia, an email is better. Plus, she wants their next contact to be face to face instead of over the phone. She wants to see how she feels, actually being with him, rather than just hearing his voice from the other side of the world. She turns on her computer and writes:

Dear David,

Thank you so much for writing. I'm sorry to be so late in replying but a few other things have come up since I returned home. I hope this delay has not messed up your plans.

I would like to see you again. What happened between us in Sydney was unexpected but nice. I'm still not quite sure myself how I feel about it all, but I do like the idea of a country trip with you.

I've organised to have next Wednesday to Sunday free, as this should fit with your need to do work on the Monday and Tuesday.

What I suggest is that, as you fly in very early Monday morning and probably need a good night's sleep to adjust to jet lag, that you stop in a hotel in London for Monday night and come out to my family's house in Reading for dinner on Tuesday. It's the address on your letter.

I know my parents will be keen to meet you, and my mum's a great cook. So there's bound to be something edible on the menu.

There's an office at the back of our house with a fold-out bed which you can use for that night if you want, to avoid another hotel room. Then we can head away for our country trip on Wednesday.

Let me know if that suits and looking forward to seeing you again.

Love, Suz

Chapter 4 – Darwin – Results of a Murder

Alan rang the laboratory about nine in the morning and got put through to Sandy. She confirmed she had done the post-mortem and had some preliminary results for him, which she thought he should see. He said he also had something to give her. They agreed to meet in the cafeteria at ten then he would accompany her back to the lab after a coffee.

Over coffee he told her about the fish and gave her the box of curry. She laughed and said, "Well I forgot lunch, so this takes its place. I'm sure it's better than my cooking; lived with my folks in Sydney until six months ago when I came here. Decided it was finally time to leave the nest, so to speak, one has to make one's own way in the big world eventually. Trouble is my mum is a great cook, and she really loves to cook. I was lazy and busy with my studies so, somehow, I never learned. Hence my cooking is terrible, so this is doubly welcome."

He had not mentioned her report and whether it would include the fish. However, it was like she was psychic, or maybe she was more attuned to the Territory than he realised. She said, "I imagine this is one detail that will never make it into either your or my report. Unless you feel it must of course?" she added with a mocking look.

He nodded. "No, not relevant, at least it'll save me one pain in the butt. Charlie is OK and I wouldn't mind mentioning it if it was only him, but God help me if Elsie and Becky get their noses out of joint. This way I know I'm good for another plate of fish curry next time, otherwise I'll never get to have that pleasure again."

Sandy nodded, sharing the joke. "I think two of us own a plate of that curry. Next chance I expect an invitation too."

Then, the professional person returned. "OK, time to get on with work. Come, see what I've found and tell me what you think."

She led him along a series of passages that opened into a room with stainless-steel benches and microscopes along one side.

There was also a light box which had three X-rays hanging from it. Sandy turned on the light- illuminating the large X-ray films. He realized these were three shots of a skull: one from above, one from the side and one from the back. Each showed several round holes punched through the skull bones on one side- which were partially matched by similar holes on the other side. Each hole was about half an inch across and circular.

"Those look like crocodile teeth marks, not unexpected from what we saw there," she said. "The interesting thing, for the ones in the skull, is that there was no bleeding into the brain around them. It looks like, when these happened, he was already dead."

Then, she pointed to an area of about three inches by three inches on the left side located high up towards the back of the skull. Here a big round circular crack ran. Within this crack, the bones were broken into several pieces and were pushed down towards the inside.

"As I thought at the site, he has a fractured skull and it's not associated with any obvious crocodile tooth damage. In fact, it looks like he was hit with something on that part of his head. That skull fracture almost certainly killed him. He was alive when it happened as there's bleeding inside the brain associated with it. Even if he didn't die immediately- he would've been unconscious after that blow.

"It was done by striking his head with a large solid object with a contact point about three inches across- based on the size of the fracture. Without knowing for sure, I think something like a club or a baseball bat could cause that sort of injury."

Then, she led him over to a microscope to show him some dark brown pieces of material from a sample jar sitting next to it. "What do you think that is?" she asked, handing the jar to him.

He examined it carefully. It looked like some broken splintered pieces of wood. There were about five or six of them with the longest being almost an inch long. He shrugged. "Perhaps that's a trick question, but I would've said splinters of wood."

"That's what I found embedded in the skin and bone over the skull fracture," she said. "I agree, it looks like bits of wood to me, too. I've looked under a microscope at the pieces. I'm almost certain that is what we're looking at. Here-take a look."

There were two microscopes sitting side by side. "Number One is samples I collected from a dead broken branch of an old tree outside this building. Number Two is what came out of his head," she said.

He studied both. They looked very alike, though he had to admit a microscope was something he knew little about.

She pointed out the features such as the timber grain to compare, then said, "I'll send the samples off for more advice or tests, but I think it's highly likely that our man was hit hard by a broken branch or similar piece of wood to the side of the head. While it could've been due to a piece of dead wood falling from a tree, the angle at which the impact occurred makes it very likely that someone else was holding it and swung it sideways to hit him. With this, I think you have enough evidence to begin a murder investigation. That's my opinion.

"I've sent off tissue samples from the head for DNA testing. I've also tested the soil samples for blood. The initial test results suggest it is blood but, it's yet to be verified. We'll also do DNA analysis on this blood to see if it matches the skull tissue.

"I've also taken a set of dental X-rays as they may assist in getting an identification. It'll take a couple of days before the DNA results come through. In the meantime I can write a preliminary report for you this afternoon if that helps."

Then, she added with a mischievous smile, "If you like I'll drop it in to your office this afternoon on my way home, though of course I can email you a copy if you prefer."

It was agreed she would call with the report that afternoon about four-thirty. In the meantime, he knew he needed to get the full murder investigation underway.

Alan drove to Berrimah police station where his desk was. He arranged a meeting with his commanding officer. He thought, with regret, *a senior detective will take over the case from here.*

With a bit of luck, he hoped he would still stay involved. Unless they had a lucky break, there was plenty of work to do. Identification of the body was the next stage. After finding the victim's identity, they could begin to try to trace the person's known associates and movements.

As a first step, Sandy said she would email him high-resolution images of the X-rays of the teeth and skull.

As expected, the case was handed over to a Senior Detective to run the murder investigation. He was made second-in-charge and given the job of focusing on the person's identification. He would begin with the dental records. Then, he would see if the DNA yielded anything to assist in determining who this man was. Another team would focus on the site, in order to comprehensively search it over the next week, to see if it gave any more clues.

There would be little he could do with the dentists until Monday due to most not working on the weekend. Perhaps tomorrow he could go back and have another look at the site. Just maybe they would turn up something significant that would help with an ID. He could also ask at the roadhouses along that part of the Arnhem Highway. There was always the chance someone had noted anything of value: perhaps two men arguing in a car while going fishing or descriptions of people not known to the locals who had been seen around a month ago. It was a long shot. But he knew from experience that each little bit, the negative as well as the positive, built the picture.

Alan got to work on finishing his initial report, documenting all he had found, ensuring all the photographs and other evidence were catalogued. It was tedious yet exciting work.

He knew if they could put it all together it would go a long way toward pushing his career to a new level. Truth be told, he hoped it would give him an excuse for a few more meetings with Sandy. She was seriously cute. And also, like himself, she seemed unattached. He would park that thought for a few days, however, as there was a mountain of work to be done first.

He was so absorbed he almost forgot her promise to bring the report. His phone rang announcing her arrival at the front desk.

He advised he would be out directly. He only had two more lines to finish his report. It was now late Friday afternoon- perhaps they could have a drink together once he handed over his report. And, he thought, he should at least read what she had written and attach it to his own.

With these thoughts, he went out and invited her in. He had not seen her out of working clothes before, but, she had obviously changed before leaving work. He had to admit she really did look good: smiley eyes and mouth, light-brown hair and curvy shape. He tried not to let it distract him.

Alan suggested Sandy come in, "I am just about finished my report. I figure it is worth comparing notes with what you have written before I do. Then, I will pass it on to my boss. If that's OK with you, that is?"

"Sure, I always wanted to see the inside of this place."

She seemed in no rush. It took half an hour, but he could see how her little touches improved what he had written. Now it was as good as possible at this early stage. Maybe, because of their prickly start, they had a real sense of teamwork.

As they walked out together, the day's work done, he realised he had left his private car at home. He said, "I was going to invite you for a drink, but I need to leave the police car here as I'm not on duty tonight. Sadly, my private car is at home."

She looked at him with a new seriousness. "Well, isn't it lucky that I came in my own car so you can come with me. That's assuming you meant it and the car wasn't just an excuse to get out of us doing it."

It was agreed and they went together. He wondered what doing it meant: just a drink or maybe something more. They drove towards the city, having both agreed it was the place to head for a Friday night. As they came down Bagot Road, Alan had a sudden thought. "Do you mind if we make a short detour?" he asked.

"Of course not," she replied, looking at him with an unspoken question. He directed her to turn off the main road and through the back streets to Charlie's place.

It was only half past five and they would not stop long. It should be early enough not to interrupt the engagement party.

He said, "Someone lives here I'd like you to meet."

Another questioning look was her only reply. Charlie was sitting on the verandah with a beer, again. This time, however, he was sharing it with a young, fit-looking man, sitting in the chair next to him.

Alan walked over. Charlie pretended to hide his face again. He said, "Jack, this is the policeman I was telling you about, the one who caught me out over the fish yesterday. Now he's come again. I think he want to take me away to jail." He laughed uproariously.

Alan joined in the mirth. "You wish, old fella, you're just trying to run away from that Elsie, you know she'll give you much bigger trouble than me tonight."

He did the introductions, saying, "This is the lady you should thank for finding out about the fish. She's much cleverer than me and saw what you'd done straightaway."

They all laughed and agreed that all women were much smarter than their men folks.

In the end, they did stay there for the night and ended up becoming extra guests at the party. It was a case of the more the merrier. Even though the 'doing it' was only telling stories, drinking and laughing together- by the end they really were the best of friends. Alan hoped, in their own time, there would be much more to doing "it" together. They were already planning lots more "doing things together" which included another visit to the billabong tomorrow.

The only thing that spooked him a bit was Charlie's warning. It was given at the end of the night and warned him "to be real careful at that place to keep away from the bad crocodile spirit."

After Alan told Sandy about the weird experience of the crocodile watching him. "I'm not normally superstitious, but I got a real spooky feeling about the way that croc watched me, as if it was some ancestor spirit. It still freaks me out when I think about it."

Sandy shrugged, not understanding and a bit dismissive. He could feel her scepticism but let it be. He did not want to spoil the enjoyment of her company or of their night together.

VICTIM					GRAHAM WILSON

Chapter 5 – Crocodile Communion

It was mid-morning before Alan called to collect Sandy in the police car. He first went to the office to talk with the investigation leader who was sitting by the radio listening to the early-morning account of the onsite investigation and confirming arrangements.

Last night, the police had booked a truck to take a five-metre cube-shaped steel cage to the site. A crane which came with the truck had an extensible arm which would allow it get out to about 12–15 meters from the bank. This setup allowed the cage to be lifted and placed in various locations with the diver still inside being protected from the crocodiles. Once it was on the bottom, the diver could systematically search the billabong bottom area between the metal grids which were 200 millimetres apart.

It was not perfect, however they thought a diver inside could do a good search of the billabong bottom for the 15 meters from the shoreline in the area adjacent to where the head was found.

Then, based on the findings in this area, they could decide whether to widen the search area. They could do this either by using boats to support and move the cage or by moving the location of the crane along the riverbank.

The diver had two-way communication from inside the cage with the crane driver. This meant the cage could be raised, lowered or moved sideways as was required. Since most of the water was 3–5 meters deep, depth was not an issue. Now, they had two equipped divers on site. They expected to start in the next half hour and use them on rotation doing one hour long turnabouts.

By the end of tomorrow, they should have completely covered the accessible area from this crane's site. At that point, they could decide whether to widen the search area or not.

DNA results were back on the blood stains taken from the ground and on the head tissue. They showed they were from the same person. However, there were no matches with their existing

DNA database- meaning the identity of the person was still unknown. They also had foot imprints and tire tracks found at the site which may be significant. Apart from these things, the site was remarkably free of anything that might give clues.

Since it did not look like there would be much more found outside the water, the senior detective's view was they would try to wrap up the site investigation by the end of tomorrow. He agreed Alan and the pathologist should return to the site. He felt this visit should look for anything that might be a weapon and also allow an onsite review of anything significant retrieved from the water.

They may also get some further information about the most likely time for the event. And, even though it seemed a low chance to get useful information, he agreed it was worth talking to the staff at the two roadhouses located between Humpty Doo and the billabong turnoff from the Arnhem Highway.

Alan put his swag and a spare one on the back-telling himself that it was just in case something really significant turned up which required them to stop overnight. To be honest, a part of him hoped there would be a reason for them to stay in the bush-perhaps even share the same swag for a night together. But the gentleman side of him said- Sandy must be given the choice of whether to stay over and the option of her own bed if she did.

He collected her from the address she had given, a block of flats in Nightcliff. She was waiting for him out in front with a small overnight bag. He asked, "Do you need to be back tonight?"

"No. I have no commitments until work on Monday."

He told her he had put in his swag and an extra one- just in case something major arose which meant they should stay out. She nodded but, otherwise, showed nothing of her thoughts.

Now, having got his head around the state of the investigation, he filled her in on details as he drove along the Arnhem Highway. Sandy sat curled up in the passenger seat of his police vehicle.

She had tied back her hair and was wearing light, functional bush clothes: shorts, a shirt with pockets, and leather sandals which not only protected her feet, but also, showed off the rest of her long legs. He could not help glancing at her from time to time. Those smooth brown legs were eye-catching- not to mention the glimpse of pale skin where her top shirt button opened. A couple of times, she arched her back and stretched like a sleepy kitten. *Must keep my mind on work*, he thought.

She had been gently digging for information about him: girlfriends, private life, interests and family. At the same time, she volunteered information about herself: she'd graduated with good marks a year ago. She had found her initial job in Glebe Coroner's Office, Sydney was a bit stultifying. As she'd no real attachments, she'd jumped at the chance when this job in the Territory came up.

He told her he was a true blue Territorian. He'd grown up as a kid in Alice Springs but, his parents moved to Newcastle for work when he was ten. As he'd always loved the NT, he'd come back and joined the police force in Alice Springs as soon as the chance arose. He'd spent ten years gradually progressing by doing many jobs in a range of locations.

In reply to her inquiries about girlfriends, he said there had been a serious girlfriend from Alice Springs when he worked there but, she had gone off to Sydney due to wanting to live in a big city. Once there she'd soon found someone else there who liked the lifestyle. Therefore, over the last few years, he'd had various short-term girlfriends but, nothing serious. He found his work consumed most of his life.

He probed a bit in return. "Surely there was some man who was sad to see you go, and tried to keep you there?"

She shrugged her shoulders. "Well, I too, was always a bit work obsessed. I didn't seem to have much time for men. I mostly turned down the dinner invitations, using work as an excuse."

Alan raised an eyebrow, "Don't you like us blokes?"

"I think I'd my mind fixed on getting away for quite a while. I didn't want to get too attached- in case it held me back. Now I'm glad to be here, but I'm still a bit cautious about the attachment thing. I do like the idea of having my own life and career."

Alan asked, "Your seemed to enjoy last night, do you go out much, you know, socially?"

"While I don't stay at home by myself whenever I'm off work, I'm not quite the party butterfly. I do love meeting the genuine people of this place- those who have a bond with the land and like to enjoy life, people like Charlie and Elsie last night."

"It's not that I'm a prude, but I think there must be more to life than being a party person. Although it sounds corny, I want to do what I do well, do my bit to make the world better somehow."

He nodded. "I'm probably a bit like that myself."

She grinned, "I know, I think that's why I like you."

With that said, she sat up straight and lightly rested her hand on his arm casually and deliberately for just a few seconds, an unspoken sign of affection that made him feel good inside.

They decided to go straight to the site and leave questioning at the road houses until the return leg of the journey. They were both unconsciously eager to see if any new discoveries had been found. It did not seem long until they were driving up to the billabong.

As they approached the bank the cage was being lifted out of the water and into the air with a diver inside. Then, the cage was being swung back to the land.

They walked across to greet those gathered around the diver as he came out. Alan knew the site supervisor, Bill, who had come out once the murder investigation was launched. He introduced Sandy.

Once the diver had removed his tank, mask and search findings, a second diver took his place and the crate was returned to the water for the search to continue.

Now they all stood around as the first diver finished removing his wet-suit and started to unpack sample containers. Bill introduced Alan as the second-in-charge of the investigation. Alan asked the diver if he had found anything he thought was of particular importance.

As if thinking how to reply, the diver screwed up his face, "Bit hard to say really. Nothing specific; there was not anything that looked like human remains or objects that particularly related to anybody. Mostly old soft drink cans and other common rubbish.

"The one thing that did fit was in the corner closest to the bank, barely a meter out. There was a pile of stuff which looked like it was from a fireplace: charcoal and grey ashy stuff in a layer a few inches thick and a couple of feet across. It started right at the edge and ran down the slope to the bottom. While I was down there, I couldn't really tell what was in it. Therefore, I scrapped up as much as I could and put it into that bucket over there," he said, indicating a large metal bucket which was about the size of a twenty-litre drum. "Someone might want to sift through that and see if anything important is there." With that he shrugged and went off to finish sorting out his diving gear.

Alan picked up the container and carried it over to a work trestle table where there was a sieve and some shallow trays. Sandy held the sieve as he first poured off the water and then poured the sludge through. It was clearly fire residue: a fine grey ash with bits of charcoal and other fragments of small detritus.

Sandy took a couple of small samples of the sludge. First she carefully separated out each significant fragment caught in the sieve and bagged each separately. It all seemed non-specific- what you would find in any fireplace. They worked their way slowly through the pile while returning all finished samples to a second bucket.

When they were three quarters of the way through the sieving Sandy saw something glint in the light. "Aha, what is this?" she said, digging out a small metal object from the sludge. It was flat and about two centimetres long by one centimetre high. It looked like brass or bronze with an emerging green tarnish.

Sandy rinsed it in clean water. It was a small brass object. It was a bit bent and twisted as if it had been cooked in a fire, but the shape was still clear. There was a pattern which looked like letters or numbers shaped in the brass on one side- perhaps 8W.

Sandy twisted it around in her fingers to look at it from different angles and turned it up the other way.

As he processed this shape in his mind Alan realized he was looking at the letters 'MB' forming a raised profile on one side, with a flat backing plate on the other side. He looked at Sandy inquiringly, saying "I'm almost sure that is an MB".

Sandy nodded, "I think so, too." She looked at it from all angles while handling it with care. "I'm sure you're right. I don't want to damage the surface. We may be able to get expert advice about how long this has been in the water to get that tarnished. I think it looks like a set of monogrammed initials which could be attached to an object like a briefcase, to identify it in a personal way. I wonder if our gentleman was Mr. MB. It looks like someone's initials, though of course, it may just be a brand."

Sandy continued checking the remaining sludge while Alan discussed the site investigation with Bill. First, they chatted in general terms about all the organizing, staff rostering and transport.

Sandy waved them both over to show them another finding. This was clearly a combination locking mechanism from a briefcase or something similar but, the lock was twisted and only a part remained in place. There were also scrape marks on the metal indicating someone had used a heavy implement like a chisel to break it. They all nodded in agreement- these looked like parts of the same bag or briefcase from which the MB had come.

They stood watching as Sandy finished her work before coming over to join them. As she reached them, Bill said to Alan, "It's funny, this place seems too tidy for what you'd expect to find. If you go on along the side of the billabong two hundred yards to the next open camping area, you start to find the usual bits of rubbish you'd expect scattered around. Nothing much, things like bits of old paper, a cigarette butt, a bottle top, an old can, all the things a fisherman might have dropped over the last few years.

"But around this camping area- there's almost nothing. It's like someone has spent a lot of time going around, tidying and cleaning up the site in order to make sure there was no evidence left to find. It has been four or five months since it last rained. So, you'd expect to find quite a bit of stuff like animal or bird tracks in the soft dirt patches- especially this close to the water. There are the odd bits, like a lizard track over there. But, once again, if you compare it to other places nearby: there should be more. As well as picking up rubbish and other things, it's like someone has swept the dirt surface- possibly using a branch. There are even a couple of places where it looks like a person scraped the surface to remove marks. Also, there is a place where someone broke off branches a month or two ago. It could all be part of the same thing."

Sandy joined in. She was nodding as he described the swept and cleaned look. "Yes, I wondered about that when I was here two days ago. I couldn't put my finger on it clearly, the way you have now, but it did all seem a bit too tidy."

The man continued, "There's something else, and it's curious too." He led them to the edge of the water a few meters along, where the soil was soft and damp. A low branch from a bush partly obscured the view from behind. Less than half a meter back from the edge, in the soft dirt, were two well-formed footprints heavily imprinted into the soil.

"Those are the only male-sized footprints we've found older than the last couple of days. There are a few more recent ones which we assume belong to your fisherman friend, Charlie. There are also some recent tire marks which match the wheels in the photo of his car.

"I think these footprints were made by someone who was next to the water's edge between one and two months ago. You can tell they're old from the dirt, twigs and leaves which have gathered in them. They're remarkably distinct for something of that age. Also, the heel imprints are much heavier than the toe imprints- as if someone stood here looking out for a long time without moving or, more likely considering the weight distribution, they were squatting on their haunches for an extended time."

Next he led them to the depression which they noted the other day- the place where they thought the former fireplace had been. It was now covered in a plastic sheet and taped off.

"We need to protect this place- I think it could be important." He removed the sheet, pointing to a place on the ground. "I know you looked at this the other day, but then it was covered with a fine layer of dust and leaves. Now we've carefully taken that away."

Alan whistled. "I think you are right- this is really something!" Indented into the dirt, right at the edge of the fireplace depression, was a single footprint.

Bill continued. "Unless I'm mistaken- it's the footprint of a smallish woman. I would almost swear it was made at the time the fireplace was dug out. If you look carefully, you'll see the ground at the edges, where it was not dug out, has a different look to other ground around. It's like they chucked a bucket of water on the ground and then stepped on the wet ground with one foot. If it happened at another time- even a day later- the ground would've been dry and there'd be no imprint.

"My guess about what happened is that this person or persons, when they had finished using the fire to burn whatever they wanted to destroy, took a bucket of water and threw it on the fire so it was out enough to shovel the ashes into the water. Maybe they even washed themselves off in the same place too. In the process, they left us a clear footprint of a right foot. I suspect at least one of the people here was a woman. If we can find this woman, I would bet her foot will be an exact match of this imprint.

"Perhaps it was a woman who killed the man in a lover's tiff. Before she drove away, she decided to feed his body to the crocodiles and hide or destroy any other evidence, so no one knew she'd been here. I won't hang my hat on it, not just yet, but it's an explanation of sorts."

It was both food for thought and a new angle to anything Alan had considered thus far.

As they walked back to the table, where a person with a notepad was cataloguing all the diver's finds, Bill said, "I've just one more thing to show you, a couple of tire track marks, a bit limited but still worth a look."

He led them out of the clearing and back up the road for fifty yards. The road made a sharp turn around a big tree and across a drainage line similar to a small creek. The earth in this area was still slightly damp. It was a road driven over by many during the last few days. At the very extreme left edge, as they walked towards it, someone had placed an orange road marker. "Just to ensure no one else drives over the exact same place," Bill said.

Under the marker, in slightly damp soil, was a footlong tread pattern which was half a tire wide. Bill said, "This is a standard Land Cruiser tire tread- nothing remarkable about it. There are about ten million of these tires in the NT. But- note that place just there. See the hole in the tread pattern? It is like a bit of the rubber has come away from the outside of the tire. It looks like a back tire track made when someone, who was driving away, cut this corner a bit hard. Someone unfamiliar with the place or vehicle could easily do it- particularly if driving at night when they weren't quite sure where the road went.

"Even though the tracks look about the right age, there's nothing to prove this was made by that specific car. In reality, it looks like very few people come in here due to the closed gate. From your description of Charlie's vehicle, this track wasn't made by it. Not to mention, the track age is wrong. If you can find the vehicle in which these people came here, I would say it's a fair bet this track will let us tie it to the scene."

After telling this, Bill gave a big, expansive grin. "God, I love this job! We get all the clever ones like this: people who think that no one will ever know. Yet, there's always something they miss. I love to find it! Especially once I get the scent of a clever murderer in my nostrils….. or perhaps it could be a murderess in this case?"

By the time Bill finished his tour, it was abundantly clear he had gleaned everything anyone would find from this site. And, if there was anything more, he would find it, too. The real challenge would be to identify this person who came from the water. For this, they now had the initials MB as a maybe starting point. It was not much but, perhaps, it would take them somewhere.

As they came back, the diving cage was returning with the second diver emerging. He had collected a bit more detritus, but nothing was deemed significant. They would now break for lunch for half an hour. Afterwards, they would move out from the edge. This was the central part of the billabong closest to where the head had been found. Bill thought this meant it was the most likely area to find other body parts.

Sandy and Alan decided they would wait for the results of this next dive before heading back to town. Therefore, after sharing a sandwich with the rest of the work crew, they started walking along the edge of the billabong- making sure to stay in the shade of thick paperbark trees located a few meters away from the water.

They walked side by side while enjoying the shade, the cool and each other's company. This was the first time they had been alone together with nothing specific to do. Sandy moved in close as they walked, almost touching, as if inviting more. Alan felt an impulse to take her hand or rest his arm on her shoulder. His hand brushed hers as he went to take it. His foot caught a root- tipping him off balance. She reached out to steady him. Without any thought, he pulled back to rebalance and, in the process, straightened his body away from her.

Sandy stepped away in order to put her own distance back in place. Now, there was an awkwardness between them which hadn't existed before. Alan felt a desire to progress their relationship but, was uncertain how to do so. They walked on a few hundred yards until they were well out of sight of the others. Alan felt he should say something. However, he was not sure how to begin.

They stopped under a huge shady tree with an open gap leading to the water to survey the absolute stillness together for a minute. There was not a single breath of air, not a ripple on the water, nor the sound of a bird or an insect. In an eerie way, it was both placid and beautiful.

Alan said, indicating to the water, "It's hard to believe a place so apparently calm and lovely can be so dangerous."

Sandy walked around in front of him, in order to face him, while looking up at his face. "Yes, I see what you mean. Standing here in this place gives an illusion of calm, but there is a whole other world living under the surface. I am glad to share this place with you. It feels good being here with you- just the two of us."

As they walked back towards camp, he put his arm around her shoulders and she put her arm around his waist. *It's such a lovely companionable feeling,* he thought. When they were about halfway there, she stopped and separated from him. She then came up to him on tiptoes and kissed him on the lips. "That's a first step to a beginning of a promise for another day," she said.

"I hope so," he replied, wanting to return the kiss but holding back. As he looked over her head towards the water, he sensed something was watching them. Off in the distance, far across the billabong, and directly opposite where they stood, were the same set of eyes he had seen watching him last time.

Alan thought the creature would stay in the distance, watching them. Then he noticed the eyes were getting closer. First, they were far out, much closer to the other side. Soon they had moved halfway across the billabong, heading directly towards them.

By now most of the head and the scale tips from the body and tail were becoming visible. The tail was lazily waving from side to side. It steadily continued getting closer and bigger. Originally, Alan thought it was large, but now he knew it was absolutely huge. In his life, he had seen many crocodiles- including some that others had referred to as big. This one, however, was much larger. Its head was twice the size of all the others he had seen. He could only just glimpse the body as it followed behind the enormous head.

By now it was barely 20 meters from where they stood and was still powering towards them. Alan took Sandy's arm to pull her back several paces into the trees. At the same time, he unclipped his revolver. It was done in reflex- although he had no confidence about its stopping power against this huge behemoth of a monster.

He was considering grabbing Sandy's hand and running with her well back in the trees until he realised it had finally slowed and was turning to swim along the bank. A bare five meters from the water's edge, it passed by them. As it did it slowed, until it was stationary. Motionless in the water, this giant creature stayed there while seeming to slowly drift towards the edge.

It was directly opposite now. They were ten meters back from the water and the monster was a mere one to two metres from the edge. Alan tried to estimate its length. It was surely more than twenty feet long. Picturing its length laid out on a roadway alongside a car, he guessed nearer to 25 feet would be a closer estimate. That figure seemed about right.

Its girth was even more striking than its length. He imagined the volume of three or four 200 litre drums set end to end. There was more bulk to its body than those drums- without even allowing for the head and tail. His best guess was he was looking at two tons of crocodile measuring around 25 feet in length.

It seemed very aware of their presence. A couple of times it half turned its head so it could look at them with both eyes. Despite all this, it did not show aggressive intent towards them. Even though it was still, he sensed it was communicating soundlessly. He could have sworn it had a spirit which was trying to send him a message.

Sandy whispered to him, "It's feels like it's trying to talk to us. I am getting pictures inside my mind of a life force coming from it, saying, 'This body which you've found belongs to me. Taking it is taking part of my spirit.' It's like it's asking us to return to it what belongs to it."

Alan felt something similar inside his own mind, too. Whenever he looked across at the crocodile, it was still there like a huge, immobile presence. He knew he could reach out to touch it if he went to the water's edge. His found his mind wondering, if he did, would it have a solid form with hard knobbed skin and scales under his hand? Or was it just something conjured from the light and shadows which sat at the joining place of the water and air.

Twice it opened its mouth in an apparent huge yawn which showed row upon row of yellow peg like structures. Each one was a tooth an inch across and several inches apart. A few times, it blinked a slit eye or made tiny twitches of nostrils, as if it was tasting the air.

Finally, as they were starting to wonder where this would all end, it slowly submerged until only the barest tip of nostrils was showing. With slow purpose, the nostrils began to move away from them. After a few more meters, they vanished, too.

Barely believing the reality of what they had seen, Alan and Sandy stood motionless for a minute. Then they walked slowly back to camp in awed silence.

As they came close to camp, Alan said to Sandy, "It's like Charlie told me; there's a huge crocodile in this place which has a spirit which can leave its body. I'm not normally superstitious- but there's more to this than just a huge crocodile. It's as if we've met an ancient creature of the dreamtime, some original ancestor spirit being from which came all other crocodiles. If it's OK with you, I don't plan to say anything about this to the others back at camp. I feel we were imparted with a private secret from this creature- whatever it means."

Sandy nodded. "I'm with you. I don't think anyone who hadn't seen it would believe us anyway. Maybe they might almost believe you, but if I said it, I reckon they'd think I had an overactive imagination. Instead it will be a story to tell our children one day."

Alan laughed. "So, we'll have children to tell- I like it!"

Sandy blushed. "It was just a figure of speech."

"I'll choose to consider it prophetic," Alan mocked.

As they came back to the camp, the cage was in again. However, nothing further had been found.

As there was really nothing further for them to do, they could have chosen to leave at this stage. But, somehow, it seemed this place had more to reveal and so they should not leave yet.

Alan checked with Bill whether it was okay for them to camp out with the rest of the crew for the night. Bill replied, "We're doing the last dive for today now- that's three for each diver. Then, we're planning to go into the Bark Hut Inn for dinner and a cold beer before returning here for our sleep. The divers have rooms in the Inn for the night, in order to get a good night's sleep away from the mosquitoes.

"You're welcome to come with us for dinner. We'll leave one of the men, our most junior constable, to maintain camp security while we're away. So you can either stay with him or come in with us. If you want to stay, there's beer and steaks in the camp fridge."

Alan said, "Why don't you take all the crew to the pub for dinner. We'll stay and keep guard."

Bill said, "Well, if you don't mind, that sounds like a great idea. I know young James is less than thrilled in the idea of staying here while we're gone: something about seeing crocodiles in his mind. I told him to sit in the car if he got scared."

Another cage came up empty and soon all the men had packed up to go. Now it was just Alan and Sandy. They enjoyed the still evening while eating a steak washed down by a couple of beers, taking pleasure in each other's company. It was like a dinner date except it was here. They talked at leisure with no pressure for anything more.

About nine pm, both began to yawn. Alan unrolled the two swags and set up two mosquito nets, pitched from the side of the car, but a couple of yards apart. He half-wished Sandy would offer to let him share her swag, but he knew he had to give her space.

Soon they heard an engine noise and saw a flicker of lights through the trees. The others were back. Bill walked over and said, "Some of the lads wanted to kick on but I told them they need to be up and fresh in the morning. With luck, we'll be finished here by around lunchtime and can be back in our own beds tomorrow night. So, with only a small bit of grumbling, they all came back and our divers headed off to bed so they can make an early start."

Bill joshed Alan, "Two swags, eh? I thought you two might be an item, but looks more likely not."

Alan replied, "Not this one, she's a cut above my class- or at least for a one-nighter. Maybe, she's a keeper."

Bill winked. "Well, I'll be leaving you for my own swag." He walked off with a torch towards the other side of the clearing where the others had made their camp.

Sandy had retired to her own mosquito net, so Alan climbed under his net. He lay for a few minutes listening to the night noises.

He must have slept for several hours because, when he awoke, the camp was fully dark. The fire had died down and all the other lights were off. It had an almost morning feeling.

He realized Sandy was outside his net, whispering, "Alan, can I come in? I've had a most scary, terrible dream. I'm feeling freaked."

He lifted the side of the net and she slid in next to him. She was wearing satiny pyjamas which felt incredibly sheer. As she slid down beside him, her top slipped up in the shadowy light. He could see the faint outline of breasts just in front of his face. He pushed his face into them while sliding his hands up her back under her night top.

She wrapped her arms around him and pushed her body against his. "Just hold me close until this awful dream goes away."

They lay together, side by side, with the full length of their bodies touching and her face pushed into his neck. She was shivering even though it was not cold. He ran his fingers through

62

her hair, along her back and down the bare skin of her buttock by sliding his hand under her nightie bottoms.

As her shivering abated, she said, "I must tell you while it's clear in my mind- lest I forget tomorrow. I dreamt I was a girl who knew this man we found and I was at this same place at night. I loved this man even though he terrified me.

"I dreamt I was lying here, tied up and captive. I saw the man over by the water talking to that huge crocodile we saw today. He promised it that, in the morning when the sun began to rise, it would be given its next meal. I was sure the meal was me. I knew I was tied up so, when morning came, he'd give me to the crocodile.

"The man and crocodile were like brothers- sharing one spirit. I knew it would be daylight soon. Then, I'd go into the belly of that awful creature. I was so, so scared. A knot of terror was running through my whole body. I couldn't cry. I couldn't think. I was just so afraid.

"Then, thankfully, I woke up. I saw your outline and heard your breathing as you slept. I wanted to come next to you and feel you hold me tight. So just hold me please until the horrible terror goes away."

Alan cuddled and stroked her in the same way he would to soothe a child. He was very aware of her body next to him. He also knew she was aware of his arousal. However, this was a moment too precious to spoil by seeking more. Therefore, he just held her close while he whispered comforting nothings in her ear. At last, he felt her body relax and her breathing return to a slow sleep state. Listening to her breathing created a trance- like state in which he fell asleep, too.

He woke when the daylight was barely lighting the eastern sky. Sandy had just moved her body inside the circle of his arms which is what had roused him.

He looked at her intently. She opened her eyes and looked at him. In the early light, she seemed both beautiful and vulnerable. He stroked her hair. She kissed him lightly on the cheek.

"Thank you for minding me in the night. It is good to feel safe when something like that happens. I must return to my own swag. The night is past. Whatever is between us will have to wait for another time."

When Alan woke next time, the sun was breaking the horizon. Sandy was rolling up her swag. He started to wonder if he'd imagined her late-night visit.

He called out, "Hello."

She crossed the distance between them while wearing a bright smile. She lifted the net and kissed him on the mouth before sitting down alongside him. "Thank you so much for minding me carefully in the night. I felt so safe sleeping alongside you. Also, thank you for being such a gentleman."

This statement made him realize it had not been a dream.

Sandy continued, "I think the dream came from walking along the river and seeing that huge crocodile yesterday. The water surface was so calm and yet something dangerous was just beneath the surface.

I suppose, in a way, that sort of describes us too. On the surface, we're placid like the water. In our work, we get on beautifully together. That's all on the outside. Underneath it all, there's a dangerous place we have to cross- that path from friends to maybe something more.

"Some people seem to find it easy. It's like they can take that step without having to give anything real of themselves. But- I'm not like that. I want to take that next step, but that part of me is scared. I've always run away from men when it got to this stage before. The fear in my mind tells me to run from you, too.

"But, since last night, my body calls me to stay. My emotions say to stay, too. So, I must decide and I need you to help me. I want to go the next step with you and perhaps be your lover. I desire to be your lover, but I don't want to give my body to you just for sex.

"So, I want you to tell me- is it just a physical thing you want with me? Or is there something real and deeper in what we have together? Please be honest with me as I've tried to be with you."

Alan was sort of blown away. This was all much deeper and much faster than he could have imagined. *Did he want to have sex with her? Yes-most definitely! Did he want something more with her?* He thought so, but it was only two days since they had met. Maybe it was a bridge too far to get to that place yet. First and foremost, however, he could not mislead her. He had to give her truth for truth.

Therefore, he told her what he knew for a fact. He wanted her for both her body and her mind. "You are beautiful and I do really want the physical part with you, to make love to you."

I feel that in just two days, we have already crossed many bridges together. If we are going to spend more of their lives being together, however long it ends up being, this is yet one more bridge we have to cross, the sex part. Every time I look at you or touch you, I really want to share this part too, to join our bodies and make love to you.

But I only want to do it when you are ready too, this is the thing I am most sure of, after only two days with you.

She smiled a beatific smile at him and said, "I asked for truth and I have truth- that's enough. If you had promised me eternal love and happiness- I would've known that was not the truth.

"My mind says that neither of us is sure enough to cross that bridge yet. So we should wait. The future will be what the future will be: but it will have begun with the truth."

Then, she looked at him very directly and said, "Can you wait a bit longer until my mind is as ready as my body?"

In a strange way, Alan was relieved. It was not, in any way, that his desire for her had diminished. Instead, her intensity of emotion and honesty conveyed something more powerful and significant than what he had experienced with other women before.

In response to her question, he gave her a light punch on the shoulder. "First of all: we're friends since you caught me out about the fish and did not tell. Secondly, we're workmates who can do great work together. Then, last of all, there is something else between us. It's feels like a spark which has quickly grown into a small fire. One day, it may grow into a raging bushfire which will have to be satisfied. For now, however, it can be fed with small things: such as a wish, a kiss and a promise for another day."

The morning passed with an edge of unreality. He was so aware of Sandy and knew she was the same with him. It was like the night before had sealed a pact between them.

Yet, they waited quietly while seeking any other offerings from the crocodile god- this is how they both now thought of the huge creature. The first cage search came up empty. There were three more planned until they had covered the full area the crane could reach. Once that was done they would have to decide whether to move along the bank or go further out from it.

Ten minutes into the next dive, there was suddenly a shout from the crane driver. He lifted the cage clear.

"Look what I've found," the diver called out while freeing his head from the mask. He held up a white elongated object.

They realized it was a lower human arm. It looked like it began at the elbow and went down from there. The skin and most of the muscle was gone, but sinews and bones remained. The ends of fingers, in contrast, were mostly missing. It almost looked like a curiosity one would find in a junk shop- like some strange sort of weird voodoo back scratcher. There was no mistaking, though, the fact this was part of a person: probably the same person the head belonged to.

Sandy made a cursory examination before bagging it and putting it in an esky with ice. "Well, it looks like I should get this back to the lab. I expect it belongs to the same person. It's the right size for the man to whom the head belonged. Interestingly, there's a bump on one of the bones of the forearm, the ulna. It could be an indication of an old break which healed unevenly."

Then, Sandy turned to Alan. She gave him a funny little smile and asked, "Any chance of a girl getting a lift home so that she can get on with her other job?"

In five minutes, they were driving away after having said a hasty goodbye to all. Once they were out of sight of the camp, Sandy said, "I know that was a bit sudden, but once we'd found the arm I knew that was all that we're going to get. What I wanted was for you to bring me home. We can call quickly to the lab to drop off the sample. After that I want you to come with me to my little flat and stay with me for the rest of the day and night. I've been thinking about the feel of your body next to mine ever since I woke up. I don't want to wait a minute longer to feel your body next to me again. So, if you still want me, I want you too. Just be kind to me as I don't know much about what we're going to do. I do know I want it to be with you- whatever happens after today."

As they drove back to Darwin, Sandy cuddled into his side with his arm around her. Once she placed his hand on her breast.

In the bedroom he discovered she'd never been with a man before. It felt like a first time for him too. It was the first time he had made love to this woman who he was totally hooked on. It was the best afternoon and night of his life. At dawn, as they lay together in a tangle of bodies and sheets, he told her this fact.

Chapter 6 – Crocodile Dreams

Susan fell asleep on the Saturday night feeling as if the day had been a huge roller coaster. She replayed all the events in her mind.

A day when she'd woken in the morning feeling good about herself, enjoying September sunshine spilling through her bedroom window as she woke dreamily from the night, feeling warm and mellow as she savoured the first flush of a weekend off work.

Then, came the jolt of shocked realisation concerning the absence of her period. This was quickly followed by her looking into the mirror where she saw the unmistakable changes in her body that showed her what was happening. With it came a dawning revelation: she knew she was almost certainly pregnant with that awful man's child.

She'd driven to the chemist to get a pregnancy test kit and watched as the definite line emerged. Seeing that there'd been no doubting it: she was indeed pregnant. Her horror had caused her to think through the meaning and consequences of such a pregnancy. It led her to what seemed like a clear plan for a termination.

But before she'd acted, she'd made an impulsive decision to read David's letter- which had sat unopened in her room for almost a month. The letter informed her David would be in England next week. *Was it even remotely possible he could be the father instead?*

She'd sent a quickly typed email suggesting they could meet up on Tuesday. Within a minute, her mobile phone was ringing with David on the line. She'd thought he would email back. Obviously, he was nothing if not direct and determined.

He said, "I'm struggling to believe it's really you after over a month of silence. I wanted to hear your voice again, to know it's really you. I'm still pinching myself with surprise to hear from you at this late stage and to know I'll be seeing you in a couple of days. I can't wait."

There was something so utterly delightful about his call. When she put down the phone, she was smiling all over. There was a warmness and immediacy to his voice. He sounded so, well, like himself: a mixture of charm and courtesy combined with an edge of Aussie humour and directness. He did not really chastise her for being tardy- just a slight ribbing. However, he did tell her he had been sitting on the edge of his seat for a month hoping to hear from her. As days and weeks continued to drift by, he had been starting to feel discouraged.

He said, "Since I have verified you are actually there and available to meet with me, I don't intend to leave anything to chance. I won't let you get away from me again so easily this time. I intend to wow and dazzle you with lots of good times. I promise the best of everything money and attention can buy."

She had said, "Slow down, David. It sounds great but let me catch my breath. I'm overwhelmed. It's unexpected- but very nice."

His reply, "It's so English to say 'Nice' to refer to the blast we will surely soon have!"

She sensed he would throw all his effervescent life force at making the best of this opportunity, in order to sweep her off her feet and win her over with a fun time. She loved the sense of her value and level of attraction to this man which led him to give her all this attention.

It was a buzz being courted by such a devastatingly charming man: one who intended to lavish personal and material charms on her. She felt flattered. She liked the idea of being the object of an unconstrained willingness to treat her this way.

She could still feel herself glowing as she got off the phone. Her mind was consumed with digesting his slightly brash plans. He'd even convinced her to meet him for dinner on Monday night in the city. He'd said he would arrange for a chauffeur to collect her when she finished work for the day.

After wanting to see her so much during the past seven weeks, he said her he did not plan to waste another day. He would only be fobbed off if she admitted to having a prior engagement. If this was the case, he would be happy to meet her later in the evening. Secretly, she felt delighted anyone wanted to be with her this much. After a bland month at home, his determination to delight her was a breath of fresh air.

By evening, her family all knew of his plans to visit- even her gran! Susan asked them all come to a family dinner on Tuesday to meet David. Without being specific, she gave enough details to let them understand his importance. He was more than just a casual friend from Australia. After all, she'd agreed to go travelling with him for a week in the English countryside- not quite something one would do with casual acquaintances or almost strangers.

As if to put the icing on the cake, David immediately told Susan's cousin, Ruth, in Australia. It must have been after midnight there. Ruth had called immediately to express her approval. The news was directly given to Susan's mum, who had picked up the call from her favourite niece. So, even before Susan mentioned David's existence to her parents, the cat was out of the bag.

The ribbing from Tim was ferocious. "What Sis- I asked you at the airport where the Aussie boyfriend was? Nothing was in sight and no mention was said then. Suddenly, a month later, he appears out of thin air. He's obviously of great importance if you can take a week out of a busy life just for him. He must be a real 'Mr. Special' to get you to give up a whole week of your precious time. Not something I remember you doing for any of the others!"

Susan could only laugh. It was hard to get cross with others trying to tease her when she felt so unexpectedly upbeat. It seemed as if the idea of an unwanted pregnancy was now buried in one of the deepest recesses of her mind. All she could think about now was seeing David again and simply spending time with him. She loved the mind image this invited: the two of them happily driving through green England with the blowing wind sweeping her hair back from her face.

Only after she'd settled into bed and lay there for a minute, thinking of the day, did she come down slightly from the top of the roller coaster. A brief image came of driving in another place of terror with another man- which she quickly pushed away. England was not that place of terror- it was a safe place. And David was not that man either- he was fully trustworthy, decent and known. Her cousin Ruth had vouched for his good character.

In her dreamy state, she also briefly remembered another whole other reality she still must confront soon. After this thought, she pushed her concerns back out of her mind. She was determined not to look further at this future problem until necessity required it. Susan drifted off to sleep with a smile on her face.

She knew, without a doubt, she was asleep in her bed in England. It felt so safe, snug and secure. Then, all of a sudden, there was another creature or being in her dream. It had a powerful determination to bring her away from this place. She protested weakly but, for some unknown reason, could not organize her mind or body to actively resist. She felt strong arms lift and carry her into the sky above her house. She looked down. Her body lay sleeping in her bed.

She felt herself being carried across the world. She headed through the early dark of England into a deeper and deeper night as she travelled east across the globe. They followed a path which led mostly over water while the distant shapes of countries of the Mediterranean, Arabian Gulf and Indian Ocean passed to the sides. The tip of India flashed by while far north she glimpsed high, snow covered mountains on the roof of the world. Then, they skirted along the vast island chain of Indonesia. It was a moonless sky with only the faintest starlight illuminating their passage.

As they began to descend, she sensed night was almost over here. It was still dark, but with an almost imperceptible lightening of the furthest eastern sky. It was as if dawn was only another hour or two away. Sunshine was shining in a more distant place now- somewhere out over another ocean. In the dark, she could sense rather than see the fact they had left behind ocean and were now over land. Street lights glittered briefly before fading. They were descending over a large slow-flowing river. Susan realized it was full of crocodiles due to seeing their eyes reflecting starlight. She was not really frightened even though she felt a prickle of anxiety at the edge of her consciousness.

At last the awful place from before came into view. She knew this billabong. She'd never seen it from above- yet she knew it. It exuded a presence which left no uncertainty. Without a doubt in her mind, this was the place of the fatal last night. A night including both hope and devastation which ended with ripping and tearing clarity as the new day rose. She felt the terror of the last time she'd been here rising to meet her. She had been chained and restrained while he brooded with his crocodile soul to perform an unholy twinning. She sensed this monstrous spirit rise to meet the spirit which carried her. It felt like a meeting of kindred souls, which were bonded together as one, through a distant ancestor ritual.

Now, however, there were others in this place. She saw a large crane rising into the sky and several Toyotas parked around the area. Why were they here? There was even one Toyota, white like the other one, but without the box and cage. She was drawn towards it. At its farthest side, there were two mosquito nets. She sensed two bodies slumbering. They were a man and a woman who were connected but still separate- not yet lovers. The woman reached out her mind from her own dream. In response, Susan went to her, linked mind to mind.

Memories flooded back to her: the terror of captivity, the delight of final lovemaking, empty eyes and the knife. These were followed by ones of a new day involving unbelievable desolation, terror, rage and hate all mingled with such an overwhelming loss.

She realized these memories were flowing directly from her mind into this woman she was seeing in the bed. Now this woman was living within Susan's own terror as these memories washed through her. In this memory, a giant crocodile rose to tear the body from the others, in order to claim its own possession.

Susan came to an abrupt realization: she must not inflict these memories on the other woman. By opening the view into this part of her mind, she'd exposed the madness which lay there.

She tore her mind away immediately. In doing so, the girl awoke from her dream into real life terror- essentially turning reality into a nightmare. Susan saw her stumble out of her own bed and go into the comforting arms of her soon- to- be lover. Susan felt an uncomplicated goodness in this embrace along with a burning regret at her own loss.

However, the arms which held her now would not leave her there. They were also comforting arms. She could sense these arms belonged to a yearning spirit which sought to bring her into its own embrace. There was indeed a part of her which wanted nothing but to fall into the depth of this embrace. She could feel the kindred yearning within her own spirit to retaste this prior love. As she started to slide into this comfort place, however, she realized it was not just one spirit: but two. Both spirits were trying to hold and own her- one was a man and one was a crocodile. Both of them were currently grieving. The man spirit was grieving for the loss of her while the crocodile spirit was grieving for the loss of the man. They were bonded and yet, at the same time, trying to pull apart. She was the prize in the middle of an eternal love triangle where none of them could possibly reach peace.

Eventually, Susan felt the connection snap. It felt as if the force of her will had resisted these powerful entreaties to the point in which she had now been able to break free. With this freedom, however, came a profound sense of loss returning. Although separate, a part of her was left behind in the embrace- creating a forever lost part. She ached to be held by this man and loved by this man- if only just once more. Without a doubt, though, she knew if she went back into the embrace of this man- she could never return.

At this point, Susan woke in her bed with the dream still fresh in her mind. With certainty, she knew the powerful arms which had carried her in the dream were those of Mark. In the dark of night, her body suddenly craved to feel his touch again. She wondered if he'd sensed the new life within her even from the beyond. After all, it was a part continuance of his spirit.

She felt she needed to tell him this new life was a part of him that lived on. He was fading now and she did not think he'd heard her or knew of it at all. As it was still the dark of night, she kept on dreaming. This time, in contrast, she followed a different path from when they had first met which led to them living a happy life together, one involving small children playing noisily at their feet.

She stirred again. This dream had faded way too fast. In its wake, there remained only an aching loneliness. She could feel wet tears on her cheeks. She fervently wished to wake up tomorrow in a happy place, one where all this night had been simply a dream which existed no more, blown to nothingness by a new day's light.

GRAHAM WILSON

Chapter 7 – David – England

Susan wakes on Sunday morning with very mixed emotions. She is surprised how far she has come up and down the roller coaster of emotion over last night. Now she feels full of anticipation at seeing David again. In the morning light, her dream is a distant and unreal memory. It's left a faint edge of anxiety but, otherwise, seems very far away. However, it has changed something inside her. She now has glimpsed a future that is no longer a safe place, but somewhere full of many dark shadows.

She tries to think through what her reservations are. She realises they are mainly to do with her own honesty about the situation. She does not believe, at all, in her heart, this child she's carrying could be David's child. With near certainty, she knows Mark is the father. Yesterday, she'd tried to delude herself into believing a lie. She'd been crafting a fiction to allow for David being the father as a significant possibility. Reality, however, would surely prove it otherwise.

She has a sense she'd been very fickle in her relationships with both David and Mark. More honesty is required, at least within herself. It's as if the dream has released her from being unable to think clearly of Mark. Since she's returned, she's blocked all traces of him from her life and her mind. While there have been vague dreams of crocodiles and terror, Mark has been missing.

This clearly can't continue now. Not only because of the child she's carrying but because it is untrue to her real emotions. She had fallen in love with him as a real person. She can no longer pretend this emotion was not real. She knows, despite all which has transpired, a large part of her loves him still. She also knows a part of him loved her, although it appears his emotions were defective. Dismissing all of this to simply turn him into an imaginary monster does not do justice to either his or her true feelings.

Mark was a torn person. He had been torn between crocodile and human love along with being torn between gentle kindness and danger. But Mark was a real person which meant he was made of both the good and bad parts. She must accept who he was in order to reconcile her life beyond him.

At the same time, her mind also tells her he needs to be left aside. This belief is not out of anger or hatred: it is simply because her life has moved on. She has to try to deal with David honestly. She needs to see if there is something real and based on truth between the two of them which can grow into something more. She knows, without any doubt, her pregnancy must come out to him. She does not intend to reveal it to him in their first minute together: but the truth of her current state needs to be told before he leaves. She must be honest enough to tell him the odds are almost certain the child is not his. However, she does not see how Mark can be discussed at all. Regardless, she needs to be open about having had another relationship while she was in Australia and the likelihood the child had arisen from this other relationship.

Having reached this clear place in her mind, Susan feels better about David coming to visit. She knows he really seems to like her and she feels a great affection for him. She remembers again her evaluation of him in Sydney, concluding he was a good and honourable man who was a hunk. Therefore, it is now time to just enjoy the visit.

At lunchtime on Monday, David rings her to confirm the time and place to collect her after work. As his broad Aussie accent booms out, Susan can't help but become excited at the thought of dinner with him in only a few hours.

After she has changed out of her work clothes into her favourite evening dress, the phone rings to announce the car's arrival at precisely the agreed upon time. A chauffeur-driven Rolls waits in the driveway. David is not in the car due to his meeting having another half hour left. Despite this fact, she and he should both arrive at the restaurant at about the same time. Susan sits back into the plush leather, soaking in its luxurious ambience as they glide smoothly through London traffic. The restaurant is in a five-star hotel. The doorman welcomes her and shows her to the bar where he precedes to serve her a drink.

She's just starting her drink when David stands before her holding a dozen red roses. He is wearing a dinner suit and looks mind-blowingly fabulous: bronzed and fit, tousled sun-bleached hair above a trademark grin. Her smile of delight is spontaneous.

The evening is truly lovely. They have plenty to talk about and news to tell one another without making more than a passing mention of the prior Australian outback trip. Even when talking about the trip, Susan finds she can tell of the places she has seen, such as Uluru, without any need for Mark to intrude. At the end of the night it seems like, by some mutual decision, they decide not rush to intimacy, to let whatever this thing is between them evolve on its own, in its own time, assuming it is meant to evolve at all. By midnight, Susan is home in her own bed.

Dinner on the following night is equally enjoyable. David arrives early and Susan greets him. Her mother is busy in the kitchen and the others are yet to come home. Susan shows him to the spare back room. David professes his delight with having a simple room in a home rather than a five-star luxury hotel room. They sit on a couch in the living room for a few minutes chatting while he lightly holds her hand. There is a warm simplicity in his company. She impulsively likes being with him.

Soon she hears her father and Gran come in together. She brings David out and introduces him around. Her father opens by saying he wondered who owned the flash show room car in the drive. He first thought a car salesman had come to visit.

David, unabashed, roars laughing. "It's the same as my car in Sydney- which I love. It's great to drive even if some of my mates take the Mickey out of me for being uppity. They tell me I'm from country bunyip aristocracy coming to lord it over the city folks. However, you are right: I rented it straight off the showroom floor.

It's my attempt to impress Susan when we go travelling. I'm equally happy driving a beat-up old four-wheel drive on the farm."

Then, David tosses her father the keys and says, "Well how about it? Let's take it for a spin. I'm sure you must know your way around this neighbourhood so you should drive."

They all pile into the car. Susan and her gran are in the back while David sits alongside her dad in the front in order to give a few simple instructions about the controls. They roar off into a balmy September evening with the top open. They do a whole circuit of the town before returning home, finishing with a drive alongside the Thames River.

Her father is laughing in delight as they return to their house. "I understand why you enjoy it so much," he says with a huge grin.

David and her father seem to have more natural affinity than there was with her ex-boyfriend, Edward. Good-humoured banter seems to come naturally between them. Her mum is thoroughly charmed too due to the fact he has brought her flowers tonight. Tim seems a bit in awe of this successful but convivial man. And her gran and David are trading Aussie tales of farm and country life like it is second nature. Her gran tells how she began life as a farmer's daughter. As such, she visited some Australian cattle and sheep stations in her early years- giving her a sense of the place. Over dinner, all of them take part in the planning of Susan and David's travel itinerary. It includes visiting a succession of historic places through the Midlands, Wales and Cornwall before being back for Sunday evening dinner.

At the end of the night, she is tempted to follow David into his room, wanting to spend the night with him. David wants it as well, as shown by the way he looks at her. Despite their shared desire, she reminds herself not to rush anything. Tomorrow night they will be on their own. Their first night alone again seems like it will be the right time to return to physical intimacy. Therefore, she kisses him lightly as he goes off to bed; saying, "Just one more night."

On Wednesday morning, they head off on their trip early, waving goodbye to all after a quick breakfast. It begins with a leisurely drive though autumn colours heading west from London. They are planning to visit Stonehenge in the morning and a castle in the afternoon.

The morning drifts along in bright sunshine as they wander through the ancient stones and drive with wind in their hair. Susan feels the physical chemistry of attraction passing between them. A tiny, nagging part of her mind says this is fickle, too fast and too soon. However, a big part says- *We've already been lovers, why not again?* Her body confirms this with a big 'Yes' as she steals sidelong glances at this gorgeous man.

While eating lunch at a pub, Susan says she does not require her own room for the night because she is looking forward to a night where the two of them are together again. As they drive towards the fading afternoon sun, she lightly rests a hand on David's arm or shoulder every so often. A couple of times, he stops the car at high places and they walk out across hillsides together with his arm around her.

In the late afternoon, as they look out towards a rolling hillside landscape, Susan says, "I think it's time we find a place to spend the night. I want to eat a slow dinner looking at you. Then, I want a slow night of making love to you."

David said, "Wow, that thought blows my mind."

They stop at the next village. It has a quaint country pub with climbing roses and ivy rambling over stone walls. They are given an upstairs room with a view out the back showing rolling fields of sheep. The hotelier departs to leave them to the room.

Susan closes the door, saying, "I've changed my mind. I hope it's OK with you."

David looks uncertain and a bit disappointed. "Do you want your own room tonight?"

"No, silly goose, I don't want to wait any longer. I want you to make love to me right now. You looked so handsome in your Tweed Jacket in the afternoon sunlight. I want you now."

It is beautiful and tender lovemaking. His strong body covers hers while he is taking her slowly, caressing her to build her pleasure. He feels huge and exquisite inside her. They move with increasing urgency until they climax together. They order room service before another period of lovemaking. After their second round, they fall into a deep and satisfied sleep.

In the early morning light, Susan admires David's naked body which already has an erection. He sleeps on in a dreamy sleep. She places herself over it and slides it within her. This wakes him and they ride the pleasure wave together: she above him with his strong hands gripping and pushing her buttocks in rhythm until they spend themselves again. This is followed by more sleep.

The days and nights pass in something of a blur. It is a week of glorious autumn weather with the countryside showing off a mass of autumn colours. The days, despite being cool, are mostly filled with sunshine with only brief showers and clouds. For Susan, it is like a rediscovery of her homeland as seen through another's eyes.

David is full of appreciation for both her and the country. He says he appreciates this land for its natural beauty and history. Towards her he shows a sort of puppy love which she finds winsome in this mature and accomplished man. As they drive, David tells her how some of the hill vistas remind him of his home at the back of the Blue Mountains, a place of wild mountainsides and lush sheltered valleys.

They walk in high mountains, visit coastal towns and villages with Welsh signs and go to a performance of a Welsh choir in a historic mining town. They chat to local farmers and fishermen who are delighted with David's accent- even though many words on both sides are foreign to one another. Their second night, in a cottage high in the Brecon Beacons National Park, in the mountains of Wales gives them comfort, privacy and intimacy all in one space. Their togetherness, comfort with one another and the naturalness of their lovemaking all grow strongly in this superb natural setting.

Next morning they return back across the Severn River and drive into Bristol. They explore this bustling city for a couple of hours then go on to Bath, renowned for its Roman architecture, where they stop for lunch and sightseeing. In the early afternoon, they head to Cheddar, a beautiful little town set within the lush hills of Somerset.

It is a major tourist centre known for its famous cheddar cheese and limestone gorge and caves. Susan tells David it is one of the most significant sites of prehistory due to a 9,000-year-old Cheddar man being found there and deemed the oldest human skeleton found in Britain. She knows this information from having studied this find and other early English finds while at university. However, she has never been to this place and has always wanted to see it with her own eyes. David seems equally interested. He admits to previously toying with the idea of studying archaeology or anthropology, too. Since then, he has maintained an active private interest in these topics. This means they can converse on all the technical detail with ease. They end their day with wine and cheese tasting which includes the authentic Cheddar product before booking into an upmarket hotel in the town.

The next day is Saturday – which means there remains just one final night before they are set to return to Reading for Sunday night. Their plan is to go to the tip of Cornwall, to Land's End. There they will stand and survey endless Atlantic breakers rolling across the horizon while looking out, past the bottom of Ireland, on to America.

They drive directly to Cornwall and first find a place to stay. It is a delightful stone pub in a local village. They have the afternoon free to explore as they wish. It is a mostly clear day but with bursts of showers coming in off the Atlantic. A big sea is running, breaking on the rocky offshore islands and firing up spumes of spray. The wind is cold and bracing as it rips in from the vast oceans to the west

After an hour of walking and exploring the exposed rocky coast, they are left chilled and wind blasted. They decide to travel on to the sheltered east side of the peninsula for the afternoon. Here, despite it being a few short miles away, they come to an entirely different world. It is a place of quaint fishing villages and bustling commerce. They discover the town of Penzance, famous for the Gilbert and Sullivan pirate opera- with not a pirate to be seen. They book seats in the local theatre for an afternoon performance of the classic opera. In the late afternoon, a man with a fiddle and repertoire of bawdy songs has them in stitches in a local pub. It is light and entertaining. Wine and warm food give them a glow of well-being. They eat dinner in an intimate restaurant, quiet despite the town bustle- just candlelight and them.

During the dinner, a pensive mood descends. Susan feels reluctance to admit the obvious: that this time of delightful solitude is near an end. It means she needs to think past this place.

She lays a hand on David's arm, saying, "Thank you for a most wonderful time. I'd forgotten how beautiful my own country is. I got such enjoyment out of sharing it with you and seeing it through your eyes as well as my own. I wish we could put tomorrow off and delay our return for another week. But, tonight, let there not be a shadow: we should party, dance and push away all else."

David nods. "You've a knack for saying what I was thinking."

They finish their meal, have an extra drink and head out into the Penzance night. They find a nightclub where the music is booming and soak it in: slow dances, fast dances and a buzz of excited conversation. It is well after midnight when they, and their many new found friends, are sharing last drinks. At last, waving and calling out to each other, they stumble off to their respective beds.

Even though they have shared many drinks, it has been over many hours and neither of them feels drunk. As they drive up the hillside, they suddenly emerge into a cutting and blasting wind. It buffets their car, pushing it sideways. It's the same wind they fled from before, but now it has redoubled with a wild roaring and keening sound.

David says, "Perhaps we should've got a place in Penzance- but I rather like returning to the wild Atlantic in the late night. Its untamed rawness appeals to my soul; a wildness for brave hearts."

Susan nods, but shivers slightly. She pushes herself in against him- a solidity against the outside storm. The pub is completely dark as they use their key to let themselves in. Despite the windows rattling and the wind moaning, it feels safe and secure within.

In the soft bed-lamp light, Susan wants to give this man a night to remember her by. She sings a song her cousins taught her from the bawdy pubs of the north entitled "Patricia the Stripper." As she is singing, she acts out the seductive poses while removing layers of her clothes. David scoops her up and swings her around. Now, they are laughing and giggling together as they touch each other's intimate places. It feels wild and joyous.

Susan wakes in the early predawn. It is too dark for shadows. David sleeps on, but she can hear his steady breathing. She sees a faint shape to his body's outline. Something else is in here, too.

She senses another presence. It feels ancient yet familiar. It is a presence reeking of crocodiles, swamps, blowflies and rotting flesh, a presence of utter terror!

Is she dreaming? Or is it real? She is no longer sure. Her sense of being with David in this hotel room seems right but, at the same time, other things seem all wrong. There is a strange smell: the smell of a swamp combined with a rotten putrefaction of decaying bodies. There is also a buzzing sound in her ears which must be a blowfly of the dead. There are even hands reaching out to touch her. They first reach for her as if in a gentle caress but, when she draws away from them, they start trying to grab her. Now, she can feel this creature clawing at her- as if it is trying to take over her body and to seize her.

She pulls away, while pulling the covers over her head. She pushes her body against David in order to try to block out the other being. She feels David's arms wrap around her and pull her close even though she feels no sense of his waking. She buries her face in his chest and tries to block out the other, while telling herself over and over again, "It's just a dream." However, she knows an ancient predatory spirit waits hungrily nearby- wanting to take her. Her mind frames it as 'a thing that has escaped from the time of the Dreaming.' As David holds her close, her sense of the numinous evil fades. She dares not move away-even an inch- lest the beast return.

Susan suddenly realises David is shaking her awake. He is up and dressed. A wintery sunshine is trying to light the grey horizon. He says, "It's coming up to ten o'clock so I thought I should wake you. They've promised a late breakfast if we come soon."

Emerging from the hotel to pack up the car, they step into a new blustery wet day. Last night's Atlantic weather front has settled over the south of England. The weather's gloom seems to match the end of their holiday- telling them of the need to return to the real and much less exciting world.

On a dreary Sunday afternoon of wind and rain, it is a slow and subdued drive back towards London as they follow a heavy stream of traffic returning to the city. Despite this, they are both in an upbeat mood. They're feeling good about the time they've spent together and about what might still come.

Somehow, the pregnancy has completely gone from Susan's mind. When it does return for an odd fleeting second, she pushes it far away, determined it be left as a subject of another time. Instead of breaching this dreaded topic, they discuss mutual interests in history, archaeology and politics. They also discuss their medical and biotechnology work.

Susan says she will absolutely have to go in to work for a while tomorrow- but she will try to arrange to have the rest of the time off until David flies out. They agree they will spend the upcoming

Tuesday together. She also tells David she is hoping and expecting him to stay on with her for the next nights since his fold out bed in the office is not big enough for two to share.

David said, "Yes, but my proviso is that for our final night we share a five-star suite in one of the city's top hotels."

Susan nods assent. Even though the balance is very much on his side, as always, it seems only fair to agree.

On returning from work the next day, Susan proposes the two of them go for an intimate dinner at a small place she knows alongside the Thames located at the back of Reading. She's been able to clear the two days off work until David's plane departs late on Wednesday. She tells David she intends tonight to be on her.

Despite her reluctance, she knows the time has come for some honesty about her situation. She does not want to leave it until the very last minute. Once they are sitting with their drinks and orders placed, she takes a deep breath and launches into it.

"David, there's something I need to say before we get in any deeper and particularly before we start talking about any ongoing relationship or whatever follows from this week.

"First, I want to tell you how wonderful this week has been for me. I can't quite understand what leads you to like me, but I've had one of the best times of my life since you arrived. I love being with you and doing things with you. I love making love to you. I love your manners and charm with others- particularly with my family- and your sense of fun and courtesy.

"So, whatever follows from here, I don't want to lose that. I most want to thank you for the good time you've given me."

David nods while being strangely silent. It is as if he knows there is more to follow.

"Now I have to tell you something which is difficult for me to say. I don't want it to cause you hurt- though I think it may.

"Two days before you arrived, I did a pregnancy test and found out I was going to have a baby. I've only made love to two men in the last six months. One was you and the other was another man in Australia. I really wish the baby was yours- but I think it's very likely that it's the other man's child. However, I can't say for sure and there's still a small chance that you're the father.

"When I read your letter on Saturday, I had just found out about my pregnancy and had already decided to have an abortion. I don't want the child of this other man and I know I won't be seeing him again.

"After you leave, I'll have to deal with this. I didn't want it to spoil our time together for the last week which is why I didn't tell you when you arrived. But now, I don't want any talk or promises for a future between us without you knowing this. I'm sorry I can't tell you anything about the other man, so please don't ask."

David sits looking at her with a kind and steady face. When she told of the baby, she thought his face might change- but it did not. For long seconds after she finishes, he sits and looks at her without speaking. At last he picks up her hand, kisses it and then squeezes it. The fingers of his other hand gently stroke her cheek. There's a something poignant in his kindness and gentleness which brings tears to her eyes.

"We've both been in relationships and had lovers before," he said. "In my heart of hearts- I knew I wasn't the only one in Australia. From the way you were in Sydney, I sensed you had, not long before, met someone else who was still important to you. Yet it didn't stop what I felt for you then and it won't stop what I feel for you now. I like the idea of you with a baby. I also like the idea of being a father to your baby. I appreciate you've told me this now instead of just having a termination the day after I leave and telling no one about it.

"I haven't told you about the girl, Nicki, I was with until about a year before I met you. She was from my town and we'd been childhood sweethearts since school. We both came to Sydney for University and then started our careers together. Through all this time, we stayed best friends and lovers, even though we both agreed we needed to associate and go out with other people, so as to experience a wider life.

"Then, a couple of years ago, we started to drift apart. I'd always thought we'd be together for life and get married in due course. I think she thought so, too. But, in Sydney, there were so many girls who threw themselves at me and it was a bit the same for Nicki.

"Gradually, we started to form different circles of friends and enter different relationships, but neither of us would admit it to ourselves or each other. It was like we needed to keep pretending and didn't want to admit that our dream was coming apart.

"Then, one day Nicki came to me and told me that she was in a relationship with another man and must end what she had with me. She said she wouldn't two-time with him.

"While I'd been with other girls, I'd always thought of them as temporary dalliances which meant nothing as she was the one for me. Nicki was more straight-forward: she didn't like the 'me being with other women thing'. She'd been hurt when I'd been with other girls- even though we lived separately. Even though we'd decided, when we came to Sydney, that our relationships with one another shouldn't be exclusive: Nicki was never truly happy about it. She'd just pretended to agree. I realized this, deep down, but continued on anyway- thinking she'd understand and wait there for me to come back.

"I was devastated when she left me for someone else. Over the year since, I've come to realize that, if one's in a serious relationship, one has to be true to it. In the year after she left, there were lots of girls at first. About halfway through the year, however, I realised there was something unsatisfying in that. I started to keep more to myself. There were two girls I kept seeing. However, it was more like meeting a need for both of us than it was love.

"From the night I first met you, I've have been completely captivated by the girl with the blue eyes and the bewitching smile who sits in front of me. So, while I didn't want to rush you with a hasty proposal, now I find that's what I want to say.

"If you will have me, I want to stay with you for as far into the future as I can see. I want to be the father of your child and, hopefully, of more to come. Simply because it is your child, I will love it in the same way I love you. Basically, what I'm saying is that I want you and me to go on together: lovers, living together and whatever more you want. From here on, it must be you and me in an exclusive relationship together if you agree to be with me."

She'd thought her revelation would rock David. Instead, it seems to make him stronger. What is she to make of his proposal, though? It sounds like marriage though he has not quite said the word. While she very much likes David, is attracted to him and likes being with him for his company and sex: she's not sure if love is quite the right word to use for her feelings.

However, this relationship is good and she doesn't want to set it aside in a search for a perfection she might never find. Love is a very dangerous place. Perhaps this strong liking she feels is better- a more solid platform on which to build something enduring.

She looks at his serious eyes. "David, thank you so much for what you've said. I can't pretend I'm not physically attracted to you and I really like being with you and doing things with you.

"But I don't want to decide my life on the basis of this baby or a week with you. I'm not saying no- but I've not yet reached a place where I can honestly say yes, either. It has all happened so fast. I want us to keep going but, I need some time to come to terms with all of this and to know better for myself what I think I should do."

David screws up his face slightly. "It's funny- I knew how I felt after the first night I met you. I'd hoped, for you, it would be as clear-no ifs or buts. I can understand what you're saying, though. What I ask is that you don't decide to terminate the baby until you've fully thought through what you want."

Susan looks at him, puzzled. "Don't you care whether the baby is yours or not? I thought this might be important to you. It is something we could probably find out if you want."

He thinks for a moment and says, "You know, it is funny, I feel I should care more than I do. It's like it belongs to a part of your past life and, although we were together for two nights in Sydney when it could have happened, that does not seem important. From here it feels like my real relationship with you began when I came to England. The other was something lovely but temporary- in another place and time. Even though I loved you then, you were only beginning to like me.

"Now I feel our life together has really begun, in a public, exclusive way. The child who grows inside you is a real part of you. So, while part of me would love the thought that it was my own child from the outset: if we stay together, it will be mine anyway. I'll watch a baby being born and I'll hold it once it's born- that feels like my child to me. From here on, it's just part of what makes up you: the Susan I love.

"So, I don't need to know if it is mine biologically and I'm sure I don't want you to have any tests which pose a risk to the baby. If I married you and you already had a child, it would be a child I would love simply because it came from you. If we could not have children together and we adopted a child, I would love that child in the same way as my own child.

"Anyway, as you say, that's not to be decided now. But, like you, I definitely want our relationship to continue. Since time will run along quickly, I want you to come back to Australia with me as soon as you're able, in order to meet my family and spend some more time with me, while you decide what you want to do. How about that for an idea?

"Sadly, I can't change my plans to fly back Wednesday night. However, as soon as you can manage, I'd like you to come back to Australia for two or three weeks to spend time with me. After that, we can decide what to do. In the short term, I need to stay in Australia for my work.

But if it's important to you, we can come back to England to live here together before the baby is born. Most of my work can be done from anywhere in the world. I'm actually here for the purpose of expanding my business into the UK."

Chapter 8 – Return to Australia

Just over three weeks has passed since David left. Susan again finds herself in a plane heading for Australia. David has bought her the ticket and insisted it be business class. Susan has to admit that the extra comfort and space is nice. She thinks she could come to like the little luxuries which seem to flow from David.

Their final two days in London had a dreamy idyllic quality as she looks back on them. They went shopping in Oxford Street and other fashionable parts of London. They also visited historic sites such as the Tower of London. On the final night, they shared a wonderful dinner with her family and close friends, which was hosted by David, in an upmarket West End Restaurant.

Anne came along and was now unattached. She'd looked sensational, a flaming mass of red curls combining perfectly with her peaches and cream complexion. Not to mention how the low-cut green dress worked perfectly with her green eyes. David was visibly struck by her. They'd even joked that, if he had not met Susan first- then her English friend may have been the one.

Anne herself had also seemed a bit wowed. She'd exclaimed, "My God, Susan, I thought you were going for a holiday. Here you bring back this amazing Aussie hunk. Is there a brother for me?"

It was a lovely night. While not an engagement party, it was obviously about Susan and David sharing hopes for a long-term relationship together. David told those gathered he and Susan had made plans for her to come out to Australia very soon. He added he was hoping to see a lot more of them all- not just Susan.

Susan knew, without a doubt, that both her parents and her gran really liked him. She could also tell her other family and friends seemed to like him, too. Her only reservations are: it was so fast and he seemed to be a bit too perfect. It was the same sense she'd had on the morning in Sydney, after their first night together. Then he had looked almost too beautiful to be real.

It is not really a reservation- just the sense that things could never be perfect for ever. There must be a flaw or a crack in the glass somewhere. She remembers a Leonard Cohen song with a line about 'the cracks letting the light in.' This line seems to capture what she is feeling the best. Perhaps finding one or two flaws in David's perfection will bring her a comforting sense of reality.

Over the last two days David was in London, she had found herself more and more caught up imagining a new, glamorous, and stylish life with him. In this imagined world, her previous visit to Australia belongs to someone else- including the baby. This is a person she can leave behind. Now, the time has come for her to move into a new persona which will provide a new reality.

On their final day in London, they had visited some upmarket jewellers. David had said he wanted to buy her a ring. Even though if she had not yet said "Yes" to wearing it, she liked the idea of seeing what rings and other things they both liked.

She had caught his mood of enthusiasm. After trying on many rings, they'd both agreed on a choice. In fact, the word "Yes" had been on the tip of her tongue since their dinner together when she'd told him about the baby. As he slid the chosen ring onto her third left finger, she had an even more overpowering urge to say "Yes." It even got right to the very tip of her tongue: but somehow it stopped there.

At the airport, right before he left, she'd told him with each passing day she was getting more certain and would be able to give him an answer when she came to Australia. She said she just needed some free-thinking time between the two visits, to get a clear head, so she could decide properly.

David, seeing this was as close as he could get to an answer, agreed to being able to wait a bit longer. In fact, he told her he had originally come to London with only a slim hope of anything happening between them. Having just found out there was a real possibility of something more between them, he found himself almost bursting with excitement. He said he'd enjoy savouring the pleasure of imagining their life together while he waited. Susan could not repress a smile at his puppy-like enthusiasm.

Now she is on a plane about to cross the world, again. She is filled with anticipation at seeing him again in a day's time. Nothing's happened to raise questions about whether she should go forward with this plan- except her dreams.

After the family dinner on their last night together in London, they'd gone to bed late and a little tipsy. This caused them both to fall straight to sleep, knowing the time for lovemaking would come later in the night.

Susan found herself immersed in a dream which felt so incredibly real. It was a dream of lovemaking. At first it was just of her and a man's body in the night, so intimate and passionate, but totally silent. It felt like Mark to her. She found she overwhelmingly wanted it to be Mark. As the ecstasy was building, she had tried to look at the man's face- but it was hidden in shadows.

Then, a street light flashed, illuminating the face, and it was Mark. She had felt so happy. Their pleasure together had been so intense. His mind was telling her: he was really there, he loved her still and both she and the child inside her belonged to him. She felt tears of unbelievable happiness flowing down her cheeks.

As the passion waned, somehow her mind left the dream behind and she opened her eyes to look at the man beside her. She knew she should have been happy. After all, it was David! The joining of their bodies had been wildly beautiful. However, her first unbidden reaction was of an intense loss and disappointment when seeing the fact- Mark was no longer there. Her body and mind both ached for Mark's touch- not the touch of the man who held her currently. She tried to hide it from him and felt she had overall succeeded. Despite this, it sat there like a stone at the bottom of a deeply buried pool of longing.

During David's absence, several more versions of this dream have reoccurred. Each one of them was a little different and none of them included full sexual consummation. What the dreams had in common were: it was always Mark who held her in her dreams and his message always stayed the same. His message was simply this- she and her child belonged to him. It began to feel like her life walked in two parallel paths. There was the real, daytime part of her life in which she had given herself to David fully and loved the idea of their future together. However, at night and in her subconscious, she walked the other path in her dreams. In these dreams, she belonged to Mark because his half-crocodile form and spirit had captured her. This dream part of her had given over her soul to him completely.

She wonders if it was a form of dissociative personality disorder- where her mind was splitting her into two people living separate lives in her own body. This sense of dual possession is not really scary. Yet it is always there buried deep down inside her. And, as it continued on, night after night, she felt as if a part of her being was tearing into two. However, as each new day began, she would push the split existence of the night before aside.

Now, as she flies to meet David, she is feeling a deep longing to be with him once again. She can't help but hope that, once there, the actuality of his presence, of him being with her all the time, will finally banish this other presence. She doesn't really hate this duality. But she knows there can only be space for the one person in her heart and that place must belong only to the living one who is actually real.

Susan relaxes into her soft seat as the aircraft ceases its climb. She enjoys the service provided to her as the hours drift away. She eats well but resists the urge for a second glass of wine with her dinner, now being conscious of a need to protect this baby: no matter who the father ends up being. At this point, she is not quite ready to give it any affection- but at least it has ceased being viewed by her as an evil object which deserved to be cut out.

Even if she and David do not work out in the long run, she is starting to feel she should keep the child. It is not its fault what kind of person its father was, when amongst the living. It is like that biblical saying of 'not visiting the sins of the father on the children.' Even though the pregnancy was not planned, she no longer thinks of it as a terrible catastrophe. David's willingness to accept the child has helped her to see this viewpoint.

After what seems like a very short night, it is becoming light again. She is looking below at the mountains across the centre of Asia which are massive snowy ridges. She remembers those same lucent white peaks from glimpsing them in the dark night of her first dream. In remembering this, she feels a strangely familiar déjà vu kinship with this place. The plane continues to incessantly carry her east. They are now approaching Bangkok for a brief evening stopover before they go on to Sydney for a five am arrival.

It feels as if the world is moving around her while she sits alone in a still place at its centre, waiting for life to move to another phase- perhaps with this man in Australia whose company brings her pleasure. She sleeps very little on this second night, as it is really only afternoon in London. Instead of sleeping, she watches the map as the plane slowly and inexorably comes down over Australia, slicing its path through the black sky above the red heart.

As they come over Australia, she realises her mind is made up. If David still wants her- she will marry him. The ending of the plane trip brings a sense of closure on a past life. She can now see herself with a new life in Australia.

David is there alone to meet her in the early dawn. She had wondered if he would bring Ruth to join the welcome. She is glad it is only David, since it's just him she's come to see. She hugs him tightly. He hugs her back. It feels good to be back together.

As they part, he looks at her quizzically.

She looks back at him with a serious expression for a second before she flashes him a brilliant smile. She knows what he wants to know and she does not want to keep him in suspense any longer.

She exclaims, before he speaks, "If you still want me, the answer is: Yes, YES, YES, YES!"

He hugs her to him again. She could swear she sees his eyes glisten with unshed tears. She feels his hands cup her face as he pushes it away from his just far enough to kiss. It feels truly good.

Luckily, in the early morning traffic, it is only a short drive to David's apartment. They spend a long hour of passionate lovemaking before drifting off to sleep for a couple of hours.

As Susan is awakening, in bright light, to the smell of coffee, David comes in and says, "If you're up to it, I've just organised another lunch at Watsons Bay. You can call it an impromptu engagement party. It will be the same gang as last time along with some of my other friends- one's who I think you'll like."

It is another lovely afternoon. The weather is warmer than last time with a strong balminess to the day. It is hard to believe barely two months have passed since she'd last sat here with all these people because it seems a lifetime ago. David has not told the others about Susan and his plan. He simply told them he was crazy about her and she has returned to spend three more wonderful weeks with him.

As they are clearing the plates, David suddenly looks serious and clears his throat. The table falls silent.

He turns towards Susan, sitting alongside himself, and she looks at his earnest face with a tingle of excitement. Next, he removes a small box from his pocket and opens it to her. It is the beautiful ring they both agreed upon in London: a magnificent pale sapphire flanked by two smaller diamonds and set in white gold.

He turns to all assembled and says, "Before I left London, I asked Susan to marry me. She told me she'd give me an answer when she came to Australia. This morning she said 'Yes'. So, in front of you all, I would like to put this ring on her finger and ask her once again."

Then, looking back at her, he said, "Susan, I'm asking you to marry me. What do you say?"

"Yes, I want to and will do," she replies. She holds out her hand and he places the ring on her finger. She can feel tears form in her own eyes.

Everyone else is laughing, giggling, excitedly amazed and offering congratulations. As they admire the ring, they all say how perfectly it matches the blue of her eyes. It feels good- even though it seems to happen way too fast.

The three weeks fly by in an excited blur. She is with David constantly, so she has very little time for reflection on what she has decided. He is fun and good company. He introduces her to many of his friends and family. They drive over the mountains to meet his family the next day. All of them are very welcoming to her.

His father is not unlike Susan's own father: slightly crusty and no-nonsense, yet with a wicked sense of humour. She isn't surprised to see David does indeed have a younger brother named Stephen. He is dark to David's fair- but otherwise similarly handsome. Susan thinks of Anne immediately. She will be invited to the wedding and…. who knows? She knows she shouldn't play matchmaker- but Anne suggested this 'brother thing' after all.

David also has a younger sister, Rachel, who clearly thinks he is wonderful. At first, she is slightly standoffish with Susan. However, they discover a shared love of riding and become firm friends. Soon enough, Rachel is telling Susan about her friends, love life and hopes for the future.

David is a competent rider meaning he is around Susan's level of skill. They both enjoy riding across the trails out behind the farm, land where the mountains rise steadily into a blue wall. It has something of the feel of the "Man from Snowy River" country- even though it is part of the Blue Mountains. It is a place somewhere between Lithgow and Oberon, local people tell her. In the early mornings, frost still crackles white under the horse's feet even though it is gone within an hour of the sun rising.

The farm is considered large and prosperous for this area. It has a stud of black, Angus cattle and fields of fine wool sheep.

They also own another farm two hours' drive away, out on the western slopes where they crop wheat, barley and canola. The crops make up most of their farming income. The family has also built up a range of other investments from many years of successful farming which contribute to family finances.

In the words of David's father, they are prosperous with more than enough for all the family' needs, without being extremely rich. Really, they are rich compared to most other people Susan knows.

The only person who is not totally welcoming is David's mother. She is not unfriendly, per say, but holds a certain reserve towards Susan. Over a cup of tea on the second day, when it is just the two of them, she tells Susan her version of the story of David's break-up with Nicki. She tells Susan how devastated David was when Nicki went off with someone else.

Therefore, her motherly concern is to protect David from another heartbreak. It is as if she has an internal womanly sense concerning this new relationship being a bit too easy and moving a bit too fast.

She says, "I do not want David, on the rebound, getting in too deep with someone else until you are both really sure. David's impulsive and part of me fears this may be that- not that he would let me say so.

"Please be sure before you commit your life to my son. Don't let yourself be swept up by the excitement and rush of it all- unless you're really sure that it's what you want too."

Susan understands fully what David's mother means. She has her own sense of the rush of it all, of moving so fast. She says, "It seems hard for me to believe, too. It has happened so quickly! Sometimes, I pinch myself and tell myself, 'It can't all be real.' But then, when I think of David and look at him- I am glad it is. It makes me feel really happy. Now, I only want to make him happy too."

His mother seems to accept what Susan says. After this chat occurs, it is like the air between them has been cleared.

Privately, Susan still thinks about this conversation and tries to satisfy herself that she is indeed sure of her decision. She completely understands where David's mother is coming from with her concerns. Sometimes, she wonders, herself, if she has been just too caught up in the whole romantic impulse of it all: boy meets girl from the other side of the world and, with great haste, they are getting married.

Once she tries to talk about these concerns with David, saying she does not want him to rush to marriage solely because she is pregnant. She suggests, maybe, they should slow down the pace a bit and give their relationship more unhurried time. She emphasizes she is not saying to break off their engagement, but to let the baby and wedding each operate on their own timelines.

David is at his eloquent and persuasive best, saying, "We have decided already- why delay?" He appeals to the logic: it is just as easy to get married quickly as it is to be married slowly.

In the end she can do nothing but agree. She decides she'll return to England to pack up her things. She'll spend just over a month tidying up things and saying her goodbyes to her extended family and friends before returning with her family to Australia for the wedding.

Even though the tradition would typically be to have the wedding in England, they both agree they want it in Sydney, specifically at Watsons Bay, since it is the place where they started to get to know each other and enjoy each other's company. There is a lovely sandstone church a few hundred yards from the restaurant. It feels like the right place to get married.

The reception is a short walk from the church, in a place where beautiful afternoon and evening views can be seen out across Sydney Harbour. They will be looking towards the city skyscrapers and have vistas of sailing boats sweep by in front of them throughout the reception.

Susan knows her own family can afford the trip to Australia and Anne has promised to come as her bridesmaid. She knows they are all looking forward to a holiday in Australia. So, without delay, the wedding date is set for December. Most guests are notified of their invitations as soon as the decision is made. The church and reception areas have been booked already.

On her final weekend in Australia, they jointly throw a big family and friends' engagement party which is held over the mountains at David's family's place. It is a truly lovely day. There are many well-wishers, with neighbours coming from miles around the farm and from the local village. A lot of David's extended family come too, travelling from across country NSW and from a mix of Australian cities.

Susan charms them all and enjoys their company. She realises she likes the charm and courtesy of Australian country people. They seem to live life at a slower, more polite pace than their city cousins.

She and David both agree to say nothing of the baby at this stage. Most of the time, Susan is barely conscious of it and is not showing yet. There is a good chance the baby bump will be barely evident at the wedding- though Susan decides to chouse a loose fitting dress in case it becomes obvious by then. *Time enough for people to hear this piece of news when they need to know- it's of little importance just now,* she thinks.

Almost before Susan knows where the time has all gone, she is boarding the plane back to England. She proudly wears her engagement ring, giving David a last hug and promising to ring him every day: "at least almost always," she qualifies.

The door closes. Suddenly she is back in her own world again. She settles into her seat and picks up her passport- noting there is now another visitor exit stamp. She will need to sort out some more permanent residency arrangements. This is something they've both largely forgotten about in the rush of the last three weeks together. However, she must get working on it as soon as she is back in England. She should probably begin with a trip to the Australian embassy next week. There is no doubt it will mean endless form filling and proof of their relationship. Perhaps she can return on her existing visa which is still valid for the year.

As she is thinking about this she begins to aimlessly flick through various pieces of paper in her plastic travel wallet. She realises it's the one she'd used when she first came to Australia four months ago. That seems part of another lifetime.

Sure enough, there is her boarding pass from London to Tokyo and another to Cairns. She decides, since she's many hours to kill, along with lots of arranging to do once she gets back home, she will start by going through this wallet and discarding the rubbish from it. It's symbolic of her moving on- this cleaning away of another part of her past life. Then, after she has done that, she decides she'll make a list of all the things she has to do once she is back in London. That will help her hit the ground running.

She starts by discarding the boarding passes from her first trip to Australia. Then she pulls out other scraps of paper which sit beside them. One is a folded sheet with the names Janet Davison and Maggie Richards written down, along with London addresses, phone numbers and emails.

At first, this information does not ring any bells. Then it comes to her: Maggie's the girl she met on the boat in Cairns then went to Kuranda with. Janet is Maggie's friend who she'd travelled with, not someone Susan has met.

When they parted, Maggie had given her this slip of paper to get in touch with her again once Susan returned home from her holiday. She can't remember any reason for Janet's name being listed. Maybe it was already on the paper when Maggie tore it out of her notebook.

Thinking of Maggie brings a smile to Susan's face. She recalls the great night out they had in Cairns. It would be fun to catch up in London- if they can squeeze it in.

She puts this slip of paper aside to keep and picks up the next bit, a double folded piece which she has no remembrance of seeing before, maybe it was picked it up by mistake. A memory flashes into her mind. This slip of paper was handed to her by the man behind her in the queue at the passport checking place. It was just before she left Darwin on that flight out of Australia. She slipped it in here without looking- planning to check it later. Then she'd promptly forgotten it.

It could be it doesn't belong to her. It is a sheet torn from a notebook, having one jagged edge and faint ruled lines. Its origin is not something which triggers a memory.

She turns it over as she looks at it. On its other side 'Susan' is written in small, neat handwriting. So, it really is hers. Something about the way her name is written set alarm bells jangling in her brain. It is not her own writing, but there is a very familiar look about it.

She opens the sheet and almost drops the paper. It feels like it is on fire, burning into her hand.

Dear Susan,

If you are reading this, it almost certainly means I am dead. I know now that is the only way forward from here. One of us must vanish and I could not bear for it to be you.

I have written this because I wanted to say goodbye.

It is important to me to tell you I love you and not just vanish with those words never said.

They are words I have wanted to say to you since that first day on the boat when I met you face to face. I had already been entranced by your image, glimpsed distantly on the Cairns shoreline with your feet in the shallow water and hair flung back embracing the sun.

My parting message is I have loved you utterly since before I first met you. It was only when brought to a place of no other choice I could say it honestly.

A page of close-spaced, dense handwriting follows.

At the bottom is a signature she knew so well,

Mark B.

Chapter 9 – Identification of a Body

Alan had been racking his brains for two weeks about how to identify this person from the billabong using just a forearm and a skull. He had picked Sandy's brains for all her ideas. He had done the same with many of his work colleagues. The same ideas came from everyone: check for missing persons, follow any leads, wait for a lucky break.

He'd visited all the dentists in Darwin and Katherine looking for dental records which matched but came up with nothing. In reality, there was not much to match: a couple of minor fillings which could have been done anywhere and a complete set of teeth. On the X-rays they looked normal and unremarkable. Although the experts told him that each person's teeth were unique and distinctive, there was hardly a database of teeth images for a computer to search through. Without other identity clues, he was unrewarded after going through hundreds of dental X-ray images in a range of surgeries in order to see if they had any which resembled his specimen. He'd almost abandoned the idea of using dental records to identify the victim. He'd left a copy of the image with each Darwin dentist he visited, just in case something turned up. However, he suspected it was a big waste of time.

On the other hand, the forearm was slightly more interesting. They had evidence of a healed forearm fracture. They also had evidence of an associated gunshot injury in the form of several small fragments of lead present in the adjacent tissue. They looked like they had come from a projectile which had disintegrated when it smashed into the bone. All the big pieces of projectile were gone and the remaining pieces were only 1–2 mm in size. They would have been easy to miss due to their size, but Sandy had picked up the white flecks on the X-ray and gone digging for them. She did this only after taking pictures from a range of angles. Three pieces had been retrieved and analysed. All had a metal profile of lead along with traces of other specific metals. The metals were present in a combination which suggested Soviet military ammunition. The scar tissue around the injury indicated the wound had been properly cleaned and, perhaps, sutured- but without any internal surgical fixation of the fracture itself. This said it was likely to have been done in a third world country because, in a developed country, such an injury would normally have been repaired with a plate and screws. This information came from a surgeon Sandy talked to in Darwin Hospital.

Based on the lower arm bone and skull shape, the information they had to go on suggested the victim was most likely a Caucasian male who was of medium to strong build. The age range estimated for the victim was 25 to 45. This age range was based on the fact the arm indicated full growth plate closure with no evidence of degenerative changes which typically accompany advancing years. Isotopic bone and tissue analysis suggested the person had mostly lived life in Northern Australia, perhaps with time spent in Africa and or the Middle East- but this was not definite. The level of healing of the bone injury suggested it had occurred when the person was an adult and at least 3 years ago. The injury had broken the mid ulna bone. Most likely, it was repaired by wound cleaning and a plaster cast, the kind of repair that might have occurred in a field military hospital. Hence, a period as a mercenary in a conflict where one side used Soviet military ammunition, in an African or Middle Eastern location seemed a reasonable surmise.

Despite these interesting facts, they brought Alan no closer to knowing the person's identity. He felt a bit stumped at this juncture and had now largely moved onto other cases. However, he was still waiting and hoping something would turn up on this case.

Sandy had finished her tests and reports. They proved all the tissues found in and around the billabong belonged to the same person. The most likely cause of death was a fractured skull caused by a blow from a piece of broken timber to the side of the head.

The police had made a cast of a back left tyre missing the piece of tread and also of the two different human footprints found. One appeared to be of a mid-sized female and the other of a medium to large man- whose size appeared consistent with the victim.

They also had evidence indicating the site had been deliberately cleaned up after the event. This cleaning included dirt scraping and brushing and the fire-ash deposited in the billabong. The ash had a few interesting, small fragments which they may yet identify: those most significant were an MB monogram and broken lock from what looked like a leather briefcase. The make of the briefcase was unknown at this time. The tarnish present on the brass monogram and lock fittings suggested a one to two month period in the water.

There were also other odd snips of information which may or may not be relevant. One such bit of information was a report from a local fisherman, who routinely came to fish further along this billabong most weekends. It was of an unknown person driving a white, utility type vehicle around the billabong campgrounds in a way which suggested the person was unsure where they were going. He reported this occurred at about eight pm on a Saturday night, right around the likely time period of this event. The description of the vehicle was imprecise- although it was probably a tray back, Toyota. The man thought he had seen something white on the back which looked like an esky box.

It was possible this was indeed a description of the vehicle used by the murderer to leave the scene- particularly if they were unfamiliar with the locality and were searching for a way out. Alan remembered how confusing all the tracks around the billabongs were in the daytime- let alone at night.

Unfortunately, the fisherman was not quite sure which weekend it had happened since he had been out there almost every weekend since June. However, he thought it had been around mid to late August. All of these facts may tie a person or persons and a specific vehicle to this location. First, however, they had to make an identification of either the victim or vehicle for the other information to become useful.

The case fascinated and challenged Alan. He worked on it every minute he could spare. He also spent hours discussing it with Sandy. He did this despite the fact he felt she had withdrawn from her desire to catch the killer.

She told Alan, during the dream, she'd felt great terror coming from the woman. It was such intense terror that it made her not want to do anything to harm this person further. Also, if she had killed the man, Sandy felt sure it was for a good reason.

At first, Alan teased her about these statements, saying: "it was only a dream, you couldn't possibly know anything real from it."

Sandy said she was as sure as she could be from what she had seen; that she'd been inside the mind of this woman and she was certain she was intended as the victim of a crocodile.

In response to his teasing, Sandy challenged him about the sense of loss he'd experienced coming from the crocodile the day the remains were found: "How could such a dumb predator communicate with you?"

As Alan relived this memory, he found he was no longer sure it was rubbish and stopped mocking her dream. After this, they called it a truce. While they still talked a lot about the case, it was only about any ways he could find to identify who this man was.

Outside of work, he and Sandy were getting on wonderfully. They were still in the first delicious period of loving infatuation when all they wanted to do was go to bed together- any time or any place. Without a doubt, the sex was great. Much more importantly, however, they really liked each other and enjoyed doing things together. Their days at work were busy and they saw little of each other besides an occasional quick "hello" call. In contrast, the evenings and nights were wonderful due to them spending them together most of the time.

They still both kept their own places but now, it was a matter of deciding which would be their joint abode for the night. He liked Sandy's place best to sleep in. It was full of her feminine knick- knacks, smells and mess. Even when she went out and left him alone there- it still felt like her. His place was more masculine and ordered with better furniture and a longer term feel to it. Sandy's preference was to stay at his place. Her reasoning was his place had better creature comforts and because of something similar in reverse, that "it was imbued with him." She stated she liked the sense of him which seemed to pervade the place.

On balance their living situation was about a fifty-fifty split between both places. Now they were having conversations about getting a larger place to share. He was sure it would happen in time, but for now it was not a burning priority. It made sense to only have the one place- both for money saving and convenience.

Everyone at the office already knew they were an item, so the novelty gossip value was fading. And it felt good to have this part of their life settled. They were now planning a short Christmas trip south to meet both sets of parents. Alan found he always felt good about being with Sandy. He even thought, maybe, on New Year's Eve, he'd pop the question. If she said yes, they would really have something to celebrate. One question still there out was: how to manage both careers if any babies came. However, they did not need to go there yet.

Alan was doodling on his pad as he scanned reports on a series of break and enters around Nightcliff- even though part of his mind was still on Sandy and last night. He was trying to get a feel for whether there was any common pattern to these events or instead just random delinquent larceny, but his attention was only half with it. His phone's sudden ringing startled him.

It was Eddie from the Vehicles Section. He said, "It may turn out to be nothing-but I've had a call from a patrol car out near Marrara. They were called to investigate an abandoned Toyota parked in the service road beside Macmillan's Road. It's been there for quite a while and nobody has paid it any attention until recently, when the house owner opposite where it was left, began wondering who owned it.

"The night before last, someone smashed its windscreen. It has remained untouched since. As a result, finally, the owner of this house rang to report it as vandalised and possibly abandoned.

A patrol car is there now looking at it. It's a Land Cruiser tray back with a cooler box and cage on the back. We've just run the plates and it shows up registered to a Mark Bennet from Alice Springs. There's only a postal address listed. I've looked up this person and can't locate him on any of our systems. I can't find any phone number or any other contact details- though the address appears to be valid. Therefore, I've asked the Alice Springs' police to call round and see if they can locate him.

"Then, a minute ago, I remembered my conversation with you over a drink last Friday. I remembered you telling me about a weird crocodile murder victim case where you'd recovered briefcase parts with the monogram of 'MB.' It may be nothing- but who knows."

Alan could feel excitement surge through him. It was in part due to the initials, but also the way the vehicle description matched that given by the regular fisherman. Could this be the break he'd been waiting for?

He brought himself back to the phone. "Definitely interested, Eddie. Thanks a lot. Is the patrol car still there?"

"Yeah. Asked him to stand by for five while I ran a few checks. I was about to tell him to leave and that we would call a tow truck to take it to a garage. Then, your conversation popped into my mind. I can call the patrol car back, ask it to hang around, if you want to go there."

Alan replied, "On my way as we speak and thanks again. I owe you one. This could be the big clue we've been waiting for."

He called out to the constable at the desk beside his, and asked "Are you good to go? We have an abandoned vehicle that may be linked to our Crocodile Man. It is out near Marrara."

In five minutes, they were there, looking at a Toyota as described. Judging by the accumulation of dust on its outside, it had been there for a couple of months. In contrast, other than a shower of glass scattered across the inside of the cab, the rest of the inside of the vehicle looked remarkably clean- way too clean for a bush vehicle.

He peered through the side window into the gloom within. It was hard to see clearly but, as best he could tell, the interior was spotless. Not what one would really expect from an abandoned bush basher. He climbed up onto the back. It was also clean except for a few leaves and a film of dust. He opened the cooler. It was spotless, too.

As he was opening the cooler, it released a faint aroma of cleaning chemicals. It was almost as if it had been closed up after being cleaned-while it was still not completely dry. It seemed this had caused these smells to still linger- even though the moisture was long gone. More than anything, this cleanness set the bells ringing in his brain. There was such similarity to the way the campsite was systematically cleaned. He felt almost sure this was the break they needed.

He looked at the back passenger side tire. He could not see any evidence of a piece of missing tread on it. It could be due to the fact the missing tread was on the inside of the tire and half the tyre was hidden up in the under-body. Looking for the missing tread would be a thing to check once the vehicle was up on a hoist.

He asked the beat police officers what they thought. One said, "Well at first- nothing. I figured it was just a car of someone who has gone on holidays overseas and parked close to the airport before getting on a plane. Then, I thought, *'If a bushie is going to leave his car here for a month or two while away- why would he clean it so well first?'* It's like it's been detailed right before it was left.

"I looked underneath. While the top is almost spotless, underneath hasn't been cleaned at all. If you were having a vehicle professionally cleaned and detailed, why not clean the under-body as well, using a high-pressure hose? Instead, the under-body still has all the crud and lumps of mud which come from months of driving in the bush. Five minutes with a high-pressure hose would shift most of it. The tires also look like someone has tried to wash them a little bit. It's definitely odd that only the topside has been cleaned so well."

The second officer continued, "It also looks like somebody smeared mud on the number plates to make them really hard to read. I needed a couple of goes, cross-checking between front and back, before I was fully sure I had the registration right.

"I can't say I'm surprised you find this as an interesting possibility for your crocodile case. You have a nose on you for these things like a foxhound on the trail of his fox. I'm guessing now that you'll want our vehicle recovery crew to take it to the police workshop before anything else is disturbed, so we can take it apart systematically."

Alan nodded. "You got it. While I'd love to pop a door and have a proper look inside, I think this is one for the pros to do. We don't want to run the risk of stuffing up any evidence which still remains. I don't suppose you've seen any keys."

The patrol men both shook their heads.

Alan asked his constable to stay with the vehicle and make sure no one disturbed it until the vehicle recovery team came along. He said for him to accompany it to the workshop and tell them what was required. Alan wanted it totally pulled apart to look for any evidence of previous users and to make a careful check of anywhere where there may be DNA, to see if it matched the "Crocodile Man" victim. They should also check to see if the tire tread matched the cast currently in his office.

He left the vehicle and asked the patrol car to drop him back at the station. He could see a lot of work flowing out of this single find. He started to wonder if he should book a flight to Alice Springs, so as to try to get some information on this 'Mark Bennet.'

Once back at the office, he rang Sandy to give her an update.

"Wow," she said, "Sounds like you've struck gold."

Then, it was off to talk to his boss about the "where to go from here" question.

They agreed they would hold off on any media about the vehicle for a day or two. In the meantime, Alan would get to Alice Springs, either to see if they could locate Mark Bennet or get further information from people who knew him. If he hurried, he could just make the mid-afternoon Qantas flight there today.

Chapter 10 – Who and Where is Mark Bennet

Alan touched down in Alice Springs in the late afternoon- just as the heat was going out of the day. He caught a taxi to the Alice Springs Police HQ where he talked to the officer who had visited the address earlier in the day. This man, Richard, told him it was an unremarkable third-floor flat with a locked garage to the side. There was no sign of anyone living there currently or of any recent use. There was also no mail, other than a small amount of junk mail, in the letter box, which suggested the box was emptied by someone from time to time. He had knocked on the doors of all the immediate neighbours, but no one had answered. Without any other options at that time, he'd departed the property at that point. He knew there would be someone coming from Darwin for a more detailed investigation.

Richard had also called to the motor registration authority and had obtained a photo from a licence issued to a 'Mark Bennet.' While it was not very detailed, it was an image of a man who looked to be in his mid-thirties. From what could be seen on the photo, he had medium- brown hair and a pleasant, if not highly handsome, face. He had no distinctive features which would obviously stand out in a crowd. Alan slipped a copy of the photo into his wallet.

As it was now late afternoon and people would be coming home, Alan asked Richard if he could accompany him for a repeat visit to the flat's neighbours.

Even though Alan could only tell him a limited amount about the investigation, Richard seemed keen to help. He had heard of the 'Crocodile Man' and Alan indicated that this individual they were trying to locate may be linked to that investigation.

The flat was located in a nondescript, relatively new, but still dingy, building on the east side of the town. Richard said it was comprised of 12 two-bedroom flats. He said the flat listed as Mark

Bennet's address shared a common entrance with some other flats. The entrance was compromised of two flights of stairs which ended in a top level and this level included his flat along with three other flats all opening off the top of the stairs. To the side of the building, there was a car park area with a row of numbered garages which matched the flat numbers.

Mark's flat was Number Eleven. Sure enough, the garage door was locked. They walked around the back. A tiny window, up high, let in a small amount of light. When Alan climbed up to look in, it was too dark to see anything clearly inside. Next, they climbed the stairs to the front door of the flat. They knocked loudly for a minute with no answer. It was a heavy security door, with no internal facing windows to look in through. They went back downstairs and outside to see if anything was evident from street level. They saw a small verandah with an iron railing which seemed to correspond to the flat. It was bare except for two old looking metal chairs. They could not get a view of the inside. There was no sign of life at the flat from what they could tell.

They returned to the neighbours' doors at the same level. Only one was home. When Alan showed him the licence photo, he said he was not sure- but he thought it may be the man from that flat. He said he'd rented his flat for about a year now. In that time, he'd very rarely seen his neighbour from Number 11. This person was seldom there and kept to himself. He'd never seen him in the company of anyone else.

They spent another hour working their way around the rest of the building with similarly little results. Only two other building residents had ever seen the resident of this flat. They also said they were not really sure if he was the person on the driver's licence. "He looks a bit similar" was all any of them would say. No one knew if he was the owner or a renter. The longest-term resident had been here since the flats were built five years ago. He said this person had used the flat for at least three years now. He also said, while this man was not rude, he showed no inclination to socialize and was barely there.

Nobody could recall having seen him here in the last three months. However, they said this was not unusual since he seemed to be at home for only a few days at a time and this happened, at most, about two or three times a year.

There was a general view from neighbours that he probably worked out in the bush due to him having a white Toyota four-wheel drive and what appeared to be tools on the back. No one remembered a built-in cooler box on the back of the truck.

The one useful piece of information was that some neighbours had observed another person collecting Mark's mail and throwing away the junk mail every week or two. This person seemed to have a mailbox key. He was described as a man around his fifties who walked with a limp. He came on a Thursday or Friday in the late afternoon. As it was Wednesday, it was likely he'd come tomorrow or the next day.

This seemed like the best lead to date. So Alan decided he'd return and wait near the mail box area, during the late afternoon, for the next two days. Tomorrow, he'd see if he could find out anything else useful about a Mark Bennet from around the town.

As he'd worked in the Alice on several previous occasions, he had many friends and work colleagues he knew well working there. Tonight he'd made an impromptu arrangement to meet some of these people for a drink at Bojangles Restaurant and Nightclub, a long-time haunt. Richard was invited but said he'd have to take a raincheck due to family commitments involving two small children.

Up early next day, Alan returned to the Police Headquarters. He'd been assigned an office and a vehicle for use while in town. Richard was working day shift for the next two days and would be available to assist him if needed.

Once Alan settled at his desk and had given a phone update to Darwin, he decided it was time to give Richard a proper briefing on the case. He was now committed to spend the next two days here trying to get leads and wanted Richard's help. Experience had taught him most investigations worked better if everyone was fully briefed.

Alan found a small conference room and asked Richard to join him. Here he asked Richard to keep everything confidential and, with that agreed, he walked him through everything he had found out up until now. Then, he asked Richard what ideas he had about how to try to track this man down, since he was more familiar with this town. His trust in Richard was well rewarded. Within five minutes, they had made a list of more tasks than they could do in the next two days. To aid in this endeavour, they divided up these tasks between the two of them.

Richard would focus on the flat and its ownership. The plan was for him to find out from the land titles office who was its owner. If Mark was a renter, he would get details from the real estate agent of any rental agreement. The agreement could include references and other potentially relevant information. He would also prepare a warrant to gain entry to the flat tomorrow. This warrant would provide a back-up plan if their mail contact did not turn up at all or simply did not have access to the flat.

Alan would focus on the vehicle itself. He would investigate details of its age, original purchaser and any previous known locations. He would also look for records of fines, breaches or insurance claims. In addition, he would seek information from Darwin about the accessories and fittings done to the truck along with any garages where it had been serviced. Alan would also look for anything else which would pin down its usage and perhaps give a clue as to where Mark went when he was out of town.

He would also try to obtain information on any local people with the name of Mark Bennet from different record sources such as listed bank accounts and the Registrar of Births, Deaths and Marriages. The trouble was Mark Bennet was a common name, meaning there may be more than one person with this name in a town like Alice Springs. At least it was a small town from a business sense. This meant there would be less places to check.

Alan and Richard planned to reconvene for lunch. At this time, they would jointly ring the vehicle investigation team in Darwin to see if they had anything definite at their end. Then they'd plan their afternoon's activities which would include surveillance of the post box for any sign of a mail collector. They decided they should cover the full afternoon in the event the person came early.

They reconvened at lunchtime over a steak sandwich at a café. Alan bought both meals on his expense account. They both agreed it had been a frustrating morning. They were equally amazed at the level of invisibility which seemed to surround this Mark Bennet.

The flat was owned by a corporation which had a Sydney post box address. It had not yet proved possible to trace back to the owner or owners behind this corporation as it appeared to have a complex legal structure relating to the ownership of it.

Nothing useful had come from the investigation of the vehicle. The purchaser was verified to be a Mark Bennet. He had purchased it new three years ago from the Toyota agent in Alice Springs. He had given his address as the flat they had already visited but gave no other contact details. He had paid cash for it with a bank cheque drawn to Westpac, Alice Springs. They may be able to trace this transaction through to bank accounts or other identity information in due course. The vehicle had returned for its first two warranty services, but then the vehicle vanished from their system. The owner had paid cash for the costs incurred during both of these warranty services. Alan had also traced the supplier of the bull bar and winch fitted to the vehicle. They had been fitted just after purchase in Alice Springs. In both cases, Mark had provided no information except the same residential address. They had shown these vehicle suppliers Mark's photo. While all of them thought it could be him- none of them was positive. As one of them pointed out, "it was three years ago, after all."

After lunch, they rang the vehicle yard in Darwin on Alan's mobile phone while sitting in the police car. They talked to a constable who'd spent the morning alongside the workshop crew while they started to take the vehicle apart.

All agreed on the fact the vehicle was far too clean. The cabin had been stripped of all its regular contents. Then, it had been cleaned using both detergents and solvents, to get it to an extraordinary level of cleanness. So far there was little to indicate they would find any DNA or other useful evidence about former occupants. However, they were yet to pull out all the seats and other fittings which may reveal something. The back tray and the cooler box had a similar level of cleanliness but not as thorough, as evidenced by a few fibres and other minor residue in its corners.

However, there was one really significant piece of news and it was a jackpot. The back passenger side tire matched the cast taken from the track near the billabong - including the piece of missing rubber from the inside of the tread.

At this time, the head of the workshop's voice came over the top. "Well, Alan, if we get nothing else- I think this will nail it. It as good as says this vehicle was the one which made the track next to the Mary River billabong: where you found your Crocodile Man. If I was a betting man, I'd say there are great odds on a 'Mr. Mark Bennet' being your Crocodile Man. If it's not him, he was at least there with the Crocodile Man. All we need now is some of his DNA from the car- or better still, from his flat- for it to be an absolute dead certainty of his identity."

As they now had an excellent basis for getting a search warrant of the flat, Richard said he would organize this if Alan wanted to go and start surveillance at the letter box.

It was turning into a stinking hot afternoon, with thundery clouds rising over the West McDonnell Ranges and Alan suspected Richard's suggestion was as much about a strong desire for some air-conditioned comfort. This suited him.

Alan liked the idea of parking himself in an obscure corner of the flats where he could see what transpired. He often got ideas for further inquiries while doing surveillance of this type. He did not mind the heat- although he preferred typical Alice Springs days when the air was dry, not today with bubbling layers of humidity.

Alan said, "Can you try to organize entry for ten tomorrow morning, when most people are at work? I'd rather keep it low key for now though it's likely to make it into Saturday's newspapers. One way or another, we'll have to do a news conference before the end of tomorrow, or we'll be accused of a cover-up."

Richard nodded.

Alan asked him to drop him to the flats before he went back into town to get a search warrant and entry team organised.

It was just after two pm when Richard left him off and drove away. Alan had a bottle of water and a newspaper to help pass away the long afternoon. There was a courtyard where he could sit to watch the post boxes. It had two seats and a table under a shady tree. It was located just inside the entrance from the street to the flats and gave a good view across to the post boxes.

Alan settled himself on a seat with his paper open. An hour passed with the only sounds being the hum of air conditioners and the buzz of an occasional fly willing to brave the heat. Alan felt feel his shirt sticking to his back. It was bloody hot and more than a bit humid- not exactly the best day for a stakeout. Still the heat meant he had no company and this suited him just fine.

About three-thirty, he heard the noise of a car coming along the street towards him. It was a beat-up old Ford Falcon- the sort loved across aboriginal communities. A weather-beaten man, who appeared to be in his fifties, got out of the vehicle and walked purposefully to the mailboxes with key in hand. He went directly to Mailbox Number 11: Mark's flat. He opened it and proceeded to sort through its contents. It looked like a dozen items of junk mail and three actual letters. The man tossed the junk mail into a bin. He started to walk back towards his car, carrying these three letters.

It was time for Alan to act. He got up and walked across to where the man's car was parked. He reached it a second before the man did. He put his body between the man and the car door. Up until this point, the man had seemed completely unaware of Alan. Suddenly, though, he realized his path was blocked.

He looked up. "Excuse me," he said in a surprisingly polite manner, "I need to get into my car."

Alan flipped open his police identification, nodded and replied, "Sure, but I need to ask a few questions before you do."

The man looked perplexed and annoyed. "You think I'm nicking his mail, don't you? Well, you're wrong. See, I've got the key," he spat out, waving it in Alan's face, his hostility rising.

Alan held up a hand to calm him. He could tell this guy was a heavy drinker and prone to a bit of temper, bloodshot eyes and a waft of beer confirming this. He said, "Calm down, old fella, no one is accusing you of anything. We're just trying to track down the man who owns those letters. We figured you may be able to help us. It would be even better if you would come and sit with me, under that shady tree, and talk with me. I'd like you to tell me how you know Mark Bennett and why you collect his mail. When we have the story straight, you'll be free to go. We might need to check those letters for any addresses, and later, we may need you to come to the police station to make a statement- but that's it."

In five minutes, Alan had the story straight. The man, Fred, mostly came around five pm on a Thursday to pick up any mail. He'd come early today because he was meeting some mates later to have a drink and needed his money. He was on a disability pension since he had hurt his back over three years ago. He said he'd only met Mark the one time. Then Fred had met him in a bar right after he got out of the hospital. They had chatted over a drink. This had occurred three years ago- soon after his accident had happened.

Mark had told him he worked out of town a lot and was needing someone to check his mail each week. This person would need to throw the junk mail away and put the real stuff into an envelope to send on to a post box address in Katherine. In return, Mark would pay him sixty dollars a month. This money would come to him in this mailbox along with the other mail.

Fred had now been doing this for three years. Each month, without fail, the letter with his money had come. For the entire first year, he received sixty dollars a month, as promised. The next year, however, he received seventy a month and now it had increased to eighty dollars a month, earlier this year. There had also been the odd bit extra, at the end of the year- almost like a Christmas bonus.

He showed Alan the letters he had collected. Two were letters addressed to Mark Bennet: one looked like an electricity bill and the other looked like a promotional letter from the Desert Sails Resort at Yulara. Alan thought this second letter was probably just junk mail- a bulk mail-out from one of those resold mail lists. He decided he would reserve full judgement until it was opened.

The third letter was addressed to the man who sat in front of him. It included his name, care of this address, printed on a sticky label which was stuck on the front of the envelope along with a standard postage stamp. There was no other clue or writing contained on the outside of the envelope.

Alan handled all the mail carefully by touching only the very corners. He realised now he would have to have to bring this man down to the police station to make a statement. He would also have to take the envelope, money and other letters for analysis.

Alan turned to Fred and said, "Listen, I'm very sorry- but we think something bad may have happened to Mark. We are trying to trace him. Despite what I said earlier, I do have to ask you to come to the police station now. We'll also have to analyse those letters, but don't worry, though, I'll give you the eighty dollars you're said you're expecting along with an extra twenty for your trouble. It'll only take half an hour before you're on your way again."

He thought the man would grumble but was surprised when he flashed him a toothy smile. "Well, I have to admit, it sounds fair so long as I get my money. I promised me mates that I'd buy the drinks this week. It's my turn, so I need the cash."

He continued, "While I only met that Mark bloke once, he seemed very fair. I think it was more than reasonable to give me a raise each year. So, if he needs a bit of help in return from me, 'tis the least I can do. Do you need the key? Or shall I keep doing what I've been doing?"

Alan looked at him and grinned back. "If you reckon money will keep coming, you should keep the key- at least for now. Just drop in any new mail to the local police station each week- even the junk mail. Make sure you pick it out carefully and put it in a clean plastic bag without touching the sides of each letter."

The man grinned back, liking this idea. "Right you are."

Alan walked over and collected the junk mail from the bin where the man had dropped it. "I need to check this too, just in case there's anything that helps us find him," he said. "One more thing, in return for the extra twenty I promised, how about you give me a drive back to the station? I'll call it a taxi fare. It's too bloody hot today to walk that far. It will also save me having to call a patrol car or taxi to come to get us."

The man nodded and grunted. "More than fair, I reckon."

Richard looked up with surprise when Alan returned with his hobo friend. Alan quickly told Richard the story. Then, he asked Richard to witness his payment of a hundred dollars to the man in order to allow him to make an expense claim.

Alan took one hundred dollars from his wallet and passed it over to Fred. Then he wrote a short statement and read it back to Fred. When Fred nodded in agreement, Alan asked him to sign the bottom of the statement. Last, Alan and Richard countersigned. Fred was now free to go and left with a cheery wave.

Alan called out, "No driving that car until tomorrow if you have a skin full." The man nodded and doffed his hat.

As Fred disappeared, Richard turned to Alan and said, "Seems like you have a different way of doing things than how I'm allowed.

Here I'd have to take the money as evidence- even though I know it belongs to the man. Then, I'm sure he would've been seriously annoyed not to have his drinking money."

Alan nodded. "It's definitely better this way: he's happy and we got what we needed along with some goodwill. The worst thing which can happen now is I'll be down a hundred if they don't refund my claim. But, at the end of the day, I'm sure there'll be the eighty in the envelope and a taxi would've cost another twenty, anyways. Due to all this, I'm sure my boss will approve my claim.

"Though, I did ask you to sign it with me. That way no one can say I'm putting my hand in the honey pot. How about we get gloves so we can open those letters and see if there's anything useful in them?"

The first letter was the money as expected. There was nothing else included in the envelope but the four new-looking twenty-dollar notes. "Off for some fingerprinting, I reckon," said Richard, "though I doubt we'll find anything."

Also, as expected, the second envelope was an electricity account. The usage was miniscule which suggested Mark Bennet had barely been home in the previous quarter of the year. "Something to follow up, the account information. I doubt it'll take us anywhere either," said Alan.

The third letter was much more interesting. It was a customer follow-up inquiry, along with a bonus voucher, sent from the Desert Sails Resort in Yulara. Alan knew the place well as he had stayed there more than once.

The letter indicated, following Mr Bennet's recent stay in their facility, they were seeking feedback on his experience and satisfaction. In return for him taking the time to complete the survey and send it back (or fill it out online), a bonus discount voucher giving 30 percent off his next stay was enclosed.

The letter did not give a date of stay but it had a reference number. By the time Richard had finished reading, Alan was on the phone to Desert Sails. In just a few minutes, the desk clerk had confirmed there had been a Mark Bennet who had stayed there in a luxury double room for one night in early August and gave Alan the exact date. The lady who answered his call also told him their records indicated Mr Bennet had a companion with him during his stay. She based this on a room service order which included two portions of an entrée and main course for a late dinner, along with a payment for two buffet breakfasts the next morning.

Alan's next question was the clincher. "Do you have any CCTV footage of either the reception or the breakfast buffet area?"

The lady answered, "Certainly, sir, we have it for both areas- at least for the buffet entrance. The footage is kept for 3 months. Therefore, footage for this date should still be available. I will of course need to sight your actual police authority before I'm able to allow you to view it. In the meantime, I'll ensure it's held securely."

Now, Alan had to decide which to take care of first: Yulara or the search of the flat. He wanted to be there for both. He asked Richard what he thought.

Richard responded immediately by saying, "Definitely Yulara. I know they've promised to keep the footage, but you know how it is with these things- Murphy's law being alive and well and with great potential for stuff-ups. That flat's not going anywhere, we can easily put it back a day. I know that makes it on the weekend but it doesn't really matter. Perhaps we can get the locksmith to try to get the door open tomorrow without smashing the lock. If that doesn't work, we'll go in with the heavy gear the next day."

It was agreed upon: they would make the run out to Yulara tonight, to seek to view the footage first thing in the morning. Alan raised his eyebrows at Richard's enthusiasm to include himself in the trip. "Don't you have any family commitments tonight?"

Richard grimaced a bit. "I know, should go home, let someone else go with you. But I wouldn't miss it for quids: a real live murder investigation when we may get to see our victim's head in the flesh. I'll have to treat the family to a special dinner Saturday night to make up. Cathy will be sweet once I explain. She's a nurse and has the night off. Tomorrow the kids will be at school anyways."

It was ten pm when they arrived at Yulara. They were both bleary-eyed from 450 kilometres of driving. As expected, the duty manager met them upon their arrival.

Alan gave him a brief explanation. "We're trying to trace all the movements of a man who appears to have gone missing. His stay here appears to be his last known location."

The duty manager passed over room key cards and told them he had organised for the resort manager to meet them soon after nine am tomorrow, to go through the CCTV footage with them.

Alan asked if it was possible now for one of the staff to spend a few minutes showing him the layout of the buildings. He asked this tour to include where their former guest's room was, the route from reception to the room and the location of any cameras which may have picked up the images of the former occupants.

After ten minutes, they had it mapped out. They were hopeful there would be images from three or four cameras. It should be fairly straightforward as they had an exact time of check in.

After an early morning walk the next morning, Alan found himself twitching with impatience as he ate a leisurely breakfast. However, he could not complain. The resort was being very helpful as they were obviously keen to handle such a sensitive inquiry in a low-key way. He knew the resort needed to deal with the early morning checkout rush and getting people out onto tour coaches, before it was reasonable to have the manager's time for himself.

After finishing his breakfast, at around a quarter to nine, he advised the receptionist he was ready and waiting for the manager meeting. Five minutes later, Alan and Richard were introduced to the Resort Manager and a technician. They were taken to a viewing room which included several monitors. The technician quickly scrolled through the footage until they came to the appropriate booking date.

Since they had a check-in time of 8:54 pm, they fast-forwarded the footage again until around eight pm. Then, they slowed the footage to rapid view. There were three cameras running on adjacent screens, all showing concurrent feeds. One camera showed the driveway and resort entrance in a wide view, another showed the reception area. The last showed the final passage way heading towards the room in question. The time was displayed on all feeds.

At 8:50 pm, a white four-wheel drive tray-back flashed past along the driveway before passing from view. Alan felt his heart skip a beat upon seeing it. He was nearly certain this was the vehicle found. Even in the dim light of the evening, the cooler box was clearly visible.

He put up his hand to indicate this finding. The technician stopped and backed up the feed, then started a copying machine. The images restarted again at normal speed. Now, they could watch the footage in full detail. It was definitely the same Toyota located in Darwin. They watched as it passed from view and saw its brake lights come on as it turned sideways into the car park entrance before vanishing from sight.

A couple of minutes later, this same camera picked up a man who looked like the photo of Mark Bennet. He walked towards and went through the entrance, holding hands with a medium-sized girl with shoulder length dark hair. Their manner appeared to be affectionate. The light and detail were not very good, but it was enough to clearly see this was Mark with an unknown lady.

A few seconds later, Mark came clearly into view in the second camera feed. He was approaching reception while holding a booking slip. The girl could be seen back at the edge of the screen. They could not see her well. It looked like she was waiting behind as he did the formalities. A third camera picked them up a minute later, walking down the passage way towards the room with their arms around each other in an intimate manner. This time it gave a full-face picture of the girl. The technician zoomed in on her face and it was fully clear and sharp.

Richard whistled. "She's a sweet-looking thing! Wonder what they'll be doing tonight? With that dark hair she could be Spanish or Italian." They disappeared from view as they passed the camera.

A few minutes later, Mark reappeared by himself. They tracked him back outside using the cameras. Then, he went back in again carrying an overnight bag and a backpack.

Alan asked to pause and zoom in on the backpack. It looked like luggage belonging to the girl. Maybe she was a backpacker Mark Bennet had picked up for a night of fun. Perhaps the detail of the pack could help work out where she came from originally.

However, this image was not nearly sharp enough for any kind of specific description of the backpack. Maybe police technicians back in Darwin could work it up more. They started the tape again as Mark continued on walking. There was a period of a couple of minutes when he vanished. Then, he came back towards reception and soon returned back towards the room now carrying a bottle of champagne. Once he passed the camera, neither Mark nor the woman were seen again for the rest of the night. The only further thing on the night's footage was of a waiter carrying room service to the room a couple of hours later.

They moved to next morning's footage of the passage near their room. They skipped through this quickly for the most part. Whenever people appeared, the technician would slow down the footage in order to work out their identities.

About eight am, Mark and the girl reappeared. They were very lovey-dovey. She looked radiant and fresh. She was half skipping as she walked beside him while chatting excitedly. This was much different from her relatively subdued manner of last night. The cameras followed them both going in and out of the breakfast café. Then, half an hour later, they were checking out of the resort.

Everyone leaned back and relaxed for a minute. Alan and Richard felt stunned. The footage was brilliant! Some parts of it were sharp enough for a TV broadcast. While they did not know if the girl had stayed with Mark beyond this day, she was clearly more

VICTIM   GRAHAM WILSON

than a casual acquaintance. This conclusion was indicated by the footage in the morning where it looked like they knew each other well and were travelling together.

Alan knew he would not be surprised if she turned up again later in the story- perhaps even as the source of the footprint at the billabong. There was something in her manner which seemed to fit with the person in Sandy's dream. He'd love to show Sandy the footage, see what she thought. Perhaps, if he got home to Darwin tonight, he could. This was in spite the fact he knew his speculation was way in front of the evidence they had seen so far.

The real questions were: who was she and how did she know Mark? Had he just picked her up on her travels? In a day or two, would she be gone on her own way again?

Suddenly, Alan realised the resort manager was talking to him. He switched his attention back to him. The resort manager said, "I trust that this is useful to you. We'll be able to give you a copy in about five minutes- once we burn it to a DVD. It's just copied to our computer's memory for now. I ask that you're discreet at this stage in your usage of it. I'd prefer not to give an impression that we spy on our guests."

Alan reassured him by saying, "Police eyes only at this stage. We do need to try to identify the girl, though. It's highly possible we'll need to use a couple of close-up stills of her face in the media in order to do so. In the meantime, I need you to hold the original footage in a secure place until we determine if we need it further."

The manager nodded. "Yes, can do that. The original section for those two days will go in the resort safe until we hear from you as to what you want to do with it."

Alan agreed they had what they needed from the footage for now. The last thing they needed was a copy of all the booking details. This would need to include how it was paid for, any credit card number and the email address used in the transaction.

129

Within a few minutes, they had all they needed and were on their way back to Alice. As Alan drove, Richard lined up the search of the flat for three pm this afternoon.

After the excitement of the CCTV footage, the search of the flat was a disappointing affair. The place was effectively empty. There was not a single personal item to be found, no toiletries and not even a cake of soap in the bathroom. There was no food other than a few unopened tins in a cupboard. There weren't even any papers except one old newspaper. There was nothing in the flat but the following: a stripped bed with clean folded sheets, a towel sitting on top of the bed and a table with two chairs. The cupboards were empty except for a small number of plates, saucepans and cutlery. They were all shining clean as if they had never even been used.

Within fifteen minutes Alan lost interest. His work in Alice Springs was now complete and he booked a seat on the next plane to Darwin leaving in just over an hour. He asked Richard to follow-up on any of the loose ends in Alice Springs while thanking him greatly for his help.

He suspected he would return next week and spend more days on the road in order to try to track the movements of Mark Bennet and this girl after they left Yulara. Right now, however, he wanted to get home to Sandy.

He particularly wanted to show her the image of the girl's face.

VICTIM   GRAHAM WILSON

Chapter 11 – The Mystery Lady

Alan arrived back in Darwin about seven pm on Friday night. He'd told Sandy at lunchtime he was unsure if he could get home tonight- but he would definitely try his best. She promised to be waiting when he did.

Alan remembered a saying of his copper mates, soon after he had first started in the police. He had been out in the bush for a week and was really looking forward to returning to his wife. He'd said, "The second bang will be when the screen door slams."

Alan really got this statement now. He'd been thinking about Sandy in an intimate way the whole flight home. His desire grew ever stronger as he willed the taxi to go quicker. As he closed the front door, they were already both tearing at each other's clothes and barely made it to the bed. Now, they lay entwined together. He looked at the tangle of clothes, sheets and limbs which represented their desire for each other.

He laughed. "Ever since I met you, I've been in a hurry to get into bed with you- but it's never happened that fast before."

Sandy had a smug, mischievous look on her face. "Well, in the month we've been together, you've never been away for a night- let alone two! I think it was making up for lost time. I really loved your desperation for me! I hope for some more later, too."

Now that the intense need had passed, Alan remembered the DVD. He got up and turned on the TV on the bedroom wall. He slotted in the DVD- saying nothing as he did so. Sandy half watched with disinterested puzzlement. For the first minute, it simply showed the empty lobby of a hotel. Then, a white Toyota came past the entrance. Sandy was still not really paying attention.

A couple came walking up to the lobby hand in hand. Abruptly, Sandy sat up in bed, a look of intense concentration on her face. She watched with full attention as the man checked in, saying a couple of times, "I wish I could see her properly."

Then, as the couple walked directly towards the camera in the passage and their faces came into sharp focus, Sandy let out a cry. "It's her! I just know, it's her! The woman in my dream at the billabong. The man looks familiar, too. He looks like the guy she was with and frightened of. Her mind picture of him is different, almost like looking at him from the inside instead of the outside.

"But it's definitely her face- I absolutely know it's her! It's strange, too, because I've never seen her face from the outside. I only know what it feels like from when I was looking through the inside of her mind. Despite this, her face is clear to me. It's like a self-awareness thing. She has this razor-sharp image of herself in her own mind and it is also how this man sees her. It's her interpretation of the image he sees when he looks at her.

I sense she's been using her body and face to seduce him. Because of that, she can see very clearly how he sees her. I liken it to a form of thought transference. It's like her image reflected through two mirrors: the first one in his mind and the second in her own mind. Despite this the image isn't distorted by these reflections- it's remains totally clear. This image is the face of the girl in this video.

"Don't ask me how I know this. Don't even ask me if the dream I had was real. Yet, when I see this lady in the video, I know without any doubt- she was the person in my dreams. It was her, filled with terror, expecting to become the victim and who then saw the crocodile cause her lover's destruction beside the billabong. The only problem is: I don't know what's real and what's just her fear or imagination interpreting things. I thought I saw her tied up at some stage. I think I even told you this on the night of the dream. Now, I don't know if it's real anymore. The images all seem to blur into one another now.

"I cannot think of her as a killer, because inside her mind is only terror and confusion leading her to seek escape. Maybe she pushed him into the water in an act of desperation as she tried to get away from him beside the river. Then, a crocodile grabbed him.

Perhaps it was self-defence. Inside her mind, she's not a murderer-only a terrified girl."

So Alan had a psychic certainty that the man and woman were together at the billabong on the fateful day. But, it was not proof. It was not even a shred of something which would lead to proof.

More importantly, he had no idea who this lady was. On top of this, despite having the name of Mark Bennet for the man, he had no real idea of who the man was either.

If anything, the man was even more mysterious than her. He'd lived in Alice Springs for at least three years yet appeared to have no friends and no one had even properly spoken to him. The exception was the mail collector who he had hired three years ago. He had to be a real person, though, because he definitely had a real body- if the body was in fact his. The Toyota was linked to the billabong and then to him. However, there was nothing to link him to the billabong, or anywhere else for that matter, except the Toyota. This link was only because Mark Bennet's name and photo was on his driver's licence. All these links to links were starting to give him a headache. Now he must get some real evidence to join all the links together.

He had already tried and failed to get any other links to the victim from around the Mary River. Because of this, he would now work his way south towards Alice Springs. He would head back towards the last known location of the man at Yulara, following down along the Stuart Highway and the other main roads, stopping at various locations. Along the way he'd try to find someone who remembered Mark or the girl. While the Toyota was well set up for cross-country travel, it would still need to follow main roads at some points and take on fuel. Taking the pictures of Mark Bennet and this girl with him, while stopping at road-houses, asking for anyone who remembered them, seemed an obvious way to go.

The next Monday Alan started his trip at the very top of the route. Once he was beyond the outskirts of Darwin, he started visiting all the roadhouses along the route. He began his inquiries at

Adelaide River. Then he proceeded on to Hayes Creek, Emerald Springs and Pine Creek. When he came to Katherine he decided it was too hard to check properly since it was a big town. So, he made only cursory inquiries in Katherine before continuing on down the highway to stop off at Mataranka and Larrimah. After all these stops, he had still found out nothing. He felt discouraged but decided he would push on anyway. At Daly Waters, he had a glimmer that his luck was changing.

The bar tender at Daly Waters had no real memory of Mark- but the picture of the pretty dark-haired woman woke something in his memory. He looked at it long and hard for a minute before saying, "Well, I wouldn't want to swear on my mother's grave, but I reckon she stopped here for breakfast with a bloke who could be your man. It was maybe a couple of months ago. I remember her because she was a real looker but still nice at the same time. She and the man were sitting up at the bar, about ten in the morning, each eating a big plate of bacon and eggs. She seemed really hungry. When I remarked on this, she said they had got up and left really early without breakfast.

I asked, 'Did you come from Katherine?'

"She said, 'No, from Heartbreak Hotel. It's such a funny name for such a lovely place.' It's those words which made her stick in my mind. I wouldn't have exactly called Heartbreak Hotel lovely myself- but it was obviously special for her."

With this new clue, Alan continued out to Heartbreak Hotel. Here he got a similarly vague description of a man and a slightly clearer description of the woman: "a lovely lass from overseas. She was very pretty and also very affectionate towards the man."

Someone else remembered she'd talked of driving across the grassy plains of the Barkly, seeing lots of cattle. From this, Alan took an educated guess concerning their travel route. Most likely, they travelled up the Tablelands Highway from Barkly Homestead- the next roadhouse at the corner of the main road to Queensland.

Next morning, Alan headed down to the Barkly Homestead. He arrived around mid-morning. Soon he hit the jackpot with a girl who'd worked there for the last few months and normally worked during the day shift. She remembered having served the man and woman in the photo on one morning around a couple of months ago. The man had also bought fuel. His purchase was more than 100 litres due to his Toyota having long-range tanks.

She said, "It was around this time in the morning. I remember them both well. We call the man Mark B. He fuels up here from time to time. He always pays cash- different from most other travellers. I've heard from others here that he does a bit of work around this area- though I don't really know him myself.

"I do remember the girl, though. She looked just the same as in the photo. I remember because we had a chat while Mark B was giving his vehicle the once-over: you know – checking oil, water, tires – all that sort of thing. Anyway, Susan- at least that was what she said her name was- asked me what the time was. She said she needed to work out the time difference to England because she wanted to ring her mum. She said she hadn't spoken to her mum in more than a week- not since before she came to Alice. She worked out it was the middle of the night in England and said that was no good, so she said she'd leave it until her next stop.

"You could tell she really liked Mark from the way she watched him work. He was an OK-looking bloke, strong and tough- but a bit hard around the edges. He seemed a real bushman, but I'd seen him before a couple times with other pretty girls. She was much classier than him- which made me curious. They seemed a strange match to me.

"I asked her how she met Mark. She told me they'd met just after she'd flown into Cairns. They'd been on a reef tour together as diving buddies. After the tour, they'd just sort of hooked up.

Now they were travelling through the outback together for a couple weeks before her plane flew out of Darwin. I could tell she was really keen on him. He came up in the end of our conversation and put his hand on her in a way which showed he felt the same way about her. That's it really. We chatted for about five minutes and that's pretty much what she told me."

Alan asked, "Did she say she was English, herself? Or just that her mother was living there currently?"

The lady thought about it for a minute. "Well, she definitely talked about the time in England and ringing her mother there. She didn't actually say she was English, but you could hardly mistake her lovely polite accent, you know. Not quite upper crust, but definitely well brought up- in that English sort of way."

Alan felt like he was finally getting somewhere. He was well on the way to identifying the girl in the photo. Her first name was Susan, she came from England, had flown into Cairns perhaps two or three weeks earlier and had gone diving on a boat tour to the outer Barrier Reef.

He rang his boss in Darwin and got his permission to go onto Cairns. There was a direct flight from Alice Springs tomorrow he could take if he hurried. It was over seven hundred kilometres from where he was to the Alice so he had a long drive ahead of him.

Alan made it to Cairns by mid-afternoon the next day. He called to the local police station shortly after arriving. To ensure Alan had the required authority for his inquiries, they offered him the assistance of a local constable for the next morning. As most tour shops had shut down already for the day, Alan decided to hit them early next day along with boat companies who ran the reef and diving tours. He'd start with the boat companies as they would have passenger lists for each day.

He had two names to look for on these lists: a Susan, with surname unknown, and a Mark. It would probably be Mark Bennet- though the person who'd checked the Katherine mailbox said a letter had turned up in the mailbox for a Mark Butler yesterday. It could be a mistake. However, just in case, he would also look out for any Mark Butler listed while he was checking the lists of passengers.

Next morning they struck lucky at the first visit. Alan happened to remember a tour on a Quicksilver boat he had done to the outer reef a couple of years ago. He remembered it had diving included and decided this sounded like the best way to narrow down the numbers.

Therefore, Alan and Constable Davey began with Quicksilver Tours. They provided a booking person to go through the records with them. He picked a three-week period starting from just before the night in Yulara and worked his way back. It was slow, tedious work. They had already gone through a couple of weeks of booking sheets before they finally found something. There it was a Mark Bennet booked on the 8:30 AM departure to the outer reef.

Alan looked for the name Susan and found four instances of the name. In addition, he found another three with only 'S' initials for the first name. They next went to check the diving group records. There they both were: Susan McDonald and Mark Bennet. Both had been divers in the second group of the day. They had ages listed next to their names, Susan was listed as being 24 and Mark as being 34. There were diving ticket numbers listed by each. They could probably get more identity information from the diving ticket numbers in due course, but it would take some time. However, Alan was in a hurry. He could see the end of the case in sight and wanted to wrap it up.

Next, they decided to try checking the international airline arrivals They started with international flights into Cairns on the previous days. There were quite a few so they began with the airline arrivals on the day before. Here there were lots more people listed, but now they had a surname to make it much easier.

In five minutes, they had an arrival match. It was on a flight out of Tokyo which got in mid-morning of the previous day. Now all they needed was a passport number and they would have an English identity. Sure enough, another half hour on the telephone got them this requested record. Alan thanked Constable Davey and agreed he could take it from there. He asked if the constable could send official copies of these documents to the Darwin office. There was a scheduled midday flight back to Darwin and Alan got on it.

Next day he prepared an official request to go via the Federal Police seeking assistance of the UK police force in locating and questioning Susan McDonald. He also wanted to see a photo, even though he had no doubt he'd identified his mystery girl.

He now had a good brief of evidence to show she was a significant person of interest in the investigation. On one hand, she may be able to assist putting together the picture of what happened. On the other she may end up being a suspect in a murder case. For now he would keep an open mind and see where the evidence led him.

After this was done, he called to the vehicle workshop where Mark's car was stored. Everything had been pulled out of it now and lots of samples had been taken for analysis. He asked to be put on to the workshop foreman, in order to get a quick rundown of what had been found. He wanted to cut to the chase rather than read lots of reports to find the information.

The foreman described how the vehicle had been carefully cleaned- at least the tray and cabin had been. The only significant fibres in these locations came from common cleaning cloths. In these areas, the car had been effectively stripped bare and nothing of value remained: but for three exceptions. The first exception was a lipstick container which had fallen below the passenger seat and rolled under the seat mounting rails. It had been sent off for fingerprint testing and DNA checking. These results were now in: a finger and thumb imprint had been found on the lipstick case along with some DNA on the lipstick itself. The second thing was a trace of human DNA found in a corner of the cooler box. It was found after they'd removed the box and cut it apart. The third thing was what appeared to be a single spot of blood. It had dripped between the passenger seat and the side door. It sat on the floor in the small gap between the vinyl floor covering and the bottom door sill.

The DNA from the blood spot, the cooler box and the lipstick were all a match. And they were different from the DNA of the recovered body. No DNA which matched the recovered body had been found to date in the vehicle. Now, they needed to get DNA and fingerprints from Susan McDonald to see if it was a match for the samples from the car.

The other significant findings related to the tyre tracks and mud found on the vehicle. The mud on the number plate, and traces found on the under-body and tyres were all a good match for the soil types around the billabong. This evidence, although not conclusive, was supportive of this being a place the truck had been to recently. Most importantly the tyre track, showing the piece of missing rubber, from near the billabong, was a perfect match to the rear passenger tyre of this vehicle. It had both an identical tread profile and an identical place where the rubber was missing. This fact alone gave a 99 percent certainty that this vehicle was at the billabong around the time of the murder.

Alan returned to the office and worked on his report. He prepared a series of questions for the UK police to ask Susan McDonald. Alan had tracked her to Barkly Homestead and probably to Daly Waters. After Daly Waters, however, she had vanished.

Therefore, the UK Police should ask her where she had first met Mark Bennet, her relationship to him and where she had gone with him. If nothing else, it would give a sense of her truthfulness. They should also request her DNA and fingerprints. They could confirm she had travelled with Mark in the car from video footage and witnesses. If they matched her DNA and fingerprints to the car samples it would be even more evidence of this fact- even though some locations were unusual, like the cooler box. If there was no match to these samples, it meant they were looking for another car passenger as well.

His judgement told him they should name Susan as a person of interest, not as a murder suspect, at this stage. They should say they were seeking her cooperation in tracking Mark's movements and determining what happened to him. The police were already under strong pressure to release the information they'd found about the vehicle along with the identities of Mark and Susan to the media.

Rumours were circulating about a girl, an overseas traveller, having been with this Crocodile Man and being involved in his murder. He did not know how such stories got out- but it was getting hard to keep a lid on it. Right now the media were on the trail of the double story of a Crocodile Man and a Mystery Girl. Soon, their names would be out.

The police could justify limiting the information released only if she was cooperating. This was on the basis she was giving them new leads in which they were looking into. Otherwise, they would need to make a statement to the press in the next few days seeking public assistance to gather more information on who these people were and where they went. Once they did this, the story would go ballistic. It had all the key ingredients: crocodiles, murder, sex and a backpacker alone with a man in the outback.

He hoped the woman would cooperate. He could feel pity for her if the media hounds were released on her. Sadly, it was out of his hands and he could only give her a couple of days to respond.

In addition, he would like to get a footprint from her, to see if it matched the print they found at the billabong. If it did, it would place her at that location. He knew the moment he asked for this print she would become highly suspicious since it was much more than routine exclusionary evidence. Therefore, they would sit on this for now and see what more they could find out.

He finished his report and cleared it with his boss. Soon after this he submitted the official request form to the Federal Police requesting they seek help from the UK police- marking it with a big urgent sticker. He would now follow up on the hundred other loose ends which surrounded this case.

He was sure he had found the key to this case, the Mystery Girl, Susan McDonald. God help her when this was made public.

Whatever she'd done, he would not want to be in her shoes now. He felt a strange affection for her. It was as if he already knew her from Sandy's dream.

Even though the evidence was not all in, his heart believed, without a doubt, she was the murderer. 'Why' was the burning question in his mind? What could have motivated her to turn on and kill this man who she had been so affectionate to beforehand? Why was she frightened of him? What was the secret hidden at the core of this? These things were what he really wanted to know. For now, however, he would have to be content with solving a murder.

VICTIM   GRAHAM WILSON

Chapter 12 – From Beyond the Grave

Susan had looked forward to a relaxing trip back to England: 22 hours of laid-back travel in her business class seat with gold class service. She intended to enjoy movies, good food and comfortable sleeps as this metal and glass bubble in the sky transported her across the world. Instead, in her hand was a message from beyond the grave. As she read these lines, she knew her life would never be the same again.

Less than five minutes ago, she was dreamily occupied in planning a comfortable life with David. She saw David, herself and a brood of tousle-haired children all living in a comfortable house in Sydney. She saw herself enjoying views out over the beautiful harbor in front of their home. She could envision occasional country trips in his sports car where they would blast along winding roads, enjoying the wind in their hair. It was a lovely mind image. She realised now she was as much in love with this image as with the person who could bring it to pass.

In the space of a minute, this life plan had become a smoking ruin. This other man could not and, most importantly, would not let her go. No matter where she went and what she did- he was determined to find his way back into her life, again and again.

First, he had taken over her body and mind. Then, when she had excised him from these, he took over her subconscious and dreams. He had even placed his seed within her during their time together. This meant it was not just himself- but the new life he had helped create which lived on in her now.

She thought she had managed to put distance between herself and everything which occurred when she was with Mark. She'd found a new man who loved her and she had promised herself to him. When David held her close in the night, the dreams with the crocodile spirit were kept at bay. She'd barely dreamt them while she slept in David's Australian bed beside him.

However, the moment David had left her side- Mark had reclaimed her. This time, though, his claim was different. It was clearly stated and felt full of his love. She had searched for this love within the words from the living man, but they had not been spoken. She had even searched for this love, even just a fragment of affection, in the eyes of the living man. The words had been kept hidden from her during all her time spent with Mark. Instead, they had only emerged now, declared by the dead man's spirit as words written on the page she now held, "I have loved you utterly since I first glimpsed you."

She stopped reading when she read these words. It was simply too painful. She did not want to hear this now. If she had a match, perhaps she could burn this page, so she'd never have to fully read it. Instead, it felt as if it were burning in her hand, expressing a demand for her full further attention- a demand driving her to read on and know it all.

Almost reluctantly, she picked the paper up and read on:

"You probably wonder why I say this now when I could not say it to your pleading eyes just a short while ago. I cannot answer as I don't know. All I know is I couldn't give you false hope for a future together in this life- to do that would have been a worse lie.

There was a time yesterday, when I was angry with you, I thought maybe I could kill you as I killed those others. But I knew, in that instant when you tried to jump in front of that truck, that it was impossible. In a choice between me and you- you must live. My life is of less importance.

I'm sorry my actions have frightened you. I've seen your fear of me in your eyes and I hate that. I understand why. Now, I must never hurt you anymore. That leaves only one way. With the first light of dawn, that time of choice has come and must be acted on.

I've just looked at your beautiful face one last time while you lie sleeping. It's peaceful. I hope your dreams are good and you dream of happy times with me. There are so many memories of you in my mind now and the joy will never go away. It will be my last memory.

I remember riding on the beach, sharing a helicopter dance and your eyes as I gave you the pendant and the ring. But most of all, I remember loving you, holding your body in my arms, your hair in my face, just loving you over and over and over again. While I've had you like this so many times, as I watch you sleep, I ache to feel you again this way- just one more time.

Before I write a final goodbye, I must tell you a few practical things. In my briefcase, combination 2153, you'll find two things which I'd like you to have. Don't give them to others- at least not until you've decided for yourself what you want to do with them. The first is a pouch of gem stones. They're mine, bought and paid for in full by me. They are all of high quality. I think their value is at least two million dollars. They now belong to you. The second is my diary. It tells of what I've done over the last five years. I ask that you read it, so you know the good and bad of me. After this, you may give it to the police or pass information in it to the families of others whose death I am responsible for. I wish I could feel guilt over them- but I don't. I didn't set out with the purpose of harming any of them. However, you must judge this statement and me with your own eyes and conscience.

I have made a will. It sits between the back leaf and cover of my diary. I inserted it and glued it closed. It's been witnessed by two friends I trust. It leaves almost all I possess to you and gives the details of how to access what I own.

Now, this is said, I must say goodbye. I leave this letter where I hope you will find it, alongside your English passport which contains a picture of your smiling face. I have just touched and kissed this picture one last time. I would kiss the real face, but that may awake you too soon.

It's time to go to the water's edge. My own crocodile totem will talk to the dreamtime crocodile spirit of this place until our spirits are one. Then, I'll swim out to join the crocodiles and offer my body to them as a gift. I'll wait until your eyes are open before I go. I'd rather not give you this pain, but you must see it to know I have truly gone. It's the only way you can have freedom from me again.

If any of me remains when it's done, I ask that you place the ashes of these parts in the place of the rainbow spirits. It is that place we looked at and loved together when first we walked out into the desert. At this place, my spirit will walk in freedom along with the many other spirits of this land. I will forever hold an image of your love amongst those twilight colours.

I wish you a good and happy life with someone else. Someone who will love you, and who you will love in return, in the same way that we have loved. I am blessed to have had this time with you.

All my love,

Mark

Susan sat there with tears streaming down her face. This total and unequivocal statement of his love was what she had wanted from him in life. Now his written words could never be spoken between them, could never be said face to face.

She felt a tide of bitter disappointment rise within her. She'd have chosen and taken him exactly as he had been in life. They could have shared the joy of their child together, lived a happy year or two together, perhaps longer, before dealing with the past.

Then, if the past still needed to be resolved, they could have tried to find a way through this together. Instead, he'd chosen self-sacrifice over opportunity. She had unwittingly aided and abetted him with his decision through her part in his murder. Despite all this, she loved him still and must honour his last wishes. She would need to read his diary and decide what to do with the information included within. It could not ever fit into a life with David.

In Mark's final sentence, he wished her to have a good and happy life with someone she loved in the same way she had loved him. She could not currently see David's face filling this space. She knew it was only stated as a wish. Nonetheless, she must seek to honour it- not just for Mark, but for herself, too. Perhaps it was also the best thing for David. It would not be fair for her to entrap him in a love less perfect than the one she'd shared with Mark.

A minute or two must have passed as Susan sat crying silently. She became aware of a stewardess looking at her with concern. She took out a tissue to wipe her eyes and nose. Then, she smiled back at the concerned stewardess saying, "It's alright, really. I was just reading something from a past life and it made me very emotional."

Chapter 13 – Wedding Plans

By the time Susan touched down in Heathrow, she was no longer sure of her decision to break off her engagement with David. It felt like she had again returned to being two people: one living in her dreams and subconscious and one who lived in day-to-day reality.

She had promised to marry David and nothing had changed her promise. The plans were now well underway for it to happen. Her family and friends were all excited about this promise of a trip to Australia. While she was still visiting in Australia, she and David had announced their wedding date to their respective families. Once it was announced, their families started busily arranging flights and holidays. Many were planning side trips to other parts of Australia, seeking her advice about places to visit and things to do while in Sydney.

It was like a juggernaut in how quickly it was off and running. She felt powerless to stop it. Her conscious mind wanted this wedding to happen and she hated the thought of derailing all these people's travel and holiday plans. On top of this, Mark had given her his blessing to be with someone else and wished her happiness in her life. Why should she not take him literally and go off to be happy with this man?

Like last time, her family was waiting to meet her at the airport. In addition, there was a smiling, vibrantly beautiful, excited Anne.

"Oh, Suz! I just can't wait to go to Australia and be your bridesmaid! Is there really a younger brother who is half as gorgeous as David?! If so, I can't wait to meet him! Will he be the best man? What dress do you want me to wear? Have you chosen your dress yet? How should we do our hair? Shall we have a girls' night before we go away?"

Susan held up her hand. "Whoa! With so many questions asked so quickly- I can't take it all in. Why don't I say yes to these things now? Then we can sit down tomorrow, talk about it properly."

Over the next week she met with Anne twice to discuss the wedding details. They more or less agreed on dresses and the other wedding things which they needed to do. Her parents had come on board easily since they both liked David, much preferring him to Edward. They said they were a bit surprised how fast it was happening but would support her in what she wanted.

At first, her father grumbled about the wedding location being in Australia, not in the local church where all her own extended family and friends could be present to witness the occasion. He said he wanted to pay for a big part of the wedding costs, as they were well off.

Susan understood this offer was partly family pride and partly his practical self. She said, "David and I are happy to have you pay a share of the wedding costs, but we want to pay our own share. David and his family are very well off too. They talk about it the same way as you- but really, they are seriously wealthy! They just don't like to boast. David has also done very well in business, himself, over the last five years, so he has his own income too."

Her father interjected at this point, "Okay- but why not get married here? It's where all the rest of your family and friends are and to have it here is our tradition."

Susan argued adamantly, "The reason we want to get married in Watson's Bay is because it's where we really got to know each other. We also love the church there and the general feel of the place. What I most want is for all my family and for as many of my friends as possible to come out to join us in our celebration of a new life together at the place we choose to begin it!"

"I'm not saying those statements are untrue, but my argument still stands as well. I suspect I won't ever be able to win this debate with you. So I think it is only fair we should be allowed to pay for at least half the cost of the wedding."

Susan suggested, "Dad, if you want to help out with money how about you help pay airfares for more of our extended family to fly there. They are not as well off as our family is. I am particularly referring to your sister, my only Scottish aunt, and cousins. We've enjoyed many trips up there, but they haven't had many here.

"Then, there is also Mum's brother, wife and his children. If Mum and you use your powers of persuasion, and a bit of your money, to get as many of them as possible on a plane here- that would be more than enough in my opinion. Perhaps, you could even rent a big house in Sydney for everyone to stay in for a week or two so everyone could have a great holiday while they are there."

In the end, she won her father and mother over. On behalf of both of them, her father gave her a cheque for ten thousand pounds stating Susan and David could spend it on whatever they liked related to the wedding. In addition to the money, he was now organising bookings for at least eight members of her extended family to come to the wedding and a big house in Sydney for them all to stay in together for a week before they went on their separate ways to have their own travels.

Susan knew it would be a lovely time with nights singing songs, telling stories and playing board or card games with all her cousins- just as they had done throughout their shared childhoods.

Since she was so busy making all the wedding plans, she'd barely thought of Mark or his letter. She did, however, remember her promise to herself to read Mark's diary. It was still there on her to do list- even though it was rather postponed for now.

She had given her notice to finish her laboratory job a week before she was due to fly out, to give herself a week to pack up and make any last-minute arrangements still needing to be completed. Then, she'd have almost a week in Sydney before the wedding. This meant she now had four weeks left until she finished with work. It did not seem like much time to complete everything, but she felt she was getting well organised and it would be time enough.

On the Friday night of her first week back in England, she met up with Maggie and her friend, Janet, in the city. Anne came with her. It was a night full of reminisces, diving in Cairns and jokes about former boyfriends. Everyone professed envy at her future.

Only one minor hiccup arose in the entire night. At one point, Maggie asked her, totally innocently, "Did you ever hear again from that Mark guy? You know the one you went diving with. You did seem keen on him? You told me that day in Kuranda that he'd asked you out the night before. You'd already gone out with us and so missed his invitation. The way he looked at you on the boat, I think he had the hots for you. Next day, the way you talked about him almost sounded like it was as if you wished you'd connected up again and had an Aussie outback affair."

After this unexpected interrogation, everyone was looking at Susan. She felt flushed and did not know what to say in reply.

Luckily, Anne came to the rescue. "She did meet her Aussie bloke, David, from Sydney. So obviously the other didn't amount to anything. Can't you tell she's embarrassed by the subject?"

With that said, everyone broke into fits of giggles and the moment passed by without another thought. The night ended with promises to keep in touch. Anne invited them both to Susan's hens' night. It was set to occur on the night she finished work.

Susan had just come home from work on the Monday night of her second week back, when the phone rang. As neither of her parents was near enough to answer, she picked it up. The voice was very familiar.

She realised with a shock it was Edward. She was surprised how it actually felt good to hear his voice. Her anger at him was long gone. First he congratulated her on her upcoming marriage. Instinctively, she knew there must be something else and he got to it in another minute.

He said, "I got a strange call today from Scotland Yard. It was from a Detective Inspector Brent. He wanted to talk to you. He said that he'd got this address and phone number from the passport office so it must still be the current address on your passport. He said he needed to talk to you urgently and left a number for me to pass on. He wouldn't say what it was about. I gave him your parents' address and phone number since I don't have your current mobile number. He may have already tried to ring, but I thought I should let you know."

Next morning, shortly after she arrived at work, she remembered and pulled out the number. *It was probably just some minor inquiry*, she thought. However, deep down, she could feel terror bubbling up inside her. *Please let it not be that!*

The number rang straight through. On the second ring, a pleasant voice answered, "Detective Brent here."

Susan identified herself. As she said her name, she felt something settle over the line- like a huge deadening weight.

He said, after a pause, "I need to talk to you with extreme urgency. It's a very serious matter. You may wish to arrange legal representation to be present during the interview. It's probably best if you come into our office here in Scotland Yard. If it's necessary, though, I could come somewhere to meet you."

Susan felt gobsmacked. Her mind was completely frozen. She needed to think for a minute to get her bearings. She said, stalling, "Could you tell me what it's about please?"

"I'm not at liberty to discuss it over the phone. All I can say is it concerns the trip you made to Australia in July and August of this year," replied the detective. "We understand you met a 'Mr. Mark Bennet' while on this trip. Would you be able to come in and see us today? It's very important we speak with you as soon as possible."

Chapter 14 – Scotland Yard

Susan declined the offer of a pick-up by a police car. She informed the detective she would rather take a taxi to Scotland Yard. She promised she would be there within an hour due to needing to organize a few critical work things first.

Currently, she was sitting in a cab as it stopped and started through busy London traffic. She needed to work on calming her panicked thoughts. Perhaps this request for an interview wasn't nearly as bad as it seemed. However, she must slow her mind and think clearly. She wondered if she should call Anne and ask her to find a lawyer to attend the interview with her. Instantly she dismissed this thought. She did not want anyone else involved in this- at least not until she had some idea what it was all about.

Mark may have been reported as missing by someone. Perhaps a person who knew they'd been together may have remembered her name from meeting her while she'd been with him. This scenario was most likely the reason they wanted to interview her.

She decided she'd say they had travelled together for a while and admit to having an affair with him. Then, she would say she'd left him at Timber Creek. She would say the reason for that was Mark was going on to Western Australia for work and she needed to head the opposite way to Darwin to catch her plane. She would say she was then given a lift to Darwin by someone she knew only by their first name. She must decide on what this name would be and commit it to memory.

She suddenly thought of her cousin, Robert Burns. The first name Robert would do as it was a really common man name. She could even say he asked her to call him simply Rob. If she was pushed hard about this person's identity, she could say she thought he might have said his second name was Burns- but she was not entirely sure. She figured by using a common first name of a relative, she could always say the last name slipped her mind since she was used to her relative's last name in relation to the overly common first name.

She hoped this would make it seem like she'd merely forgotten an inconsequential last name, opposed to her making up part of the story. She'd say he was driving a four-wheel drive station wagon. She would say she could not remember the make or model, but the colour was a dark blue. It was easy to remember this story. She could hold it together in her mind, it was simple and consistent.

She would say Rob parked outside where they had breakfast. Mark was inside for a meeting and she said goodbye to him there before walking outside to look for a way to get to Darwin. She had started chatting with Robert who revealed he lived in Darwin and had offered her a lift. As he seemed okay so she had taken him up the offer. He had dropped her off in the city very late in the afternoon. Rob had seemed like a nice guy. He told her he had a wife and two kids who lived in Darwin and was on his way back from the west. They'd chatted a bit and he was friendly, but there nothing more to really tell. This was all she knew about him. Yes, that was the story she'd tell the detective.

Then, she suddenly realized she would have to account for a whole day in Darwin. Perhaps she could give a vague description of staying at a backpacker's hostel in the middle of the city, with its name having currently escaped her. This cover story would have to do. When she got home, she'd Google some hostel names and learn the basic facts about the city. She would say she had slept most of the next day as she had been tired from the night on the Victoria River. The next morning, she'd say she flagged down a taxi in the street to take her to the airport for her ten o'clock flight. She would have to say she went early- as they would already know her check in time.

Susan was suddenly aware the taxi she was riding in was no longer moving. She'd reached her destination, so she paid the driver and got out. She realised that, during this simple ride she'd created a whole imaginary web of lies in her mind. She must be very careful as her concocted story was already getting tangled in her memory.

She took a deep, calming breath. She must stop having these flights of fancy! She needed to let the police do the talking, and thus see what they really knew and had to say. People got themselves into trouble when they started rambling.

Susan went up to the counter and asked to see Detective Brent. In less than a minute, she was shown to a meeting room. Two people came in a minute later: a smallish, solid man and a slim, stylish lady. She felt social protocol required she smile a greeting to them. There was no humour evident in their demeanour.

They introduced themselves as Detective Inspector Michael Brent and Detective Sergeant Rebecca Lacey. Susan introduced herself and then sat back to wait. She steeled herself to appear calm even though her heart was racing.

She assumed they would get this interview underway by telling her why they had asked to see her in the first place. Instead, they went through the formalities of a police interview. First, they began by telling her the entire interview was being recorded. Then, they told her whatever she said during this interview could be used as evidence for the current case. Last, they confirmed she did not wish to have a lawyer present. She shook her head at this question. After this action, there was a long pause.

Finally, Susan broke the silence. Looking at Detective Brent, she said, "You asked me to come and see you, indicating the matter was extremely urgent and not able to be dealt with on the phone. Could you please tell me why?"

Susan sensed a glance of admiration from Sergeant Lacey. Perhaps this indicated respect for her composure during such an unknown circumstance. In contrast, Detective Brent looked at her with a mildly annoyed expression. He flexed his fingers.

Finally, he replied, "Thank you for coming in, Susan. We've been asked to investigate a matter by the Australian Police. This request came specifically from the Northern Territory Police.

They've asked us to interview you and ask you a series of questions. These questions all concern your knowledge of, relationship to and movements with Mark Bennet from Alice Springs. Mr Bennet has mysteriously disappeared. The police are currently trying to ascertain his whereabouts. Therefore, on their behalf, I have a series of questions to ask you. If you're happy with this explanation, I'll go through them all one by one."

Susan nodded for him to proceed.

Detective Brent placed a sheet of paper on the table in front of him. It looked like it had about ten questions on it. Reading from this he began the interrogation, "Did you meet a Mark Bennet while in Australia?"

Susan simply answered, "Yes."

They looked at her questioningly, as if to say, 'Is that all?'

She continued to remain silent.

As if he impatient with the proceedings, Detective Brent moved restlessly. Susan remained impassive. After a long pause he moved on to the next question. "Where did you meet him?"

Susan answered, "In Cairns."

Detective Brent rolled his eyes. "Could you be more specific?"

She replied, "On a boat tour to the Great Barrier Reef. We were two of ten people on a dive together, diving buddies."

"Did you have a continuing relationship with him?"

Susan answered, "Yes."

"What was the nature of this relationship?"

Susan replied, "It was both a friendly and sexual relationship."

Susan could sense their frustration with her minimal answers. She had no intention of expanding her answers. She knew these people were not here to help her. Rather, their sole purpose was to gather evidence which they could later use against her. Knowing this she maintained her poker face.

Brent continued, "Did you go travelling with him?"

Again she answered, "Yes."

"Could you tell me where you travelled and over what period?"

Susan answered, "I met him in Alice Springs around the start of August. I travelled with him in his Toyota four-wheel drive through various parts of the Northern Territory until we came to Timber Creek. There I left him to travel to Darwin and then fly back to England. He told me he was going to Western Australia, via Kununurra, as he had work waiting for him there."

Brent continued, "Where and when did you last see him?"

Susan replied, "In Timber Creek two days before my flight."

Brent asked, "Did you two have any conflicts or arguments?"

Susan could feel this question start to make her shake inside. She tried to continue to say nothing and maintain her poker face until she felt in control again. Finally, she answered, "No."

Brent raised an eyebrow and asked with obvious disbelief, "Are you sure that's right? You travelled with a man, with whom you've admitted to having an intimate relationship, across the entire Northern Territory and had not one argument, conflict or any other heated exchange?"

Susan decided to say nothing in response to this prodding.

After a lengthy pause, Brent continued again, "Do you have any knowledge of what happened to Mark Bennet since you saw him? Have you had any further contact with him since this time?"

Susan answered, "No, to both questions."

There was another long pause. It was as if the interview had not gone as the detectives expected. They seemed almost unsure of their next step. In the meantime, they were using this silence to put pressure on her. The silence seemed to go on and on forever.

Finally, Susan broke the silence by asking, "Will that be all?"

Detective Brent replied, "We've been asked to request you provide us with a DNA and fingerprint sample."

Susan's heart sank. She knew there must be more to this inquiry if they wanted these things. However, she was determined to keep composed. She said, "You need to explain the basis on which this is requested before I agree to it. So, as of now, my answer is no."

Then, she asked, "Is the interview finished?"

At this juncture, she watched them quietly confer for a minute. Then, they both excused themselves and stood up. Sergeant Lacey asked her politely if she would wait here for a few minutes.

She nodded and they left the room.

Five minutes passed. An older lady, who looked like an orderly, came in with a jug of water and a glass.

She said, "How are you, dearie? The inspector asked if I'd offer you a glass of water and see if you'd like a cup of tea or coffee."

Susan nodded thanks while taking the proffered glass of water.

The woman waited politely for a few moments before asking again, "How about a cup of tea? I'm sure you've had a busy day."

There was something kind and motherly about the way the woman asked- almost like she actually cared. Susan could feel her hard resolve crumbling. She dared not even speak, worrying her voice would show her fear. She shook her head mutely in response to the woman's questions.

The woman said, "Right you are then," while giving her a little pat on the shoulder. Then she turned and walked out.

Susan felt tears start to form in her eyes at this simple act of kindness. She knew they were watching her, however, and was determined not to crack. She steeled herself, took a deep breath and pressed a tissue to the corners of her eyes and under her nose.

This time the silence seemed to go on and on forever, although probably it was just another ten minutes. Susan tried to keep her mind blank.

At last the door opened. Three people walked into the room, the two police officers she'd spoken with and a third, older man.

He introduced himself as Senior Detective Inspector Davidson. He said he headed this part of Scotland Yard (whatever part this was). He reminded her of her father, due to his having a weather-beaten face with kindly, yet sharp eyes.

His manner was different to the others. As soon as he sat down, he turned to her in a friendly and engaging manner.

"Susan, I watched the formal interview with you a short while ago. While you answered the questions you were asked, you were far from forthcoming with additional information other than what was directly asked. I've just been on the phone to my Australian counterparts to seek their agreement to tell you more of what this is about. We've agreed, if we want your full cooperation, it's only fair we tell you why we're questioning you and what we need to find out. Then, we will all be on the same page and not going in circles around each other.

"Therefore, I'll tell you what I can about the circumstances of this investigation. At the end of September, part of the body of a man was found by a fisherman in a billabong located in the Northern Territory. Initial examination of the body indicated it was probable he had died from a crocodile attack. However, upon further examination, it was found he had a fractured skull which occurred prior to this crocodile attack. The man's identity was unknown when he was initially found. This fact was widely reported at the time. He had been referred to as Crocodile Man by the press. As you can imagine, it soon became a sensational story- especially when it became an official murder investigation. The Northern Territory Police now believe they have identified this man as being Mark Bennet of Alice Springs. This information has not been released to the press yet.

"The police have also obtained CCTV footage showing a person sharing a room with this Mark Bennet at Yulara, near Ayers Rock. They've provided this image from the CCTV footage. I believe you will agree with me when I say: this person looks remarkedly like you," he said, passing a sheet of paper across the table to Susan.

She stared at the photo and felt an electric shock go through her. There was absolutely no way to mistake it: in front of her was a full-face photo of herself.

He continued, as if he did not notice any reaction from her, "Two days ago, the Australian police matched this photo with an image of the same person on arrival in Cairns. This match provided both a name and passport number. As a result of this person being outside of Australia's jurisdiction currently, they have sought our assistance. I think we are all able to agree, without any doubt, this person is you.

"You've just admitted you knew and travelled with Mark Bennet in the Northern Territory. When we match the timeline you've given us with the estimation of when his death occurred, it appears you were with him until shortly before he was murdered.

"At this stage in our investigation, your identity and that of the victim, Mark Bennet, are not publicly known. However, the police will have to release this information very soon. You will be named, when they release the identity of the victim, as a person of interest in his disappearance and with a possible connection to his murder.

"As I'm sure you can imagine, your photo will be on the front page of every newspaper in Australia and Britain when this announcement is made. There'll be all sorts of lurid speculation about a beautiful English girl's love tryst with the man they've termed the 'Crocodile Man'. It will become a frenzy of media interest in everything connected to you, your friends, family, boyfriends, work place, and so on.

"As well as assisting the Australian police in a murder inquiry, we're conscious of trying to protect you and your British interests in this case. You are our citizen. What we've found out about you in the last two days leads us to believe, while you had an affair with this man, for you to have been involved in his murder would out of character for you.

"What we're seeking from you, we being both us and the Australian authorities, is your full cooperation with all our inquiries. We need to know who Mark Bennet really was, who he met with while you were with him, where you two travelled and any other sorts of things which may help us with our investigation.

If you agree to assist us, then the information released to the media can be kept limited while we pursue our investigation. This means we would only name you as a person who knew him, travelled with him and is assisting the English and Australian police in tracing his movements to try to determine the identity of any people who may have been involved in his murder.

"If we don't have your full cooperation, an alternative scenario is that you will be identified in the media as a likely murderer. It would be explained there is an indication you may have killed your companion in a lovers' tiff and fed him to the crocodiles, to hide the evidence. We both know what effect such a story is likely to have on you.

"Having regard to all this, I have come in here to ask for your cooperation. I'm advised the request for DNA and fingerprints is for exclusion purposes at this stage. Such a request is routine, but that's a matter on which you may wish to seek your own legal advice before agreeing to it.

"I wanted to give you the facts related to our inquiries in the hope you will agree to give us your full cooperation in this matter." After this last statement, he finished speaking and paused for a minute- as if to let her digest the facts he had just provided.

Then, he turned to her in almost a fatherly way and said, "Well, Susan, I've placed my cards on the table as honestly as I can. I don't know what happened back then. I do know you seem like a nice girl. Personally, I wouldn't believe you to be a murderer. But the question remains: can you help us? We're seeking your help. If you give it, we'll do our best to calm down the media sensation."

Susan looked at his kindly face. She wanted to say yes, but she could not. Full cooperation would mean telling all she knew of Mark and giving over all the secrets he had given her. She could not do that. In addition, despite their image of her as being a nice girl, the murder charge was absolutely true! She was, in actuality, Mark's murderer. In her mind, to "cooperate" only to tell them another lie was absolutely pointless.

She would just have to let the cards fall where they may. All she could think about right now was buying time before her identification as a suspect was announced, to allow her to tell David, her family and friends that their marriage could not happen. It would all be out in the open soon enough anyway.

She took a deep breath, turned to face them all and said, "I wish I could help you more- but there is very little I know. As you said, I need to talk to a lawyer about giving DNA or other samples. Due to this, I ask you give me a couple of days before I reply to this request. That is, if giving me those couple days is possible for you to do."

The glass which she had drunk from earlier sat in front of her. Almost absentmindedly, she picked it up and wiped all its surfaces- both inside and out- with a tissue before she carefully placed it back on the table. The detectives were all looking at her strangely.

"That was a very strange thing to do for someone who is assisting us," said Detective Brent. She could sense his antipathy towards her. She had not done anything to get him in her corner.

Suddenly, it was all too much for her to take. She felt as if she had lost the will to fight. She could feel her body and resolve crumbling. She looked away. She was so very tired and it was all just too hard. How had it come to this? It was not what she wanted and yet she seemed to be trapped inside this never-ending horror story. She turned to the side and covered her face with her hands. She could feel her body shaking with the effort of trying not to cry.

She took a deep breath and asked, in as normal voice as she could, "Can I leave now?" She directed this to Inspector Davidson.

He replied, "If that's really what you want to do- though I think it would be better to talk it through some more. I suggest you engage a lawyer. If you don't know one, I can give you some names of ones I know of around here. I'll ask the Australian Police to hold off from releasing any information to the public for another 48 hours- but that's the best I can do.

"If we don't have your agreement and a real demonstration of your willingness to cooperate by then, I expect the Australian Police will inform the press of this information, seeking public assistance to locate Mark Bennet's killer. I think we all understand what that means.

"Susan, I know your father- not well, but we've met a few times. He's a man I have great respect for, a senior civil servant of Her Majesty's Government. I am trying to protect your interests. I'm trying to protect both your father and your family's interests along with those of this government. I'd prefer that none of us get caught up in a distasteful, extremely sensational piece of publicity. It will sell lots of newspapers, but it will help none of us.

"Of course, at a public level, our police force will help the Australian Government and to be completely impartial in relation to wherever the evidence leads. Nevertheless, I'm seeking your assistance. Having this will make it easier for us all and give us something we can offer to the Australian police."

Susan stood up and looked directly at Inspector Davidson. "Thank you for your honesty in telling me what you know. I would tell you more if I could, but I don't know what I'll do from here."

After this statement, Susan walked out the door. The lady at the front counter saw her coming out and asked whether she would like her to call a taxi. Susan shook her head and walked outside.

VICTIM   GRAHAM WILSON

Chapter 15 – A Friend

Susan found herself wandering away from Scotland Yard with her mind in a daze. Her thoughts were a jumble of endless incoherent images: Mark when she last saw him, a mangled corpse in the mouth of a crocodile, Mark holding her in his arms and loving her, his serious but half-smiling eyes, David in his tweed jacket leaning on the side of his sports car in the English countryside and the little church in Watsons Bay where she and David sat quietly together to plan their marriage. These memories were jumbled up with future images of tabloids screaming out her name, shocked faces of family and friends as she was exposed in the papers and led away in handcuffs and, finally, hideous images of a gleeful ancient crocodile spirit cackling in delight at her comeuppance.

It was a November afternoon and night was rapidly descending on top of a bleak London day. It was not raining, but the wind was blowing heavy, low clouds across the sky. She was only wearing a light jacket. She wrapped it tighter around herself. Other than this reaction to the cold wind, she was impervious to anything outside of her own mind, totally lost in a revolving maze of memories.

She walked aimlessly. She found herself going along the Thames, meandering through largely deserted city streets. A couple times she came to dead ends and was forced to retrace her steps. She did not have her handbag and couldn't recall where she last had it. Perhaps she'd left it at the police station. She knew she should contact her parents. They would be worried when she'd not come home by this time of night. There were also lots of other things she was sure she should do as soon as possible. However, she could not think clearly enough to plan or do anything.

Somehow, deep in the night, her feet led her to the part of London where Anne lived. She found herself standing in front of the building where Anne's flat was located upstairs. A few lights were on, so although Anne was probably in bed, not everyone was.

Familiarity and force of habit made her go through the motions of ringing the bell even though she had no clear-formed intention of going inside. There was a long pause of silence in which Susan waited- but did not ring again. A bleary voice came over the intercom, asking hesitantly, "Is somebody out there?"

Susan replied, almost mechanically, by just repeating her name into the speaker, "Susan."

Anne's voice came back, "Susan, what in God's name are you doing outside at this time of night?! Come on in."

The front door lock clicked open. Susan stumbled up the flight of steps to Anne's landing. Anne was there in her nightdress.

"Jeez, Susan, what happened to you? You look awful." Anne put her arm around her friend's shoulders and led her inside. As she came into the warmth, Susan started to shiver violently. Anne pushed her into a chair, picked up a blanket, draped it over her and said, "First things first: a hot cocoa for us both. Then, you can tell me what this is all about."

She heard Anne bustling in the kitchen. A minute later a hot cup was pressed into her hands. Susan tried to lift it up to her lips- but her hands were shaking too much. Anne took the cup from her and placed it on the table.

"You look like you've seen a ghost. Spit it out! What's up?"

Susan tried to think of how to say something. A mass of fragments inside her head would not connect. "I, it, they, Mark Bennet, David, a billabong in the Northern Territory. I went to work. I've lost my bag."

Susan put her hands to her face. "Oh, Anne, it's all too hard! It's such a confusing mess! My head's spinning! I've walked around for hours trying to think what to do. I didn't plan to, but somehow I ended up here and I don't want to dump this on you either."

Anne looked at her with a mix of sympathy and confused irritation. "Dump what?"

Finally, Susan got together a coherent thought. "The police asked me to come to Scotland Yard this afternoon." She stopped there, trying to think what came next.

Anne said, "And?"

The 'And' gave Susan a place to go on from. There were so many 'ands'. Now, they all came spilling out.

"When I was travelling in Australia, I met a man called Mark Bennett, and I went travelling with him in the Outback, and I'm going to have his baby and he's been murdered, and crocodiles have eaten him, and the police know I was with him, and they want me to tell them what happened, and I can't tell them, and I can't, and I can't marry David. It's not fair to him and I'll probably be in jail. Oh, Anne, it's all such a total fucked-up mess. I want to crawl into a hole and die."

Anne came over and put her arms around her. "Oh, my poor, poor Suzie. I knew there was more to the Australian story, but this is much more! So much more than even I thought possible! Just stop worrying for a minute. I'm your friend. I know you're a good person, regardless of this mess- as you call it. So, when you're ready, tell me about it. At least tell me what you can without upsetting yourself too much."

Anne picked up Susan's cocoa and gave it back to her. "Now, no more talk until you've drunk all this," she said, using her most official, school-teacher sounding voice.

Susan sipped slowly. Her hands were finally under control. She stood up and walked over to the mirror in the hall. She really did look like a ghost, hair sticking out in all directions, her eyes wild within a white-drawn face, her clothes askew and dishevelled.

Suddenly, she looked at Anne and gave her a big smile. Anne smiled back, bemused. Susan started to giggle and then laugh. Anne could not help herself- she started laughing, too. After a minute, Susan was able to control herself. "It seems so ludicrous that I only half believe it's true. It's like the last night I spent with Mark- the situation was awful and had spun out of control. Then, suddenly we started laughing together. Next thing you know, we were friends and lovers again. It solved nothing- but was wonderful anyway. This situation feels sort of the same."

She put on her serious face. "Anne, you're a good friend. I'll tell you what I can. There are parts I cannot tell you about because if you knew, you'd need to report the information to the police or you'd become an accessory to what I've done. I'll tell you all the rest, though."

Susan began her tale back in England with Edward and the split up. She knew Anne knew it, but still it was the beginning of the story. She said, "When I broke up with Edward, I didn't really miss him. I only truly missed the sex- as that part, at least, was good. Once I got to Australia, I'd more or less made up my mind to have an affair, either with another tourist or an Australian. On my first day out on the Barrier Reef, I met Mark. We were diving buddies. He wasn't quite handsome, but he had something that attracted me to him. It was a fearless vitality with a wild and dangerous edge to it. I was really attracted to him and I could tell he was to me, also. When I missed meeting him again- that night in Cairns Maggie mentioned- I felt really disappointed.

"The day after I left Cairns, I went to the Magnetic Island. It's a place on the reef about three hundred miles south of Cairns.

I checked into a backpacker hostel on the beach. As I was eating my lunch, Mark walked in. From then on, we clicked. That same afternoon, we walked into the bush to a little secluded beach and made love for the first time. The next five days, we were continuously together doing various things like: riding, swimming and sailing, but mostly having sex. I've never had anything like it with anyone else before. It was wild and completely and utterly possessed me. I could barely think of anything else when we were together. He'd only to look at me and we'd start wanting it again.

"Finally, I had to fly on to Sydney and he had to go to do some work in the Outback. I was really sad. I thought I'd never see him again. Then, he said he'd be in Alice Springs in a few days. I'd told him I might fly back that way. At this point, he gave me his mobile number, with no promises but a half offer to come travelling with him in the Outback.

"Part-way through my Sydney stay, I got in touch with Mark and I arranged to meet him and travel through the Northern Territory with him during the next week. However, at the same time, I had met David. He was really keen on me. At first, I didn't like David much. My cousin, Ruth, sort of pushed us together in the end. We spent lots of time in each other's company and I started to really like him, too. It wasn't the same way I liked Mark, but David is incredibly good-looking. Also, there is something very kind and honourable about him.

"I didn't intend to have an affair with David. I was planning on meeting Mark the next week. On the second last night before I left, it was just David and me in the pub, the others had already left. Then, it happened. I was a bit drunk. He was so handsome and charming. I ended up back at his place and then in his bed.

The sex was only okay but, still, I really liked him. After this, we kept doing things together until I left Sydney. But I was going to Alice Springs the next week to see Mark and I was still totally captivated by him.

In the end, I wasn't very nice to David. He asked me to stay longer in Sydney, even offered to fly anywhere in Australia to see me again. I wasn't interested at the time. But to spare his feelings, I gave him my phone number and address back in England, telling him to write to me. You know the story from this point.

"Once I got to Alice Springs, I forgot all about David. With Mark this time, it was even better than before! I'm not just saying the sex! There seemed to be this incredible bond growing between us. Part of him was really wild, but another part of him was like a lonely little boy. He'd lost his mother when he was little. He grew up being beaten up by his dad and others. As he grew up, he learned how to retaliate and became really dangerous.

"Mark had done really terrible things, in his past, which I gradually found out about. He said he'd killed some of those girls. I didn't know what to do with this knowledge. In the end, when you texted back, I knew I had to leave him, but was trapped! I used my body to seduce him and get away- but not without Mark's death. I flew back to London and hoped no one would ever know what had happened between us.

"Now the police have discovered what remains of his body, after it was eaten by crocodiles. They know I was with him in the Northern Territory and are running a murder investigation. The police at Scotland Yard called me in for questioning today. They have my photo on CCTV with Mark. They know we were together not long before he died. They have asked me to cooperate with the investigation they are doing on behalf of the Australian police.

"They said that, in just two days, this story will be on the front page of every Australian and English paper: "the English slut who fed her lover to the crocodiles." It's going to be terrible beyond belief! It will be bad enough for me- but it will be worse for David, my family and all my friends! Everyone will be caught up! I think they'll seek to extradite me back to Australia on a murder charge.

"To make matters worse, I'm expecting what I think is Mark's baby and I'm engaged to David with my wedding set for just over a month's time. David knows about the baby. Even though I did sleep with him during the time, I'm almost sure it's not his. I told David this. He's been so good about it: promising to love the child as if it was his own and even offering to live with me in England while I have it. He's such a good man! All of this will break his heart! I haven't told him about Mark, specifically, only I was involved with another man in Australia who I think is likely the father. I simply said I won't be seeing this person anymore.

"I have one day, two at most, before all hell breaks loose. I don't know what to do. I have to tell David and my parents. I have to cancel the wedding. Mark left me his diary which tells the story of the last five years including where he went and what he did. I must read it. I should give it to the police, but I cannot. If I tell them I have it, they'll take it away and I'll never get to know about this man who is my child's father. I first thought of having an abortion, that is before David came back- but now it's too late to even consider it.

"So that's my story in simple terms. I can't tell you more about the awful things that Mark has done. I can't tell the police either, at least for now. I can't even tell you what happened between us at the end and how he died. I really should not have told you about his diary, even, but it just sort of came out."

Susan looked at Anne with great earnestness, begging, "Please, promise me this: It has to stay our secret. You're the only person I've trusted enough to tell any of this. Perhaps one day, when I've read Mark's diary, I'll be able to tell more. For now, though, I can't.

"You see, despite all the awful things he's done, my first loyalty is to him since he's also the father of my child. I gave myself willingly to him, without any thought for the consequences, and I allowed this baby to happen. I can't casually give away information which would destroy his name and thereby, forever tarnish my child. Despite all he's done, I love him still and must be true to this.

"I feel love and great affection for David, but it's not the same as what I felt for Mark. For a while, I thought it might be enough. Now I know, without a doubt, it is not. I think I was more in love with the idea of being married to David than the reality. It's a truly awful thing to end our relationship at such a late stage- but it's better than living a lie. Also, I'll not be in any position to continue with David if I'm charged with murder. Even if he wants it to continue, there's no way I'd put him through all this with me."

She had disgorged these words in a big flow, barely taking a breath, lost in her own world of memory. However, she had run out of things to say now. It was almost as if she had to get it out or her nerve might fail her. Now, she looked up at Anne to see how she was taking it.

Anne had a bemused expression on her face as if she was struggling to understand everything she'd been told. Susan did not find this at all surprising. If the situation was reversed, six months ago, she would have found it all pretty hard to take in, too.

Anne said, "My head feels like it's spinning almost as much as yours after all that. It sounds unbelievable but I'm sure it's real since you are telling me all this yourself. It's not something you would make up and it explains tonight. I'm starting to understand the cryptic text you sent me while you were in Australia.

"My God, Susan, you're right! There are definitely more things you shouldn't tell me. If it was me, I would have already gone crazy and be locked up in an asylum right now. I promise I won't tell anyone what you've told me! However, sooner or later, what happened to those girls has got to be told to their families. Only you can reveal it and it's not fair of me to stand in judgement of you for choosing not to share this information yet.

"First, we need a plan of what's really urgent to do. The thing we must do now is let your parents know you're here. I'll ring them, myself, in a minute. There's no need for you to talk to them tonight. Tomorrow, we can decide what you need to do about warning other people about the upcoming news releases identifying you as a possible suspect and what needs done concerning your wedding. One more night will not change anything about that.

"For now, we both need a brandy nightcap to put some distance in our minds from today or we'll never get to sleep. First, let's have a hug. It's what friends should do at a time like this."

She came over while speaking and put her arms around Susan- just like a mother would do. Susan put her arms around Anne and they held each other. Susan felt so comforted. She let it all slide away from her mind, enfolded in her friend's warm embrace.

Anne ended the hug to walk into the kitchen. She returned holding two glasses filled liberally with brandy. "Here's to us: friends through all adversities. We'll get through this one, too. Though, to be honest, I'm stuffed if I know how."

Chapter 16 – Into Hiding

Susan woke up the next morning wondering where she was. Then she realised she was in the other side of Anne's king bed. After they drank the brandy, Anne had quickly called Susan's parents to let them know Susan was sleeping over. Then, Anne lent her a nightie and gave her half of the bed to sleep in. There was another small bed located in the spare room Susan could have used, but it was not very comfortable, and the room was full of junk. So, they'd agreed it was better if Susan slept in Anne's room. They'd done this lots of times before- either when they were between relationships or when they'd been on a girls' night out together.

Once in bed, they chatted for a while. Both had deliberately steered the conversation away from the momentous event of the day. Shortly after they both started to yawn and, after a few more minutes, Anne turned off the light.

Before Susan knew where the night had gone it was a new day. There was no sign of Anne anywhere in the house. She had left a note on the kitchen table which said:

Gone to work early for an hour to sort out a few things and make space in the day. I've also rung your work to say you won't be in until after lunch. Back by 9ish and will see you then.

Susan felt great welling of affection inside of her for Anne. She really loved that girl. They'd been best friends since part-way through high school. Anne was so good at organising other people's lives: lawyers at her work, boyfriends, family, the list went on. Anne clearly had the "older sister bossy gene" which Susan teased her about. This was despite the fact Susan was an older sister, too, and pretty organized overall. However, Anne left her in the cold due to her sheer efficiency. Along with this efficiency, Anne accomplished it with such an undeniable charm that others rarely got offended by her input.

As Anne had said to Susan late last night, in one of her flashes of brilliance, "I'll help you sort out some of the things that need to

174

be sorted. That way you can get on with what's most important: reading the diary of the crazy former boyfriend of yours- though why you'd want to do it beats me."

Susan looked at the clock and saw it read ten to nine. Anne would be back soon because she was rarely late. She found one of Anne's smaller dresses and showered. She felt much better with clean clothes on. Susan had just finished drying her hair when Anne walked in with fresh pastries and coffees.

Susan currently felt a strange sense of apathy about the future. Even so, she went along with most of Anne's plans. There were two things she would not agree to. The first was engaging a lawyer. In her mind she was guilty as charged. The second was her facing the music with her head held high, declaring her innocence with full confidence, saying it was all some ghastly mistake, to be followed by her stating she was cooperating with the police to the best of her ability but knew of no further information other than what she had already told them.

For her to continue to proclaim her innocence, she would have to continue on with her life. This would include staying on at work and postponing, rather than cancelling outright, her wedding.

The problem with this plan was Susan had run out of will to fight. Instead, she decided she would go away somewhere to disappear from life. She would find a new place to stay where others would not find her and break all her links with the past. She would give the fingerprint and DNA samples requested, but she would not help with their many other inquiries. She would not draw any others into this investigation or aid in discovering information which be harmful to Mark's memory.

There was almost a relief in not running or fighting anymore. She would meet her parents and tell them of the coming storm. Then, she would ring David's mother and tell her of her decision regarding the marriage and the reason why. She asked Anne to be the one to ring David and tell him about it. Susan just could not find the words to tell him about what she had done and yet, also, could not bear to lie to him either. Last, she did not have the mental energy to debate with him whether calling off the wedding was the right thing to do or even to decline his offers of help which she knew he would give. She asked Anne to say she sent her love to him, but also to say a future together was impossible and he must not waste time hoping for it. In the end, Anne reluctantly agreed she would ring David as soon as Susan left.

After this discussion her day's tasks were clear and she got ready to leave. Anne lent her fifty pounds to go to Scotland Yard to provide the requested fingerprints and a DNA sample. If the station was where she had left her purse, she would also collect it. After, she would continue to her work, tender her immediate resignation, pack up all her things, collect her car and drive home. She expected to be home by lunchtime. This was important because no one else would be there.

She planned to get out the diary and photograph all the pages. She would place the images on a microSD card. This way the diary contents would be on something too small for others to find but on something she could read on her smartphone. She would then arrange for the diary and the pouch of gemstones to be placed in secure storage where no one else could access them.

Then, she'd return home early to meet her family and tell them what was coming. Her smartphone would get a new SIM card, with the number only known to her parents, Anne and the police.

Her parents and Anne could make any statements they wished to the media, but she would refuse to talk publicly to anyone.

She would rent a tiny bedsitter in an obscure part of London, so she'd have some privacy. She would go there later tonight. She would be there on her own until either the media storm subsided, or the police charged her. She decided she would not oppose her extradition if charged. Rather, she would voluntarily return to Australia and let events run their course. She may even go back to Australia of her own volition to find out more about Mark.

At some stage, before the baby's birth, she'd change her identity. Doing this, both her baby and herself would have a new name, in order to start a new life. She had no idea what she'd do if she was in prison when her baby came. Such a concern was a worry for another day.

It was as if, in the night, something had changed inside Susan. The once joyful, funny girl was now gone. In her place a hard, relentless person had emerged. A person who would give no quarter to anyone and take no prisoners. She still loved Anne and her family dearly. She also still felt affection towards David. But, to the rest of the world, she was indifferent. She told herself she had to grow up the hard way.

Even though Susan thought she was indifferent to other things, she thought about how it had been a tough morning while she was driving to her parents' house. She felt guilt about dumping the phone call to David on Anne. But, despite the guilt, she knew it was an impossible conversation for her to have and that being on the other end of the line would not improve it in any way.

The provision of fingerprints and DNA samples at the police station had been mundane until she informed Inspector Davidson she would not provide any further information to the police. This part had made the visit hard. It was not as if she did not want to help, she just could not do so without revealing Mark's secrets. Since Inspector Davidson reminded her so much of her father, it felt like a further act of betrayal because she also could not explain why she would not do this.

Turning up at her work and announcing her resignation, effective immediately, was also a thing she considered bad form. Her colleagues had been so helpful in accommodating her recent absences. They were planning a big party to say goodbye at the end of the month. To vanish so abruptly was a shock to all. She felt like a deserter. In the end, she'd gone around and talked to people she knew, to say individual goodbyes. She could not explain the reasons for her abrupt departure, but it was still better than nothing.

Then Susan headed home, going via a real estate agent in north-west London. Here she rented an ugly and depressing little bedsitter, located on a busy street in a disgusting neighbourhood. She' glanced at the rental agreement without even seeing it first. The only requirement she was concerned about was it being in a building with a security door which separated it from the street, to help with her privacy.

Its best feature was it was inexpensive but still close to things. This meant she could get rid of her car if she needed to. She had the money to live there for up to six months. She did not expect to be there for more than a month or two at most. After paying for the first month today, she would pay for additional time each fortnight as needed.

It was now past one o'clock and she needed a couple of hours to photograph Mark's diary. She would use her underwater camera. It took high-resolution images, the batteries were fully charged, and it had an almost empty 16GB memory card. Susan figured this size of card was more than enough to hold all the images of the diary pages. From this she could easily transfer the images to her laptop. Later, she could transfer these images onto a tiny card which she could hide deep in her purse. She could then use her phone to read the entries as she desired.

Once at home, she took out the diary and the jewel pouch. After a glance to ensure the jewellery contents were still in there, she settled down in the conservatory, where the light was best, to photograph the entire diary. There were about 200 pages in this book, but the last 50 were blank. First, she wrote a page number in the corner of every page. By numbering pages, it would be much easier to keep track of separate images. She deliberately avoided reading any parts at this time. Rather it was best to pretend it was another routine document copying job.

She began with taking images of the front and back covers. After this she worked her way through the pages from start to finish. It took almost two hours before she was happy with the final product. Next, she loaded the memory card from the camera into her laptop and did a quick visual scan to ensure all the images which were sharp and clear. Then Susan copied the images to her laptop before putting the memory card from the camera in her purse. Tonight, she planned to move these files to a tiny memory card and remove them from her laptop. Susan figured it was best to do this soon should the police come visiting with a search warrant, wanting to check her computer.

With her task complete, she found herself sitting and staring at the diary. Susan wondered why she was set on keeping it secret and if everything she was doing now was just a terrible mistake.

She thought, *Now I have my own copy maybe I should just take this thing to the police and cooperate. I could plead self-defence in Mark's death.* But she knew, with his child and Mark's letter to consider, she could not let herself do this.

It would be a final act of betrayal if she turned over this evidence before she properly read the diary. She must try and understand who he was and why he had become this person.

Susan decided she must find a secure place to hide the diary. She thought of finding a place in Reading, but it was a too obvious should anyone search for it. Wokingham was the next big town on the London side of Reading and she knew it well.

There was a private company there which rented out safe deposit boxes with either key or security code access. She did not want a key. It was another thing to carry. It could also link her to this location. An access code was far better since it would do none of these things. She had an excellent memory and, for insurance, she would make a couple of backup copies of the number.

With another decision made, she drove to the facility and paid three hundred pounds to rent a box for two years. She placed the jewels, the original memory card from her camera and the diary into the box. The memory card had the photos of both the diary and from her trip to Australia on it. As an afterthought, she added in the letter Mark had written to her at the end, since it was in her purse, too. She locked the deposit box and drove home.

Her family would be home in about an hour and she must forewarn them. It was possible she'd be front page news in tomorrow's paper, so she needed to move out tonight so as to prevent there being journalists at her front door. She packed her room, leaving things she didn't need in the cupboards. Once it was done, she carried two suitcases of clothes and personal things, along with a few cardboard boxes of other items outside and loaded them into her car.

Susan heard someone come in as she was carrying the last box to the car. It was Tim. He must have heard her because, next thing, he was standing beside her car gazing at all her things.

"What's up, Sis?" he asked, indicating her car filled with her things. "I thought you were to keep on staying here until you flew to Sydney for the big wedding."

His face was bright and hopeful as he asked the question. He seemed to think her new life in Australia was an exciting adventure. She understood he was looking forward to the wedding trip and knew nothing of what was coming. She hated the idea of him knowing- not to mention all the others she would disappoint too.

Susan's bravado crumbled and she turned her face away from her brother's smiling face. Tim came closer to her and put his arm around her shoulders. She felt she would cry her heart out, now finally having to acknowledge to herself and someone else the unavoidable fact that her whole world was collapsing.

She looked up at his concerned face through her teary eyes. "Oh, Tim, it's such a God-awful mess. I can't get married. I'm in big trouble with the Australian police. I think I'm about to be charged with murder. Tomorrow, my face will probably be printed on the front page of every newspaper. I must get away from here. I couldn't bear for a thousand sleazy journalists to try to shove cameras into my face."

She looked up. There was her mother, standing a few feet behind Tim, with a totally shocked look on her face. Her mother must have heard everything she'd just revealed to Tim. Susan should have realised they'd come home together from university.

Her mother asked, bewildered, "Susan, what have you done?"

Her mother said this with total incomprehension- not condemnation. Susan found herself crying so much she was unable to speak. She had not meant to tell them like this. She had intended to be in control when she revealed the news.

Within a minute, her mother had picked up her mobile and dialled her father. "You need to get home right now. Susan needs you. Take a taxi to Paddington and catch the next fast train."

Her mother brought her into the kitchen and made a cup of tea. "No more talking until your dad gets home. Best you tell us all at once, rather than to say it over and over again to each of us."

Susan sat at the kitchen table with a cup of tea and slice of cake in front of her while her mother clucked around. She liked this domestic certainty and hated the thought it was about to end. From tomorrow on, this life would be over. She absolutely hated this fact.

As she sat and waited for her father to come home, the phone rang. Her mother picked it up. She immediately held the phone out to Susan while saying, "It's David. He demands to talk to you. I think it's a thing you must do."

Susan took the phone slowly and raised it up to her ear. His voice came down the line, saying, "Is that you, Susan?"

Susan could barely answer since she was crying so much. All she could manage to say repeatedly was, "Oh, David! I am so sorry," mixed in with a few other incoherent phrases.

In the end, her mum took back the phone and talked to David herself. She could tell her mum was trying to talk him out of flying straight to England. "No. I think she's too upset for that at the moment. She needs to try to work this out herself first. I'll ask her to talk to you when she's less upset. I promise I'll tell her you love her and that you don't want to call it off."

Finally, her mum put down the phone, while looking weary and resigned. She came over and put her arms around Susan- hugging her the way she had when she was a little girl. They stayed in a wordless embrace until they heard her father arrive.

Susan told them a story similar to what she told Anne. The key differences in the stories were that she left out the intimate parts, the existence of the diary and the missing girls. At first, nobody asked any questions and she just talked. Then, her father's practical brain started to ask for details: the how, the where and what were their options.

At first, Susan tried to answer them all. Finally, she put her hands up, exclaiming, "You need to stop this now, Dad. You can't undo this! And I can't undo this! Nobody can undo this!

The police will investigate as they normally do. I'll neither help nor hinder them. I won't resist charges they lay against me. I'll even tell the truth in court- if it comes to that. I'm so tired of running and hiding from this. I'm going to have this man's baby, no matter whether it ends up being a good or bad person due to its genes.

"The reason I need to disappear now is that I need privacy from the press. I don't want to feed all the gossip or speculation which is sure to follow, after this news is announced. You'll have my phone number and address if needed. It's best if you don't come around, in case someone follows you. I won't come back home either for now. We can meet up somewhere else for now and that way still see each other."

Her father replied, "Of course we believe in you and will help you. We are on your side. However, I think you are making a big mistake not cooperating with the police and telling them whatever you know. Please reconsider and think seriously about doing this."

Her mother nodded too, adding, "Susan, please help yourself. I refuse to believe you did anything so awful you can't say!"

Her brother looked away from her, as if unwilling to believe all the things he just heard.

Susan broke contact with her parents' eyes. "Please don't push me away, too. I won't tell them more and I can't tell you more. The more you ask me, the harder it gets to not give into your pleading. But, even if everyone asks a hundred times, I'll keep saying no. Please, don't make it harder by making me fight with you, too."

She could see hurt and disappointment on her parents' faces, but they nodded agreement, "Okay, if that is what you want."

This concluded their discussion. Afterwards, they ate a subdued family dinner during which they talked only of small things. It was very poignant as she hugged them to say goodbye.

Her father said, "You know we're all here for you, Susan. We will support you- no matter what happens."

Her mother said, "How about we meet for family dinner once a week? We can start at a restaurant until we see what happens."

Tim said, "I can't wait to read about you in the paper and discover all the awful things you're supposed to have done. I've never known a family member who's a true celebrity."

Her father cuffed his ears and, her mum tried to look outraged.

Susan laughed for the first time all day. Still laughing, she said, "Trust you to find a silver lining- you total publicity junkie."

Susan got into the car then and drove away.

She tried to feel upbeat about her future but could not stop the tears silently sliding down her cheeks.

***

As the evening passed, Anne was sitting at home alone. She could not watch TV or bring herself to read to occupy herself. Her mind looped round and round in an endless circle of remembering.

An hour ago, Susan rang briefly to give her a new phone number for use to contact her by. She also said thanks for helping last night and for agreeing to talk to David on her behalf. She gave no information about where she was or what she'd do from here. Each time Anne tried to probe for details, Susan stonewalled.

Anne recounted the phone call Susan had asked her to make earlier this morning to David. It had been awful but at least it was done. She was determined to leave that part of her day behind.

Instead, Anne found herself thinking repeatedly about her friend and how much she had changed recently. The bright and confident Susan she known before last night had been broken when she came to Anne last night. She'd still had a kind and soft centre, though.

But Anne observed, overnight, something had changed in Susan. Today, Anne felt Susan had retreated inside herself as her last line of defence. Anne was dismayed by this change. It seemed like, during the night, Susan had become autistic. Although in the morning, Susan still tried to smile at Anne with her old trademark smile, it simply felt like glitter over a steel cage.

As Susan had left in a taxi that morning, Anne felt as if she' d lost her best, most loyal friend. She felt utterly devastated at this. Regardless, Anne would do as Susan asked her. She knew, without a doubt in her mind, Susan would never survive another betrayal.

VICTIM   GRAHAM WILSON

Chapter 17 – The Diary

The flat was even more disgusting than Susan had imagined. It had a mouldy, airless smell which she attempted to reduce by opening all the windows for a minute. The air outside was freezing so she was unable to keep them open for long. It took three loads to carry all her things upstairs. She almost wished the police would lay charges tomorrow so she could get out of this hellhole. So much for any imagined pleasure in experiencing the life of a recluse!

She'd planned to do some work tonight by beginning to read the diary, while compiling her own narrative to summarise it. But she felt too depressed and apathetic to do anything. In the end, after sitting and looking around aimlessly, she just crawled into her bed. Her one real comfort was a big fluffy doona her mum insisted she take with her. Her favourite teddy bear was sitting on it and she now hugged the bear to herself. She picked up her mobile phone to check it. Three missed calls and multiple messages from Anne were listed on the screen.

She dialled the number and spent five minutes talking to Anne. David had taken it much worse than even Anne expected. Anne said it was awful and she'd ended up feeling really sorry for him.

"You're right. He really is such a decent guy," Anne said.

"David said he'll only agree to *postpone* the wedding for now. He won't call it off or break the engagement until he meets you himself. He says he needs to hear it said directly from your mouth.

But at least, it's all put on hold for now. I've promised to ring him at least once a week and give him any news about you I can. I hope that's alright with you."

Susan said this was fine and thanked her friend profusely for calling him. It had been a terrible job to give Anne and was pure cowardice on her part. At least it was done now. She told Anne about Tim's parting comments which made her laugh out loud.

After cutting Anne short each time she tried to ask questions, she said goodnight.

Awful though it all was, particularly this place she was staying in, she decided she did feel better overall. She was finally on a path to somewhere and would never again let herself be diverted by minor emotions. It felt as if she'd closed the door to the previous part of her life and could begin to look towards another part which was now starting. Even though this outlook seemed bleak from here, it was her own life to live, for which she was responsible.

She drifted off to sleep. Tonight, her dream of Mark returned. It seemed, while she was in his arms, she was temporarily free of the crocodile spirit. He told her while he was with her, he was in a happy place where he was free of his past and his crocodile spirit was pushed away. He loved her here and she loved him without limit. It was simply wonderful.

Susan told him about the child he'd made and he pushed his face against her belly, as if to hear the beating heart of this new life. She stroked the short hair on the back of his head. They made plans to live in their own secret place, somewhere in the heart of Australia where no one would ever find them and have children by the score. It was a slightly mixed-up place where they went. It had a tribe of small brown bodies running around, like the ones she'd met at the morning tea when they'd visited Seven Emus.

Susan woke up in the morning wishing the night had lasted forever. Now, she did not want to let go of sleep at all. She wished it was night again so they could resume their loving of one another.

She got up and washed. Then, she dressed herself in warm winter clothes to keep the chill at bay. It seemed strange to have a day with nothing to do. She walked down the street until she found a corner shop. At it she bought enough supplies to last a couple of days along with the morning paper. It made no mention of her on the front pages. She settled into a corner seat in a nearby café to read. On page seven, she saw a small article which gave her name:

"Australian police have sought the assistance of Scotland Yard to investigate an English connection to the likely murder of a man in the Northern Territory. This man, dubbed Crocodile Man, was first thought to have been killed by a crocodile. However, a post-mortem examination revealed he had been murdered.

This man is now identified as Mark Bennet of Alice Springs. Scotland Yard has been asked to interview an English citizen, Susan McDonald, as a person of interest. It is believed that Miss McDonald was seen travelling with Mr Bennet shortly before his murder. Susan McDonald is believed to have returned to London. Scotland Yard has declined to comment at this time."

This article proved the hounds were out and pursuing the fox. Susan was pleased to see no picture of her had been printed in the article. Once this happened, she would have to be much more careful going out in public. Perhaps she would even need a head scarf and dark glasses to use for a disguise.

After half an hour, she returned to her flat. She decided to work on transferring all the image files to her tiny memory card. One by one she checked them to ensure they all were of good quality. A couple times she found duplicates of pages- which she discarded. Some pictures needed to be rotated or cropped slightly to make them easier to read. For now, she decided she'd work and read on her laptop since it was much easier. However, she would leave no files on its hard drive- she would only work using the ones contained on the memory card.

She opened a new Word document to use to compile and keep track of what she found. She named this "The Diary" and saved the blank document. A quick scan of the diary contents showed that it appeared to be mostly chronological. Often, though, it had no specific dates to link to an entry timeline. Sometimes it would simply say things like "Saturday" or "two days later." Only occasionally was there a real date written, from which she could figure out the actual time events took place. There were also places with business notations, work orders and other information attached to the entries. These included things like, "*booked to work Argyle Mine, 23–30 August, Halls Creek 250 litres fuel, Ring Fred Smith 89887018.*" It would be hard going figuring out what was important and what wasn't.

She decided she would try to find the place where Mark first mentioned her name- or described someone who sounded like her. Then, at least, she would have some sort of narrative to work with.

She started at the end and worked backwards, scanning for her name or a description of a place which sounded like where they'd been together. She skipped back six pages, seeing occasional references or things about herself. Her eyes caught something:

Beach Girl, beautiful. She stands there with her toes in little waves, hair flung back like a Greek goddess, arms stretched to the morning sun. So enchanting. I want to know who she is. I stand on the shore path, watching her in the bright light. When she looks my way I move behind trees, now I can only glimpse her. She comes my way, I keep out of sight, it might look like I'm spying.

She has stopped at an ice cream stand. Now she walks on, licking a cone with such pleasure. Ice cream trickles down her fingers and she licks it off. I wish I was an ice cream drop. She is looking at tour signs, perhaps I can accidentally meet her on a tour. She goes into a shop and I see her discussing her choices with the man at the counter. Now she is booking, now she is finished. I must go inside and ask him to book me on the same tour. I pull on my eagle cap and some dark glasses to hide my face. She passes me at the door, leaving as I enter. Her eyes are beautiful, cornflower summer blue. I see her, I'm entranced. Even though she looks at me she sees me not.

I go inside, pretending to be rushing, running late, apologising as I go. I say – My girlfriend just made a reservation for some tours here. She was here just before I came in, the girl with the dark hair and blue eyes. Can you book me on the same tours please?

'Sure – so that will see you on the Quicksilver tour to the outer reef tomorrow.' I agree. 'How about the Kuranda Rainforest by Train tour the next day?' Two trips in two days where I run into her may seem a bit obvious. I say

'No, I'll skip that.' I pay my money but the confirmation is slow. I want to rush out and see where she goes.

By the time I come out she has vanished. Was it a dream, did I imagine something so lovely. Tomorrow I'll find out.

This entry is followed by a few doodles and notations. Then another entry after it continues his earlier musings.

I feel like I'm in love, I wonder if I have really ever felt like this so quickly before. I've had so many girls and many of them have been beautiful. But this is different. I only talked to her for half an hour over lunch and spent an hour diving with her yesterday. It was delightful, we were sharing a meal and she was telling me about her life, with that soft English charm. She told me where she was staying, the Excelsior Hotel and where she was going on to, Magnetic Island. I suggested a hostel there to stay at. Now the seed is planted in her mind. I think she will remember and go there. Her Magnetic Island stay is for three days, so I will find her even if she chooses another place, and when she sees me she will think I'm a long lost friend.

Today would have been perfect, except that, at the end of lunch, she met another English girl and they started talking like old school friends, sharing jokes I don't understand. So I left her to her friend's conversation and declined to go diving with them both together.

Tonight I went to her hotel to ask her out for a drink but she had already gone out elsewhere. Instead I left her a note.

I'm sure I will find her again. She is far too lovely to let her escape. Today I found two stones in my pouch that match her eyes. They are my two most favourite pale blue ovals. I'll send them off to be made into a pendant and a ring, which I hope to give her when I meet her next.

A couple of days later, Susan reads:

I found her again yesterday. She was staying at the hostel where I suggested she go. It was like an electric shock passed between us when I saw her again. She was wearing the skimpiest bikini, the same cornflour blue as her eyes. It barely

190

covered anything. I could not help but look. She knew I looked and liked my looking. We sat side by side and ate lunch together, gazing out to the sea. Each time our bodies lightly brushed I could feel a jolt of connection between us.

Then we walked to the beach at the end of the headland and made love in the waves. Wow, it was just so amazingly good. Then we slept together under the stars. I've just sent her to her own bed, as the first dawn light comes. Every time I look at her blue eyes my insides turn to mush. I am definitely in love. What will come of it – who knows, I'm not good to be around, and must be careful, so, so very, very careful. She is too precious to harm.

Susan put her laptop down. It was so beautiful to the point where she could not bear to read anymore right now. It was just as he had said in his letter. Did she love him as quickly as he loved her? Perhaps not quite as quickly, but it had been extraordinarily fast. It was hard to separate the joy and pleasure of the sex from the love of the man. She was certain she had been in love with him by the time she left Magnetic Island. She wished she'd told him that, then and there. Instead, she'd held it inside- fearing it would sound like over-commitment at such an early point in their relationship.

Now, Susan had proof he had purposefully set out to entrap her, the man with the eagle cap. She found she did not care it was a setup from the start. She'd want him to do it again, in just the same way as before, if the chance to relive this slice of time came again. The only difference was she would tell him how she felt straight away. She regretted all the time wasted while they had danced around their feelings for one another. It was not until that last night, when it was already too late, that all their feelings had come tumbling out.

She decided she would savour these words in Mark's diary slowly, taking in small bits each day to draw out the pleasure. She knew there would be bad bits included in the diary, too. Susan was thinking about the parts where he'd told her of the other girls and what he had done to them. However, she didn't care. In the last hour of her reading, she'd discovered the real Mark she loved had been hidden within the other.

His words were like beautiful poetry or a song of bush ballads. She had glimpsed the poetry of his mind in the stories he'd told her, but the words he wrote were much richer.

Now, she would walk amongst the late autumn leaves, savour all his words in her mind while rolling them off her tongue. Then, she'd come back to her little room and return to him in her dreams.

For the next few days, Susan only read, walked and slept, barely even eating. Her dreams were only of Mark. Her waking thoughts were only of Mark. She knew there was a storm raging in the world around and that her name was at its centre.

She glimpsed this briefly from conversations with Anne and odd meetings with her parents. Despite this, she still did not care. Her own personal world was one of only loving delight. She had not read any bad bits of the diary yet. She did not really want to go there. She wanted to drown in the delight of Mark's words. These words and their memories consumed her completely. They filled all her waking moments and then overflowed into her dreams- leaving no room for any other person to be included in her mind or heart.

VICTIM   GRAHAM WILSON

Chapter 18 – Brazen English Hussy

"Crocodile Man's Brazen English Hussy"- this was the headline the tabloids were screaming out in a few different variations. The word "Slut" was also used frequently in lieu of "Hussy." It had taken only a week to build up to this level of hysteria.

Susan's disappearance had both aided and constrained the story. The responsible journalists and newspapers merely stated allegations of this nature were circulating which could not be confirmed due to Susan having gone into hiding. These papers said they were seeking to locate Susan to get her side of the story before drawing any conclusions. On the other hand, all the trashy tabloids were not going to let truth get in the way of a good story. Where they had no information, because they could not find her either, they simply made up a story.

After a week of blocking them out of her mind, Susan started to read the range of stories and opinions on her laptop with a sort of morbid fascination. She had largely stopped going out, except at night. She adopted this habit because her face had become very well-known and did not want to take a chance of a stranger recognising her. Even if someone only thought she looked like the "English Hussy", this might still bring journalistic wolves to where she lived to commence a feeding frenzy in their effort to be involved in the hype.

She knew it was really hard for Anne and her own family. They defended her in a limited way, but mostly declined to comment. Her father merely told journalists, "The whole family loves Susan dearly. Speculation concerning her is both highly offensive and totally out of character with the person we know."

He also informed them of the fact his daughter was unwilling to answer questions because she did not want to feed the media frenzy any further. She believes it would be impossible to get a fair hearing in such a situation. He received many offers from people asking to be put in contact with Susan to tell her side of the story in a sympathetic manner. Many offers included cheques ranging all the way up to five or six figures. After the first couple days, he maintained stony silence. For Anne, it was much the same as for Susan's father. Anne handled it in the same way he did.

David and his family in Australia had been wonderful. He'd made a few statements which maintained his total support for her, refusing to discuss, in any way, what it meant for their relationship. He dismissed questions about her moral character as nonsense, saying, "Unlike you, I know her- and I know she's a good person."

Her friends had generally stuck by her, refusing to speculate on all the crazy theories and continuing to defend her decency. However, one or two cracks had appeared in her group of friends. A couple people she thought were solid friends seemed to have fallen to the inducements of cheque book journalism. These 'friends' disgorged lurid stories of her university days, such as wild parties she had attended and other similar stories. However, these stories did not have much substance. She could feel the vacuum for real news getting ever stronger and pulling harder as journalists searched for ever newer, more shocking revelations. She knew, with certainty, these new shocking revelations would not be long in coming.

The funny thing was she preferred the tabloid versions of events. In them, she was an evil hussy who seduced a man from the outback, murdered him and fed his body to the crocodiles.

At least these stories had a ring of truth to them. In contrast, she felt positive stories were trying to embellish her good character too hard. She'd grown to dislike reading about Saint Susan. She felt these journalists were fawning to her and her family, done in the hope of getting under their guard, to snare a juicy morsel.

In her private life, she still dreamed of Mark each night. In these dreams, the passion they felt was undiminished. By day, she kept reading through parts of the diary. However, their power to thrill her was declining. She had discovered some other parts written about her which were less positive than the ones she had read prior. There was a place where he said about her "that bitch keeps wanting to know about my past. It's driving me crazy."

She began to realise, even though he may have loved her, there was something a bit crazy and unhinged about his emotions.

She had also found similar expressions used about the other girls, descriptions of being incredibly smitten with them, telling of their looks and descriptions of their wonderful lovemaking. She realised some of these other women had been really special to him, too. In particular, it seemed Bel-who she thought must be the French girl, Isobel- had held a very special place. Partly she felt jealousy to those who came before her in his life and part of her wanted to see how he looked at them. She couldn't help but wonder whether he looked at them with the same deep tenderness and affection with which he had looked at her.

From what she'd read so far, there were no statements made to any other women which were the same unequivocal declaration of love he had given her. She could also see how, when other girls were not totally in line with what he wanted, a mean and darker side of him could emerge. Of one of the other women, Amanda from America, he stated, "She has started to really hassle me and try to push me around. I told her to shut her fucking mouth or I would shut it properly for her."

She found herself increasingly unable to read about the other girls, their relationships with Mark and what had happened to them. Instead, she found herself re-reading the good bits about herself and the other parts which gave voice to his private thoughts and emotions. As yet she really did not know what had happened to any others and realised she did not want to cross the bridge to obtain this knowledge. This desire to avoid negative aspects of the man she loved drove her to avoid any bits which even appeared to be about another girl.

She had come to understand this diary was a private therapy place for Mark and not everything he said in it was fully true. Some of it was written as a form of escape where he could blow off steam to give him relief from real life. She also saw it as an outlet for the thoughts of a man who thought much yet was mainly silent in real life. All the life of his mind must go somewhere, so parts of his writing flowed out as streams of thought onto the paper. There was a brilliance in places which belied his limited education.

She also began to realize, at his core, part of him was deeply lonely and searching for affection. She sensed the absence of a mother or other kind figure in his childhood left a hole which he sought to fill with temporary liaisons and infatuations with many girls. However, the hole was never really filled and he kept moving on while still looking for a new hope. In a way, she was just the newest and latest of these infatuations- the new Goddess.

Deep down, she understood he felt worthless at his core. Perhaps he thought his badness must be due to the character he inherited from his father. He seemed to believe he could not be of much value if his own mother did not treasure him or fight for him in any way.

Then, slowly she came back around to thinking she was not just one of many. The way he talked about her seemed subtly different. These descriptions had a deeper and more accurate character. It was as if he was beginning to both see and understand her in a realistic fashion. At the same time, he seemed to gain a real insight into himself and the impacts of his previous behaviours. It seemed he was trying to find ways to move beyond these and put his past behind him. Over time, she better understood she really was special in his eyes. He had not done for others what he did for her, the jewellery was for her only and the tender words were almost all for her.

The things she loved most in the diary were descriptions of the land and its people, often intermingled, written in both passages of poetry and prose. It was as though in these words- his spirit was set free to fly. A love for the land and its people flowed out. There were incredibly moving descriptions of joy in telling tales around a campfire and seeing a sunset by himself in the desert. His poetry was often simple couplets which she could feel he had rolled around his tongue until the words came out right. She now rolled them around her mind and spoke them aloud to share the pleasure. At times there would be a page of dense writing, half-way between poetry and prose, which described a place or a situation in incredible richness. She felt it was a sort of autism where written words allowed him to unlock his frozen mind.

She particularly loved his little obscure and eclectic anecdotes with which he peppered the pages, such as his description of that morning she remembered at Seven Emus:

We came to Shadforth Central, where the emus used to live. Now no self-respecting emu would be found dead in this junk heap. But out of such junk heaps grow powerboats, helicopters and little brown children. Our gift pig was taken by the old Chink. Despite appearances, he is far stronger than you or eye. His magic wand soon conjured dumplings and spiced pig meat, which we all did then eat with great relish. Susan loved this place. I loved it too but most of all I loved her blue-eyed love of it. Tonight, I'll give to her a thing to make her blue eyes shine brighter, brighter even than a desert sky.

Susan read at random. She had ceased to follow her plan to understand what happened to the other girls since she had not even fully grasped the sequence of stories he wove around her. She lived in and loved the joy of these little insights which came from his poetic soul. She felt a vague guilt for not using her days of leisure in a more purposeful way. Still, in her meanderings through his written words, she felt she was coming to understand him. This satisfied her need to begin to truly know and see who this man was.

On the tenth day, the dam finally broke. The news had been starting to die down through an absence of anything new. Now they had it. The *Times* reported:

Miss McDonald in Murder Car on day before Mark Bennet's death.

Despite a statement by Susan McDonald that she left Mark Bennet at Timber Creek and caught a lift back to Darwin, while he went on to Western Australia, the Northern Territory police have found out this version of events is untrue. A credible witness confirms that she saw Susan go into Mark Bennet's Toyota and fall asleep on the passenger seat outside Timber Creek Hotel. An hour later Mark Bennet was seen to come out and drive in the direction of Katherine with Miss McDonald still inside. This was the last time that anyone saw a living Mark Bennet.

Two days later Miss McDonald flew out of Darwin **on her own.** *Information has emerged that she drove Mr Bennet's vehicle to Darwin to catch her plane back to England after systematically cleaning both the murder site and vehicle to remove any evidence of her presence.*

It is understood that the Northern Territory Police will soon be issuing a warrant for the arrest of Miss McDonald, seeking her extradition from the United Kingdom to Darwin, Australia, to stand trial for Mr Bennet's murder.

After this was printed, the papers sought to exceed each other in their histrionics of condemnation. Susan sat inside her flat and waited for the call. It did not come the first day. Only a brief phone call came from her parents. It did not come on the second day either. She only had a brief phone call from Anne. It still had not come on the third day. Instead, the only call she received on the third day was from David. She was surprised. He admitted he had persuaded Anne to give him her number as he said he needed to talk to her in person at least once more.

She found she was glad he had called. He still remained the decent person she had known and she still enjoyed talking to him. It was a fig leaf of normalcy in a world of craziness. In the end, she was sad when he said he had to end the call. They did not discuss their relationship.

They just talked as friends- and friends were in short supply right now. He mentioned he wanted to fly to England to come and see her.

She said, "No. I will not be opposing extradition when the warrant comes, so I will be in Australia soon enough. You can come and see me there if you want."

On the fourth day, the call finally came.

VICTIM   GRAHAM WILSON

Chapter 19 – A Charge called Murder

Inspector Davidson's voice came through her mobile. "Susan, I think you know what this is all about. In response to a request made by the Australian police, the United Kingdom police have sought a warrant for your arrest. It was issued this morning.

"A police car will be arriving in about half an hour to collect you from your flat. I ask you be ready and suggest you pack a small bag with a couple of changes of clothes. You'll be held in custody for up to a day while we, working alongside the Australian police undertake initial questioning of you and further investigation of this matter. After that there will be a hearing before a magistrate where you can seek bail if you wish.

"As you've declined legal representation to date, I've arranged for a solicitor appointed by us to be at the initial questioning. This person may represent you if you wish. I strongly recommend that you use his services, that is unless you choose to engage your own legal representative."

Susan knew she should care- but she found she did not. She felt only relief that all the waiting was finally over. She also felt pleasure thinking this was the first step in her return to Australia which would bring her closer to Mark. She was glad she'd gotten rid of her laptop when the latest news broke. She did not want a search done on it. So she'd put it into the rubbish three days ago, just before the dump truck came. She watched it lift this container of trash, emptying it into its gaping maw of crushing plates. It was beyond retrieval. She felt safe.

Susan quickly rang her dad. She asked him to come and pack up her flat- even though there was not much left there. She also rang Anne to let her know. She took the tiny memory card with Mark's story, made a tiny hole in the lining of her bra and pushed it through- hiding it under the fabric. Unless they strip searched her, which seemed unlikely, no one would get to look there. Even if they did a body search, she felt sure she could continue to hide it. She knew it was unlikely she'd be able to read it unless she had a mobile phone or a computer. Despite this, she liked having this link to Mark right next to her body.

Last, she packed her overnight bag, locked the flat and went down to the street to wait. The police car pulled up and she was inside before they'd barely opened the door. As they drove off, she felt no regrets at leaving this place. It had given her a brief place of refuge but held no other significance to her. Her life was now lived within her mind and her external surroundings had become almost completely irrelevant.

Twenty minutes later, the car reached the police station. An army of reporters were clamouring to get a look at her. Despite their attempts, the car windows were tinted and stayed closed. As people pushed towards the car, a gate opened automatically. In moments, they were through it and away from the crowd.

Detective Davidson met her as she stepped from the car. He gave her a smile and she flashed him one in return. It felt nice to see him as she liked him. Despite the circumstances, she knew he had a soft spot for her. He led her inside to a small meeting room and asked her to wait for a minute. He came back in with another, younger man. He was a solicitor, Dylan Madden, to represent her if she chose. As she liked the look of him, she shrugged. This cue was taken as an equivocal consent. Inspector Davidson then excused himself, saying he would leave them together for a few minutes to discuss the case. Questioning, with the Australian police present, was due to start in about fifteen minutes.

Once the door was closed, Susan took the initiative. Her mind was quite clear. She said, "Thank you for coming, Dylan. I'm happy for you to sit with me as the questioning proceeds, but I don't really require any representation or legal advice. I'm clear on my position and what I'll say. I'll be polite to everyone, but I will not be answering any questions except confirming who I am and giving summary details about meeting Mark Bennet and travelling with him in the Northern Territory. I will not seek bail or oppose my extradition to Australia. I'm happy to return and let events run their course. I don't intend to state either my guilt or my innocence. It'll be up to others to judge this."

The lawyer looked taken aback. "Are you saying you don't want me to represent you?"

Susan replied, "No, I didn't say that. I'm happy for you to attend. I'm agreeing mainly to please Inspector Davidson, along with my family and my friends. You may speak on my behalf-provided it's in accordance with what I've said. I don't agree to anything other than that. To the extent that they ask something you consider is prejudicial or inappropriate, I am happy for you to object. But I wish to be clear that I don't want you to seek, in any way, to prevent me from returning to Australia. I want to go there to face this charge as soon as possible."

On this basis, they went together to the interview room where the Australian police were waiting. There were two officers: a Detective Sergeant Alan Richards from the Northern Territory police and Detective Inspector Margaret Ryan from the Australian Federal Police. From the moment the interview started, it was clear the real person running it was Sergeant Alan Richards from the NT police, with Inspector Ryan largely silent.

Detective Inspector Ryan was a middle-aged, solid lady with a no-nonsense manner- not unfriendly but businesslike. She had obviously been in many of these situations before and her serious face gave no clue to what she was thinking. It was clear she was here to represent the Australian Government and ensure the all the correct processes were followed.

By contrast, Detective Sergeant Alan Richards had an open, friendly face which felt familiar. There was also an indescribable 'outback' character which sat around him like an aura. It was more his mannerisms than his looks. There was also a raw honesty to his manner which reminded her of something she had seen in many of the people she had met from the far reaches of Australia.

Susan could not help but like this about him. However, she told herself, he was not here as her friend. But she subconsciously sensed he was not against her either. He seemed to simply want to find out what had happened. She wished she could just answer his questions. It would be preferable to the ongoing silent refusal she was determined to adopt.

The questions began with confirmation of her identity. She agreed she was indeed Susan McDonald and that the passport identification they cited was her. She confirmed she had travelled to and departed from Australia on the specified flights and dates they stated. She confirmed she had met Mr Bennet and travelled with him in the Northern Territory beginning in Alice Springs and continuing to Timber Creek.

With each question, as the inspectors sought further details, she would shake her head. Her lawyer would follow with the statement, "My client is not willing to answer your question."

It went on like this for over an hour. She sensed the growing frustration from all present. It was now well past lunchtime. Susan had not got around to eating or drinking anything this morning. Her back was starting to ache- perhaps an early sign of pregnancy. She was also feeling light-headed- as if the whole thing was unreal. Gradually she found she was no longer listening to the endlessly repetitive questions. She looked up blankly when she became aware of not having heard what Sergeant Richards had just said.

Susan said, "I'm sorry I'm finding it hard to concentrate. Do you think we could stop for a minute?"

Her lawyer immediately came in. "My client is now seeking a short recess. She has patiently answered your questions for over an hour, and so I think that request is reasonable."

The others nodded and all leaned back in their seats. She sensed they were about to get up and go out of the room. However, before they did this, Inspector Davidson put up a hand and said, "With your agreement, I'd like to talk off the record for just a minute."

All nodded. He said, clearly, "Please stop this recording."

A little green light went off in the centre of the table.

Now, he turned to Susan saying, "Susan, you may not believe this. But all of us here think there's more to this story than what you've told us. I, for one, having observed your character over recent weeks and, having talked to many of the people who know you well, consider it is inconceivable you deliberately set out to murder Mark Bennet.

"Something must have happened, an event to change what was an apparently affectionate relationship, one which lasted all the way to Timber Creek, into a situation where, within a period of 48 hours, Mark Bennet was dead and you were fleeing the country, doing it in a way where you sought to remove all evidence of you ever being together. There's clearly evidence for a charge of murder, but it doesn't make sense.

"So, I'm appealing to you, as if you were my own daughter. Even if you won't tell us what happened, please tell us why you're unwilling to speak about it.

"Did something happen between you and Mark Bennet, an event to change your whole relationship, something to put you in great fear of him?"

Susan could not help it- she gave a little involuntary nod of her head. Then, she shook her head violently, turned her face away and buried it in her hands. She bit on her hands until the pain became so severe she could think of nothing else. Without looking up, she forced herself to slow her breathing and regain control.

As she looked up again, she could see blood on her hands from where her teeth had broken the skin. She felt furious, blazing with anger at her giveaway. By using kindness, this man had tricked her into making an admission.

Susan looked up at them all with flaring rage. "I've sat here for an hour and patiently answered all your questions, even though you kept asking me the same pointless questions, over and over.

Now I'll make a short statement which I'd like you to record. After this, I will have nothing further to say to any of you, not now, not ever. Before I do, if you need any further DNA please take it now," she said, pointing to the blood which oozed from the teeth marks on her hands.

They shook their heads. It seemed she'd stunned them into total silence.

Susan saw the green light was back on, so she started talking again. "My name is Susan McDonald. I admit to travelling across the Northern Territory, in August this year, in the company of Mark Bennet, between Alice Springs and Timber Creek. I'm not prepared to answer any further questions in relation to this time or what happened. I will not seek bail if charged with Mr Bennet's murder. I am happy to return to Australia to stand trial for this murder if that's what the authorities determine should happen. I do not now, nor will I in the future, make admissions or pleas in relation to my guilt or innocence in this matter. Beyond that, I have nothing further to say. You may continue this interview if you wish- but I won't be answering any further questions."

Susan then turned her chair sideways, so she was looking at the wall and away from them. She was vaguely aware of consternation and of attempts made on their part to engage her. However, she was locked inside a frozen place inside her mind. Nothing but her anger was real.

After about ten minutes, she became aware they'd all left the room. In a few more minutes, a different female police officer came and took her by the arm to lead her to a cell. She checked Susan's bag, removed Susan's belt and anything else which might possibly be used for self-harm. Then, she left Susan alone.

Susan sat on her bed, immobile. The rage was still surging through her. She was determined to hold onto it- lest her self-control slip and she start crying.

An hour later, she was aware someone had placed a food tray in her cell. She picked at it listlessly. Another hour later, there was a knock on her cell. Her solicitor, Dylan, was let inside. He sat on the chair next to her bed. Even though she had not acknowledged his presence, he talked to her.

Dylan said, "I've been in a conference with the police for the last two hours. As you haven't told me to cease acting for you, I've followed your instructions in these meetings. I found it was necessary to repeat them several times. The others seem to have great difficulty accepting your instructions at face value.

"Tomorrow, you'll go before a magistrate who'll consider whether there's a reasonable basis for you to be charged with murder. At this hearing, unless you object, I plan to read out the instructions you gave today to all present. It's likely the magistrate will find a prima facie case exists for you to stand trial for murder in Australia and will agree you should be sent there for trial. If this occurs, a formal request will then be made by the Australian Federal Police for your extradition.

"I've indicated that you don't intend to object to this. However, you can change your mind at any stage. If you object to extradition, there will be a court hearing held to rule on this. Alternatively, if you agree, it's then up to the Minister for Justice to approve this request. Should the request be approved, you'll be transported to Australia in the company of these police officers.

"If this proceeds without objection by you, it's likely you'll be taken to Australia in one to two weeks. In the meantime, I've been told you'll remain in custody here until your departure. I also expect you'll be held in custody in Australia until your trial occurs."

Finally, Susan looked up at him. She tried to smile at him, for it was not his fault and he was doing his best. She said, "Thank you for what you've done. I'm happy with the arrangements you've made. I ask you continue representing me on this basis."

Then, Dylan added, "Two more things: first, do you need anything? Second, your parents and your friend Anne have sought permission to visit you- do you wish to see them?"

Susan replied, "I'm happy to see my parents and Anne tomorrow. Today, I'd prefer to be left alone. I have everything I need for today."

In the end, the extradition took three weeks to process. Susan sought no delay, but there was now a crowd of well-wishers who had started a 'Save Susan Campaign'. They were lobbying for the Minister and government to oppose her return to Darwin, citing all sorts of obscure reasons why justice wouldn't be served if she was extradited back to Australia.

Concern was expressed for her mental welfare. This was both due to her unwillingness to state her guilt or innocence along with the passive role she was taking to what happened. It led to people suggesting she was either mentally ill, profoundly depressed or suffering from some unknown physical ailment.

Examining doctors and psychiatrists were called in to evaluate her. They asked her many questions. She answered them politely about everything except the actual case. On this topic, she kept her ongoing stony silence.

She was informed that their opinion was that, while she was otherwise sane and healthy, she appeared to have been profoundly traumatised by some unknown event which had happened in the Northern Territory while she was there. One specialist gave an opinion the government should delay and treat her for PTSD before she returned to Australia.

Susan let this all go without any comment. In a way, she felt their conclusions were accurate. Her grief and mental anguish were real. But she had no intention of undertaking any treatments.

It was ironic but no one sought to test her pregnancy status or to question whether this was a possibility. This was despite two separate physical examinations being performed on her. She politely declined requests to provide blood and urine samples, saying, "My health is good. They aren't needed."

Finally, the day came. She was handcuffed to a female officer and taken to the airport in a police car. Sergeant Alan Richards sat alongside her with Inspector Davidson in the front. Approaching the boarding gate, Inspector Davidson stepped up to say goodbye.

She found her anger from the day when she was brought into custody was long since gone. She reached out, took his hand and looked directly at his face. "Thank you. I'm sorry I couldn't cooperate. I'm also sorry I got so angry with you. I do truly understand now- you were only trying to help."

"Thank you, Susan. Somehow, I know it will come out alright. Whatever you've done, you're a brave woman. I admire that."

As Susan sat on the plane, she looked at the date on her boarding pass. It was December 7th. This was the day she had been due to fly back to Australia to get married. She started to cry.

VICTIM   GRAHAM WILSON

Chapter 20 – The Blue Girl

Alan sat on the Airbus looking at this woman who sat beside him as the tears streamed down her face. Her crying was not audible- although her body shook with an occasional sob. He felt a great desire to put his arm around her shoulder and pull her towards him to comfort her.

He knew he must not. Perhaps, if it was only them, he would have. His police companion, on the other side of Susan, sat stony-faced and unmoved, as if she found such displays of emotion a bit of a bore. He'd be glad when she continued on to Sydney and he and Susan exited at Bangkok for the Darwin flight. She had hardly been an exciting companion for the last three weeks.

He looked back at Susan. She was such an enigma. Here she was, sitting and crying her heart out, despite being so resolute and in control at other times. Her rage in the interview room had been terrifying, as if a switch had flipped in her brain. In that minute, she had appeared to be capable of anything. He knew, in that instant, she could have killed someone. Also, the way she had bitten down into her hand to suppress her emotions and regain control. Nearly three weeks later, the teeth marks were still clearly evident on her hand. Despite all this, here she was now, sitting on the plane, crying her heart out like a schoolgirl whose pet dog had just died. At this moment she just seemed fragile and vulnerable.

She turned her face to him, looking slightly embarrassed. Before, he'd thought her pretty, but not anymore. With her blue eyes glistening with tears, she focused on Alan, giving him her total attention. As she gave him a watery but radiant smile, he realised she was sensationally beautiful with totally captivating eyes.

In that exact moment, he sensed another type of danger which flowed from her. It was the power of her unconscious beauty. It could captivate men's souls. It was the completely unconscious nature of it which made her so dangerous.

With her free hand, the one which was not shackled to the arm rest, she touched him lightly on the forearm and said, "I'm sorry. It was just, when I saw today's date on my boarding pass, it all came crashing down on me how my life has run off the rails. Today, I was to fly to Sydney to get married. It seemed like a fairy tale. Yet here I am now- flying to Darwin to go to jail. I'm alright again now. It's just, for a minute, it all seemed so futile."

It was funny how, in that minute, a strange deep friendship was born. If Alan was honest, he was more than a little bit captivated by her. It was good the flight was only for a single day. Then, he'd be returning to Sandy who he really wanted to see again.

However, there was something which seemed intrinsically good and decent about this girl and it tore at his heartstrings. Forever after he would remember her, as she was on the aeroplane now. He would always think of her as the 'Blue Girl' due to the blue brilliance in her eyes and the deep blueness in her soul.

Alan wished he could help mend this blueness, but such a task was for someone else. In that instant, he knew he was one of many other men who were a little bit in love with her.

As long hours drifted past, they spent more and more time talking. At first, it was little nibbles of conversation, making polite pleasantries. However, as all the hours went by, it became a deep and meaningful sharing of their souls. The strangest thing was, that part of the time, he could have sworn he was looking at and talking to Sandy. Several times during conversations, he felt sure it was Sandy, not Susan, looking at him and talking back to him. It made it even more intense, feeling like he was being entranced by two people at once.

At first Alan tried to justify it as a way of coming to understand this person who his chief murder suspect. He reasoned this might assist in properly cracking the case. Despite this rationalisation, he knew it was not the real reason for his conversation with her. There seemed to be a much deeper bond between them.

For a while Alan could feel resistance from their travelling companion, Inspector Ryan. She seemed to be giving an unspoken message stating 'fraternising with the enemy is inappropriate.' However, as time went by, he could feel Susan start to win her over, too. It was in the way she listened intently as she looked with those eyes, loveliness radiated from them, but with room for all. By the time they had reached Bangkok, they had all become friends of sorts, even though, from here on, each of their lives would take very different trajectories.

Susan seemed to have no need to sleep. At times she looked out the window at the ocean. At other times she watched TV or read a magazine. Mostly, when she was not talking or listening, she sat there living a life inside her head. Once, after a burst of intense conversation, she said, "I'm sorry for talking so much. I've mostly sat alone and silent for the last month while I was waiting for things to happen. It's as if I've stored up these words to say. Tomorrow, I'll be silent again. I promise."

Alan replied, "It's good to hear you talk. It's nice to know about a real person inside there."

She told him about her life in England and about her former boyfriend, Edward. Then she proceeded to tell him of her meeting and engagement to David, and of the recent trip to Australia to visit him and meet his family, of the wedding plans and of her friend, Anne. Last, she told him of her life as a child spent riding horses and walking with her father in the Scottish hills.

In return, Alan told her about his life in Australia- particularly his work in the Northern Territory. He told her some of the cases he had worked on, some of the communities he'd visited and many crazy tales of the aboriginal people. Finally, he told Susan of his girlfriend, Sandy, along with their hopes of a future together.

Alan was surprised of her apparent knowledge of the places he had been, the characters and history of the Northern Territory. It seemed a huge amount to have absorbed in a couple of weeks of travel. This was just another of the many things about this lady which were remarkable.

The one thing they did not talk about was the case they were both included in. He knew it was a taboo subject for her and he didn't want to spoil this brief, pleasant interlude. After Bangkok, Detective Ryan parted ways and they caught a new flight. Detective Ryan was staying on the direct flight to Sydney from Bangkok. Alan assured the detective it would be fine with just the two of them.

Honestly, Alan liked the idea of it being just Susan and him on the last leg of the flight. It would be nice to talk privately without the third person listening along. They now had a full row of seats all to themselves.

As they sat back down, he removed the handcuff from his wrist. Then, rather than clip hers to the seat rest, he indicated for her to hold it out towards him. He took the cuff off her wrist, too.

She smiled a "thanks" at him, again with those brilliant blue eyes. Alan could feel himself becoming even more smitten.

Susan took the seat next to the window. At first, Alan chose to sit next to the aisle. They ate the meal served on the flight. After it was cleared, Susan suggested, "Why don't you sit next to me? It's easier to chat if we're side by side, rather than separated by a seat."

Alan nodded and moved across to the seat Susan indicated. She took his hand and said, "I'm glad it's just the two of us now. It's better that way. I know there's something you want to tell me about. There's also something I want to tell you. I'll go first; it's easier for me to begin."

Alan said, "Ok, your turn first."

"About two months ago, when you first found the body of Mark, I had a dream. In that dream, I was carried across the ocean. I started from my house in England and ended up back at that billabong. You and Sandy slept in two separate mosquito nets, placed side by side. I sensed you and Sandy were not yet lovers but wanted to be. As I reached the billabong, I found myself inside Sandy's dream while she was also inside my mind. However, at the same time, I was being pulled towards a crocodile spirit which wanted to capture me, to keep me for itself.

"I was very frightened. Sandy could feel my fear and became terrified, too. When I realised she was feeling my terror, I made myself pull out of her mind. After I pulled out of her mind she didn't see what occurred. However, she'd already seen too much and knew much of what had happened.

"Now, she's seen my mind from the inside, and I've seen hers, too. Even now, I can feel a part of that link remains. Don't ask me to explain it- I just know it is so. It makes us like sisters. I know she didn't want you to arrest me. From the inside of her mind, I also know of her attraction to you. Through my connection with her, I feel and share some of that affection for you, too. Although I feel this affection for you, it's different from what Sandy feels for you since I love another. I can also sense you feel some of the attraction for me which you feel for her. This feeling is because she and I have become kindred spirits. However, you love her more than the simple attraction for me which you feel."

Alan said, "Yes. Sandy has told me of the same dream."

"When I was leaving that place of death, in my dream, I saw her come to you in fear of what she'd dreamed. I sensed you desired her greatly, but instead you held her close to comfort her. With the trust she felt after this experience, you became lovers soon after. After you became lovers, a part of me desired you, too, as I could feel her desire for you. At that time, our minds and desires were linked, intermingling with one another, but it has faded since Sandy saw me on the video.

"It means I trust you and we should be friends. Despite this pull of attraction for one another which we both feel, our other loyalties will keep us apart. It means simply, from here on, we'll be the closest of friends and be able to give strength to each other through our minds. Sometimes, our bodies will still desire one another. Despite this fact, our friendship will be even stronger."

Alan felt amazement at her insight. He could feel himself nodding in reply as she spoke.

"I know you want me to tell you of the night and new day which was part of the killing time. I cannot tell you what you want to know, the why and how it happened. That's for you to find out- if you can. I'll neither help nor hinder you. Much of the knowledge already lies inside Sandy's mind even though she doesn't really understand it yet. Maybe it's better if she never does since the knowledge wasn't meant to pass to either of you.

"That's why I was so angry with Detective Davidson. Through our friendship, he tricked me into revealing what wasn't rightfully mine to tell. He did it for good intentions- but it still felt to me like a betrayal. My anger over it still simmers.

"If you want to know what happened, you mustn't seek the truth from my mind- either directly or through Sandy's knowledge. If you did use her knowledge, it would only tear at her loyalties, give her a sense of betrayal. It would be just like the time when my secrets were stolen from me through my trust.

"The answer is already out there for you to discover through other means. To do so you must do your job, taking no account of me. It may end up, when this is finished, with me spending years in jail for what happened. However, such a possible ending must not influence your investigation. I don't want to end up in jail, but there is still justice in it, due to my actions. If I must, I'll pay that price.

"Since that time, I can feel part of my mind becoming crazy while it withdraws to an imaginary place where I still feel the love of the other. While I am being charged with his death, I still feel love for him right now. I know this is not good- but I'm powerless to stop it. My desire for him seems to be so overwhelming.

"There's a crocodile spirit which comes from my lover and draws me in, too. It's both good and evil in mixed parts. Parts are within me, trying to take me over. It feels like a cancer invading my soul. Perhaps the spirit will end up winning if the court trial finds me insane and I spend the rest of my life locked up. Then, I will be in a place with only dreams and memories for company.

"However, fighting against that dark spirit is a new life growing inside my womb. It's his child- the child of my deceased lover. My lover wants it to survive, grow healthy and carry his spirit forward."

With this statement, she took Alan's hand and placed it on the corresponding place on her lower belly. It was an incredibly tender and intimate thing to do. She looked deep into his eyes with those brilliant blue eyes of hers, saying, "You may not feel the movement of the baby, yet, but open your mind to feel the spirit which moves within me. It's the spirit of a new life and the continuation of the Crocodile Man."

Alan could feel something which was like a tiny bright light pushing out from within her. Right now, it was only just a little light- yet he still felt its power. They sat like this for a minute while contemplating their intimacy in this moment.

Alan could feel his body being aroused by her closeness and the feel of the soft skin on her belly. He desired to stroke her there and realised his fingers had involuntarily started to move over her skin- which was barely separated from his skin by the filmy fabric of her dress. He could feel her arousal, too, as shown by her belly pushing against his hand. Slowly, she pulled his hand downwards. He could feel private places of her body beneath his fingers. Her fingers pressed his hand down against her and her body pushed up against him. He stroked and caressed her, loving the warm softness of this private place and her aroused breathing. His fingers rested there, beneath her hand, in complete intimacy.

She turned to him and said, "Thank you. Just for one minute, I had a need to be touched like a woman when a man desires her. It may very well be the last time I get to experience it."

She slowly pulled his hand back up to the place where the life was growing inside her. After this moment of intimacy between them, she laid her head against his shoulder and cuddled into him.

He felt her joy and his own contentment. She seemed to fall asleep for a while and be transported to another place of happy dreams.

When she awoke, she kissed him lightly on the cheek and said, "Thank you for sharing this time with me. It has helped me and given me new strength. You have become like my brother now. In another life, you might have been my lover. Now, you must tell me what else is in your mind."

He said, "There's nothing more to say as you've already told it all. For me, it was to tell you how Sandy spoke of you. She knew your face when I first showed her your picture. She also knew of your love and terror. However, you already know all of this."

It was almost bittersweet for them both when the plane landed in Darwin. Susan would now go to her cell and he would go to his lover. He returned the cuffs to both of their hands. She smiled at him as he did so while saying, "Now our hands are linked again. Inside our souls will always be linked. Take care, my friend, for what you're doing and where you're going is a very dangerous place. It is a place of an ancient crocodile spirit. Remember, my love goes with you and my sister- the one who is your true lover."

Later that evening, as he lay with Sandy after their loving, he told her of his trip escorting the girl with the so, so blue eyes. He even told Sandy of Susan's power over him: the sense of irresistible attraction towards her. However, he did not share the part about their touching.

Sandy said, "I knew it already. I, too, have felt the pull of the other man who loves her. I have even felt, within myself, the desire she feels for him. You and I are the lucky ones now. We love in flesh and blood. They can only love in her dreams."

They lay for a few minutes catching up on a month of small talk and sharing all their hopes and dreams. They had planned a joint visit to Sydney and Newcastle to meet both sets of parents and their many extended family. It represented the next step in their commitment to live together

Abruptly, Sandy sat up. She slapped Alan hard on the face, twice in a row. "That's to remind you: I'm your woman of flesh and dreams. I may be her sister, but she may not share my lover! Don't forget that!"

Alan laughed while rubbing his stinging face. "You pack a mean punch. You just might be even more dangerous than she is!" Sandy laughed back, "The word is not might but definitely!"

VICTIM GRAHAM WILSON

Chapter 21- Search for the Truth

Alan knew the truth. Susan McDonald had killed Mark Bennet, but it was not based on real evidence. The biggest frustration for Alan was he did not know 'the why'. Why ate at him. He told himself there must be a solution. He decided he would gather all his evidence and lock himself away with it for a couple of days. Maybe then some new hidden insight would emerge. He hoped his analysis would impart real understanding.

Meanwhile, the trial of Susan was proceeding apace. Two days after she arrived in Darwin, a preliminary hearing was held. It was a formality and confirmed she would stand trial for the murder of Mark Bennet, the date being set for March next year.

Alan had provided his evidence to the Director of Public Prosecutions who was of the opinion that the case for Susan being the murderer was compelling and it should proceed forward to trial without delay. The use of the evidence Alan had gathered thus far was now out of his hands. They would prepare the case for the prosecution. He would be a key witness. Apart from being a witness, his role in the court case was finished.

They had now matched Susan's footprint to the one found at the billabong campfire site. It had been the final link needed to solidify the case against her. This gave clear proof of the fact a woman of her size had been at the billabong immediately after the deliberate clean-up of the site, as the footprint was made at that time into wet soil. It was not totally conclusive like a fingerprint or DNA. But her foot size and shape match were very compelling arguments of her being there. With this, the total evidence was more than adequate to go forward to trial.

Alan's role should be over. He should now move on to work on other cases and put this one aside. But he knew he could not walk away yet. There was a whole other story to be told for this to make sense. Alan was certain, if this story was told, it would lead to

Susan's exoneration and subsequent redemption. It would give her life back to her.

Since their trip together, Alan felt a tug of responsibility for all the events which had come to pass. If not for his own investigation into the case, it was likely her role would never have been discovered and she would not have been arrested. Even though he knew justice must roll on, somehow it felt like what had happened was an injustice to her. Now he was determined to do something more to right this wrong. He was the only one with sufficient understanding and commitment to find out the real story. Therefore, it was up to him, and him alone, to do this.

Since the day on the plane when he escorted her to Australia, Alan felt bound to her in a way which meant he must do all within his power to help her. He must ensure she did not spend the next twenty to thirty years in jail. He knew she would not try to help herself. Rather, he felt she had entrusted him to do this during the conversation and intimacy they shared while on the plane.

Since the day on the plane, she had shown no signs of recognition of him and no acknowledgement of the friendship which had developed on the ride. It was as if the 24 hours when they had sat side by side in such an intimate manner had only been an imagined memory. She had retreated completely inside a shell. He understood the reason. It was her way of trying to escape from something she found too horrific to even think about.

At the committal hearing, Susan had entered no plea, refused any legal representation and made no statements. She had merely listened in silence as others outlined the evidence against her.

Even though it was inescapable, he hated having to give testimony against her. Fortunately, it was brief, little more than a recitation of a few key facts. Before giving his decision, the magistrate had looked at Susan and specifically asked her if she had anything to say.

She had shaken her head to signify no. The magistrate pressed her to confirm this refusal by using her words. In answer, Susan said one simple word, "No." This summed up the entire defence contribution to her indictment to stand trial for murder.

Alan sensed the magistrate was deeply uncomfortable to proceed on this basis. However, he had no option to do any other. Therefore, he preceded to confirm the charge, acknowledge there was a case for her to answer to, and accordingly, commit her to stand trial for the murder of Mark Bennet in three months' time.

Alan observed that even the prosecution lawyers seemed uncomfortable with the way the indictment had gone. One of them said afterwards, "It felt like punching a defenceless person."

Since the hearing, Susan barely spoke to anyone, not even her friends or family. Alan felt appalled sympathy for her predicament. She was being left alone, with only her demons for company.

Alan had met briefly with Susan's parents at the hearing. He had also seen Anne and David- whom he felt he knew simply from Susan's descriptions of them. He had heard Anne and David were running their own private investigation into the murder. As part of this investigation, they were now requesting a meeting with him. Since his supervisor had strongly recommended against it, Alan had declined by using a range of excuses to avoid them.

Alan knew they were digging for information about Susan's guilt or possible motives. But, despite this, he could not talk with them about her guilt, as it was for the court to decide. They were also trying to get through to her by seeking insights as to why she was behaving this way. He understood they were trying to help Susan and he would have loved to help them by sharing his concerns and suspicions.

However, this sharing of theories was impossible. It would compromise his position if Alan was seen to be helping undermine the case. Instead, he must focus on an even more thorough examination of the evidence, so as to let this evidence do the talking, just as Susan had indicated. Despite their time together and their conversation on the plane, Susan's motives baffled him, too.

The only thing Alan could see as a likely motive was Susan having a sense of betraying Mark by revealing the full truth about him. He felt her motives may have to do with the protection of the unborn child which was, after all, a product of the joining of Susan and Mark.

Her mother, father and brother were also in Darwin. It seemed they were still trying to talk to Susan. They had also asked to meet Alan next week, which had also declined. In the end, someone put through a call from them and he ended up talking to them on the phone. From this he understood they'd met with Susan on two separate occasions and she'd barely said a word to any them, other than a couple of polite phrases assuring them she was alright, before she went back inside her head.

When they'd tried to push Susan, she had got stubborn and asked them to leave, saying, "Thank you for your concern. I know what I need to do. If you can't accept it and support me in the choice I've made, I'd rather not see you. I don't want to discuss it any further."

He found it hard to understand why these people, Susan's family, would want to see him anyway. Alan could only figure it might indicate desperation. In their place, he'd feel anger at the person responsible for pursuing Susan and obtaining the evidence outlined in the English court which led to her extradition. It now seemed likely to result in the ruin of the rest of her life.

How they thought Alan could help, he couldn't imagine. He worked for the other side. He'd been instrumental in getting her to this place. However, they seemed to sense his empathy for her. He understood their fear, not so much for the trial and its probable consequences, but because she was losing her mind. Her family and the police knew of her pregnancy- but no one else seemed to know. The thought of her giving birth in prison, only to have the baby taken from her, was also too awful to think about. Perhaps her parents could seek to adopt the child.

It was crazy stuff indeed. It was almost like her mind was living in a separate place from reality- but the harder people pushed, the greater her resistance and withdrawal became from reality itself. There were even serious discussions about whether she was mentally unfit to stand trial. When Susan heard the prosecution lawyers suggested this and had called for a psychiatric assessment, Alan was told she had become very upset- almost distraught. Susan was reported to have said to her warden, "Please don't let them go down that path. I just want it all to be over- no matter what happens. Then, at least, I'll have my life back. I'm as sane as any of the others are. I just don't want all these people trying to make me do what I will not agree to do."

Alan knew that time was fast running towards an inexorable result. He must somehow change this path, or he would be responsible for a great injustice which would destroy this lovely girl with the blue eyes- for whom he felt huge affection.

He could see the result: she convicted of murder and her child being taken away. This would cause her to have a complete nervous breakdown and be declared crazy. In a year's time, after this, all that would remain would be an empty shell. It was up to him to make sure this did not happen- but how?

Alan talked about it with Sandy. She, like him, was on Susan's side. He was also concerned for Sandy as this progressed, with him knowing she shared some of Susan's pain. This horror was living inside her mind, too. Luckily, she could barely comprehend it. He had not pushed her for more information as he kept remembering Susan's advice concerning Sandy and Susan's mind link.

However, Sandy seemed to want to talk to him about it. She had told him of fragments of memories she had: a man's body being torn apart by two crocodiles, a man squatting beside the water communing with crocodile spirits and an image of a man's startled face a split second before something momentous happened. Most of all, she remembered Susan's overflowing terror which swamped all else.

This Sunday, Alan and Sandy had agreed, when no one else was around, they would go into his office and work their way through the evidence together. There must be a clue he had missed which would get him started down a path towards finding out the full truth of what had happened.

Next Sunday, they both woke in the half light of dawn. Suddenly, neither was sleepy. They wanted to get at it. It was before six-thirty in the morning when Alan swiped his pass key. He had come in the back, so the duty officer did not see him.

Alan and Sandy went to his office. They collected all the material he had on the case and took it to where there were several desks outside the office. They arranged the evidence into groups on different desks: the pathology of the skull and arm in one place, the exhibits from the murder site on another. The third desk had a map showing Susan and Mark's probable course through the NT along with the various bits of information they had gathered at each place: photos at Yulara, the testimonies from Barkly Roadhouse, Heartbreak Hotel, Daly Waters and Timber Creek. On the last desk, they put the things they had found out about Mark Bennet: his driver's license, vehicle registration and a small pile of mail.

It was a pitifully small amount to represent the life of someone who appeared to have lived in the Northern Territory for several years. They both felt perplexed while looking at it. They knew plenty about Susan. Once they had her name, she had been easy to discover. Now, they had the full story of her life. In contrast, for Mark, they had almost nothing- even though they had known his name for longer than they had known hers. He was a complete enigma. He was a person whose only humanity was a name, a licence photo and a few video images.

"Why?" Sandy voiced what Alan was thinking. "He's the key to the puzzle. We have to unlock his life. We keep thinking Susan is the only one who can explain this. However, in a single day, she goes from being a madly adoring girlfriend to killing this man who she's still obviously in love with. Then, there is the fact of her being

227

so terrified when she did it. I know this because it's this feeling of terror which overwhelms all other emotions that I feel inside her on the day of the murder. She kills him out of terror. Why do that?

"The only explanation I can think of is that he's the cause of her terror. He did something, or she found out something about him which scared her completely witless. Therefore, she killed him in fear of what he would do to her. Then, once it was done, she became full of guilt or regret. Do these feelings of guilt or regret mean he's not really guilty of what she thought he did when she killed him? Or is her level of love and loyalty so strong that she's prepared to overlook something terrible in him. Perhaps her motivation is the fact she knows something terrible about him but cannot bear for others to find it out. She can't reveal this secret because it would betray him. However, without telling his secret, she shares this guilt and the consequences of being his murderer."

Sandy stopped talking and raised an eyebrow. "Is that all just mad speculation? Or could it somehow be an explanation?"

Alan scratched his head. "There may be something in it-although it seems a big stretch when you look at it from the outside. But there are two things which do fit with your theory. I don't think I have properly told you about the first thing.

On the day we arrested Susan, the lead English detective seemed quite friendly with her. I could sense he liked her in a sort of daughter-like way. He didn't really believe she had done this thing. He appealed to her for cooperation. When this appeal failed, he looked for another way to get through to her. Until that moment she was being pleasant.

"He asked something along the lines of what you said a minute ago. I think his words were, 'What happened on that day? Did something happen to make you change?' And, without meaning to, she gave a little nod of agreement. I could tell it had been involuntary. It would've hardly meant anything at all if not for what she did immediately after this tiny involuntary slip.

"It is the only time I've seen her completely lose it. First, she shook her head violently as if to deny her own admission. Then, she buried her face in her hands, looking as if she was crying. She was actually shaking with rage and what seemed like a sense of betrayal. Next, she bit into her hand so hard it bled and left big bite marks which were still there three weeks later. It was as if she was grief-stricken and angry for what she had just done.

"I thought she was punishing herself for her lapse. Perhaps it was meant to be partly theatrical to distract us from her admission and at the same time was a way to get her control back.

"Her self-control after this incident was formidable. She sat there for twenty or thirty seconds while biting into her hand. It must've really hurt- but she was so concentrated on getting her body to follow her mind and not let us find weakness, that she didn't seem to notice any pain. Her jaw was clenched tight and her muscles were shaking. She appeared to be locked inside her mind, in a place of rage and pain, and was completely oblivious to all else. Slowly she forced herself back to a calm place, but still with implacable rage. When she looked up again, her demeanour was like steel. After she regained control, she never said anything other than yes or no to any of us until we left the country.

"That day, her anger was terrifying. In that moment, I could easily see how she could have easily killed someone. The only difference was her anger was mostly directed towards herself for being tricked into a betrayal, which is what she told me later, on the plane ride.

"Even during the plane trip, the only thing she revealed was there was something or someone, other than herself, which caused what had happened with Mark. It was almost like, in her mind, she was first guilty of killing him and then, in the moment of her unintended reveal, she had also become guilty of betraying him. She was appalled at what she had done but also furious with us for tricking her.

"So, I think it must've been a thing done by him which caused his murder. If it wasn't something she knew about him or a thing bad he'd done, I can't see how it would've been a betrayal.

"It was only after we left England that she finally seemed to come back from the place of rage she'd been in since the interview. Then, I think this awful reality, including looking far out into her distant future to see the consequences of the thing she'd done and spurning all our help, started to sink in. First, she apologized to Inspector Davidson. It was really a quite gracious apology. Then, while on the aeroplane, she must have felt utterly lost and friendless because she started crying her heart out for the wedding she would never have. I don't think it was because she really wanted to marry David, but more it was her first actual realisation of the loss of such a future.

"She said, 'Today, I should've been leaving London to get married. Instead- I'm leaving London to go to jail.'

"The second thing was something else she said while on the plane. It was, 'You must find out the reason yourself. I will neither help nor hinder you.' I could already tell by my investigation into her that she seemed a good person- if not an innocent one. She knew I felt this way. Due to this knowledge, she was telling me, once again, there was a real reason for what she did. It seemed like she was saying she couldn't tell me the actual reason as it would be a betrayal. I could sense part of her was willing me to find out the reason to give her a way out of this. Ever since then, I have felt like she entrusted me with finding a solution. Or, at least, she was hoping I would be able to find one.

"In saying all this, let's stick with your theory that whatever caused the murder was something to do with Mark. Possibly his actions were the reason why he was killed- he provoked her into action. This was no capricious lovers' tiff. It was either something appalling or frightening enough to make her kill him- despite her obvious love of him. We can both speculate what this something might be- but that's just a guessing game at this point.

"We must find out more about him: who he was and what he's done in his life up until his untimely demise. There must be something in his life, from before he met Susan, which gives a clue to the reason for the murder. Let's start by double-checking everything we already know about him- in case we've missed anything obvious."

Sandy said, "There's one more thing to think about before we get started and it sort of fits, too. Susan's really clever and she knows a lot about DNA and pathology from working in a lab. She has also shown incredible self-control- we've all seen it.

"Once he was dead, she should've come clean and told us. That's what most other people would do. At worst, she'd have been up for manslaughter, maybe self-defence, if she could prove he'd threatened her. She didn't do any of that. Instead, she made a decision to conceal what happened: not only to hide her role in it, but to hide his identity entirely. I've wondered about it many times.

"It comes through in the way she cleaned up after she killed him. Let's assume she fractured his skull by hitting him on the head with a piece of wood. Then, he either staggered or she dragged his body to the edge of the water where the crocodiles finished the job. This is what the evidence at the site indicated from our analysis of the blood trail and the dirt she had scraped away.

"After it was all done, his body was gone. No one knew he or she was there. The day before he had been in Timber Creek along with her. If his vehicle was just found abandoned there, or even in Darwin, it would have seemed strange, but people would have just wondered where he'd gone. They'd expect him to turn up, eventually. Maybe, after months, he'd have been listed as a missing person. Perhaps the vehicle would've been checked then and her DNA found in it.

"However, finding her DNA then would've proved nothing- she never denied having travelled with him to Timber Creek. By the time they arrived in Timber Creek, she'd already spent ten days with him. It would be expected we'd find her DNA and fingerprints in lots of places in his vehicle. All she would have needed to say to explain this would be that they'd travelled together for several days in his vehicle. She could have said he must have vanished after they parted at Timber Creek. In fact, that is what she said when first asked about their travels together.

"This leads me to my question: why remove everything? Not only did she remove her things, but also every last thing which had belonged to him? He clearly had business papers- we found his briefcase with a smashed lock. Yet she burned it, and presumably, all the papers it had contained. Every single one of his belongings was destroyed, too. When travelling in the outback, he would've had a whole range of gear. We saw some of it sitting in the back of the truck on the CCTV when he came to the Desert Sails at Ayers Rock that night. The people in Alice Springs also describe the vehicle as having boxes and tools on the back. Despite this, every last bit was gone when the truck was found.

"It was as if she was determined to remove any trace of his identity which she possibly could- remove everything which connected him to her or to anywhere else. Perhaps she found something incriminating in the car and she couldn't bear for it to be found by anyone else."

This theory seemed to make sense, Alan nodded in agreement. "OK, let's accept the premise there's something about him which they both wanted to stay hidden. Now, we need to find out what it is. I fear she's done such a good job of destroying all the evidence that there may be nothing left for us to find."

Sandy said, "You don't really believe that, do you? He lived for at least three years in the NT. He had enough money to buy a brand-new car, take it wherever he wanted and pay for everything with cash. So he clearly had access to plenty of money. And he clearly was careful about revealing his identity. But-NO ONE can live in a place and earn money for three years without leaving any traces behind.

"Somewhere in the outback, there must be people who know him, know real things about him. We already have information to suggest he did regular work somewhere around the Barkly. There are not so many stations, aboriginal settlements and mines to check around there. We just have to be thorough."

Alan said, "1 will have to find a justification to keep investigating, though. I wish I could do it all on the phone while sitting at my desk. However, many people out there will only talk to other real people. Doing my own footwork has been how I've got the evidence thus far.

"Now, as far as my boss is concerned, this murder is solved. He says I should be working on other cases. I can probably fudge a day or two each week working on the loose ends. Sadly, I can't go travelling around the back of the NT on what others will call a 'wild goose chase'- unless I can think of a good reason."

Alan walked over to Mark's little pile. It was only a bare half dozen letters- most of which were junk mail. Not all had been opened and the advertising fliers had been put to one side. He looked at them, one by one. He knew it was probably futile, but he opened the unopened ones anyway. Inside them, he found only what had been expected.

The last letter had a mobile telephone logo on it and was addressed to Mark Butler. It was probably just another piece of junk mail sent to Mark Bennet in error- perhaps a telephone promotion of the sort which seemed to come in Alan's mail every other day.

Alan found himself asking in his head 'what was there to lose?' He opened it. It was indeed a phone bill. It listed a mere dozen calls and a similar number of texts in a full month's time: hardly a big user. The numbers were meaningless due to most of them being calls to other mobiles. The first ones originated from or came to his phone when he was in Queensland, two showed indications of being related to the central Queensland area and two indicated Mount Isa. The calls made later on in the month came from or went to him while in the Northern Territory, a couple from Tennant Creek and a couple from Alice Springs. This was all hardly remarkable for a person who lived in the NT.

Despite this, a bell was ringing in Alan's brain. There was a pattern somewhere which he suspected was eluding him now but had been noticed by his subconscious. He realised it was the vague story of their first meeting and subsequent travel together which he had obtained from the girl in Barkly Roadhouse. Mark Bennet had met Susan in Cairns and had then come back to the NT. The obvious route was through Mount Isa and Tennant Creek before he met her in Alice Springs. The dates on the phone bill did seem about right for this route.

After figuring this out, Alan thought, *even if it is not Mark but just a coincidence- what harm is there to check it out. I'll ring through to the numbers and see who answers.*

The first number rang through to the message bank of a company somewhere in Queensland. This one was not promising. The second was also a company, but this time a voice on a message claimed to represent a big multinational. He rang the third number and found it was a helicopter operator based out of Mount Isa. This number was at least a bit interesting and gave him something to follow up on.

Sandy had come over to stand alongside him and listen to the messages. Then, there was the same number listed four times over about a week's time. First, there was a text received from the number and later, during the same night, a text sent to the number. Next, a phone call was received. Finally, one more text was sent. He dialled the number only to hear the automated message, "I'm sorry. This phone number has been disconnected and is no longer in service."

Alan kept calling all the numbers on the phone bill. There was another helicopter operator, this time based in Borroloola. "Hello this is Vic from Carpentaria Helicopters. I'm probably out flying if I don't take your call. If you need to book my services, please ring after seven pm or send a text. I'll call back as soon as I can." Alan decided to send a text. "Vic, please ring Sergeant Alan Richards, NT Police, on this number."

There was nothing in the rest of the calls which seemed of any value- although he could not help but be intrigued by the bracket of four calls or texts to the same number in just a few days. It did not seem to fit Mark's typical call pattern and was, therefore, worth following up on. Tomorrow, he'd run a trace on that number.

Alan and Sandy spent another couple of fruitless hours looking at everything from all different angles. They were both getting hungry. They had just decided it was time to go out and eat a late breakfast when Alan's mobile phone rang.

The caller said, "It's Vic calling from Carpentaria Helicopters. Is that Alan Richards?"

Alan replied, "Yes, thanks for calling back. I'm just trying to trace a Mark Bennet. You don't know anyone by that name, do you?"

Vic replied, "Name doesn't ring a bell. Any reason it should?"

Something about Vic's response made Alan feel cagey. This guy did not seem to know about the murder so he must not see a lot of TV or newspapers. Considering this, Alan replied, "Actually I'm trying to trace his movements from around August this year. It seems he did work in your neck of the woods. He was travelling around there with a girl named Susan. Does that ring any bells?"

The moment Alan had said the name "Susan," he heard something at the other end of the line. It sounded like an indrawn breath which showed surprise.

The voice came back on the line, loud and clear. "I have a good friend called Mark Butler. I've done a load of work with him over the years. Around the time you asked about, he was indeed travelling with a girl called Susan. I remember her, she was a lovely English girl. I took them fishing out on the Calvert and Robinson Rivers. Perhaps you've got the name wrong. Does a Mark Butler sound like your man?"

Alan's heart was pounding so hard it almost caused him to drop the phone. He pulled himself together quickly. "Could be. Listen- I have this bloke's photo. It's really important I show it to you as soon as I can as I need to verify whether or not it's the same guy I'm looking for. I need to find more information on him. Where are you now?"

Vic replied, "As we speak, I'm at Mataranka. However, I'm just about to ferry into Katherine for an overnight stay before I do a job at Scott Creek first thing tomorrow morning."

Alan said, "OK. Could we meet in Katherine later today? I can be there in about three hours. Any time after that is good for me- just name the place."

Vic laughed. "Must be urgent! I'm staying at the Paraway Hotel tonight and I should be there by then. Ask for Vic, the chopper pilot. They all know me there."

Chapter 22 – The Helicopter Pilot

In only a minute, Alan and Sandy were on the Stuart Highway heading directly for Katherine. They both felt a huge hit of adrenaline. It was similar to their first discoveries together at the Mary River billabong. The difference was how much bigger the discovery felt this time.

When they reached Adelaide River, Sandy said, "We should slow down a bit, stop for something to eat. We need to think carefully about how we approach this. If he is Mark's friend and we come in too hard, we may make him cagey. We need to explain to him about our need to discover more about this unknown Mark, in order to get his trust."

Alan said, "Stuff that! We just need to know what he knows. Surely he will help us when he knows his mate is dead."

Sandy put her hand on his arm, "Slow down cowboy. It's not like you to rush into something without thinking it through. What you need to do is put your brain properly into gear. Let's stop for ten minutes, eat and gather our thoughts."

Alan nodded, albeit reluctantly, as she continued on. "Then, when we do get there- we won't barge in and make a mess of things. It's not like Vic is going anywhere today. We'll arrive in the early afternoon and we will still have the rest of the day to find everything out. People will most likely be resting in the shade when we get there, which will make it a good time for a leisurely talk.

"I suggest you first show him the photo. Then, if he agrees we're talking about the same person, you should tell it as a bit of this story to get him in. As you say, if Vic is his friend, I'm sure he'll want to help us figure out what really happened."

Vic was sitting by the pool with a cool drink in hand when Sandy and Alan arrived. He was a wiry, mid-sized man with dark skin and features. He did not appear fully aboriginal but was obviously of mixed descent. He showed a big grin on his face when he recognised them.

"I wouldn't put it past my old mate Mark, sly bugger that he is, to go by another name. What's he been up to this time? Is it a bit of cattle stealing, maybe? Once you said the name 'Susan' it was hard to believe it could be anyone else."

Alan pulled out the two photos he had brought with him. First, He held up the photo of a perfectly clear, full head shot of Mark which had been taken at Yulara. "Is this your friend, Mark?"

Vic barely glanced at the photo, "Sure. He's hard to mistake."

Then, Alan held up the photo of Susan. "How about this one? Is it the girl, Susan, who was with him?"

Vic took it from Alan. He looked at it even more intently than he had with the photo of Mark. He nodded, saying, "She's even prettier than in my memory. Although, it's not like this photo could show those gorgeous blue eyes of hers. I've seen Mark with quite a few girls. Most looked good- but this one here was special.

"When we first met, I even said to her, 'If he ever lets you go, make sure you let me know.' I meant it, too. Then, another time, I said to her, 'Why don't you trade him in for a helicopter pilot? You know- someone with a bit more class?'

"She laughed, ever so nicely, and said, 'I'm sure you've had many girls choose to join you in the mile-high club.'

"I only spent one day with them, but I could tell she thought the sun shone out of Mark. She was gorgeous- not just to look at, mind you, but in her ways and manners, too- I was a bit hooked by her myself. You know- even with Mark being my best mate and all- if she had been interested in me, it would've been hard to stop. But, on that day, he was the only one she had eyes for."

Then, suddenly, Vic became very serious as he said, "But you didn't drive all that way, in such a hurry, just for a social chat about my mate. What's this all about?"

Alan looked at him and cautiously asked, "I gather you are not a big news or TV watcher, are you?"

Vic looked a bit sheepish as he replied, "Well, the last three months I've been really busy. Haven't had any days off since I saw them. You know how it is- a frantic rush to get the mustering done before the rain comes. The end of this coming week, I'll be done, finally, have a whole fortnight off. Stations are shutting down for Christmas starting this weekend. Until then, I'm fully booked. Today's my first half day off in ages. I thought I might catch up on the news this afternoon. At the same time, a beer in a pub would be nice. Anyway- tell me what this is all about?"

Alan took a deep breath. There was no nice way to say this. "This man," he said, pointing to Mark Bennet's photo, "he was murdered less than a week after you saw him in August. This lady, Susan, is on trial in Darwin now for his murder."

Vic looked dumbfounded. For a full minute, he didn't speak. At last he asked, while pointing to the picture of Mark, "Are you sure it's him?" Then, before Alan could answer that, Vic pointed to Susan's picture and said, "That thing that you said about Susan murdering Mark- it can't possibly be true! It does not fit at all."

He looked back to Mark's photo and said, "How do you know it's him? Are you real sure it's him? I knew this man, with the name of 'Mark Butler' for almost ten years. You are saying the man you found is 'Mark Bennet.' How do you know it's the same 'Mark?' Do you have a photo of the man you found after he died which definitely matches the face of the 'Mark' I know?"

Alan said, "Why don't I start at the beginning and I'll tell you what I know." Over the next half an hour, Alan filled in the gaps as to why he now believed the 'Mark Bennet' he found was the same 'Mark Butler' Vic knew. In return for being given this confidential information, Vic told Alan how he knew his 'Mark.'

Alan admitted honestly to Vic that the only evidence identifying the body found as the person 'Mark Bennet' and not someone else was a photo on a driver's license. He explained how the car was linked to the billabong crime scene. He also explained they had discovered the car was registered to a 'Mark Bennet.'

However, all they had left of the body was a skull and a bit of forearm. For obvious reasons, they could not really tell if these matched the driving photo of 'Mark Bennet.'

In addition to being unable to conclusively match the body parts to the license photo, they could not match them to the person Vic identified as 'Mark Butler' from the photos at Yulara.

Vic asked, "Which arm was found?"

Alan said, "It's the right arm."

Vic said, "Did you find anything funny about it? For instance: an old gunshot wound?"

Sandy exclaimed with surprise, "How could you possibly know that we found such a thing in the arm?!"

"Well," replied Vic, reluctantly, "Mark had a bit of a bump on the bone of his right forearm. One day, we were working with cattle in a trap yard. A metal gate flew open and hit him directly on that lump. Mark doubled over, looking as if he was about to pass out after it happened. He was grey and shaking from the pain.

"Later in the day, I asked him what his reaction to being hit there had been about. Mark was a tough bastard who rarely reacted to any pain. So, I knew it must've really hurt. At first, when I met him, Mark would tell me nothing about his life from before. But, over time we became good friends. I told him all about my family, all the Afghan, aboriginal and Scottish relatives. Because I'd told him everything about me, I think Mark felt he should tell me at least some part about his life from before we became friends.

"Mark put my hand on the lump so I could feel it. It wasn't very big- but it was quite distinct. He told me, in a much quieter voice than he usually spoke with, 'I was working overseas as a mercenary in Africa when I took a bullet right there. It smashed out a piece of bone. The hospitals and doctors weren't very good there, so I could not have any surgery done to repair the arm. All they could really do was clean out the hole, remove as much of the bullet and rubbish as they could find and fill me up with antibiotics. Then, I strapped up my arm and went on my way. It took nearly a year before my arm was better. Even after it healed, I couldn't do much with it. I had to teach myself to write with my other hand. Now, it's as strong as ever. But although it's completely healed, that pointy bit of bone is still tender, particularly when banged directly. It's possible there's a bit of the bullet still left in there."

Sandy stated, in response to Vic's story, "You know, this is the first real confirmation which identifies the body we found as the man who goes by the names of 'Mark Bennet' and 'Mark Butler'- whichever name ends up being his real one. I've X-rayed the bone we are talking about now. I've seen the bullet fragments still located within the bone. It's definitely some kind of Russian ammunition. Finding it tells us this man has worked in Africa or the Middle East at some point in his life. With your help, we now really do know it's your friend, Mark, but I'm sorry you had to find out like this.

And now we need to know who he was, what he's done during his life and must try to understand why Susan was involved in his death. Do you think you can you help us with this?"

With the mention of Susan's name, Vic turned his attention to her. "Where is she now? Why is she being accused of his murder? How do you know it was a murder? What's she said about this?"

After this barrage of questions, Alan explained the evidence he had gathered so far. Vic listened intently. When Alan told him about Susan's complete refusal to cooperate followed by her continuing silence, Vic shook his head, saying with confusion, "It just doesn't make sense. Don't get me wrong: she was no weakling. She would probably be physically and mentally capable of killing him. But the way they acted together- it just doesn't make sense that she'd want to kill him for any reason. She was as captivated by Mark as he was by her. It sounds like she was there as it happened, alright, but I'm sure there must be another explanation!"

Alan agreed with Vic, wholeheartedly, replying, "That is exactly why we were so desperate to see you! We must find out how and why it happened. Except for Susan, you're the only person who has admitted to knowing this man during our investigation, up to this point. We need your help desperately! Please tell us everything you know about him and also if there are any others who might know more things about him?

"In three months' time Susan's trial will begin. Unless she decides to help herself, or we can find an explanation for what happened that day, one which doesn't make her a cold-blooded murderer, it'll be over in a day. The end result will be her spending most of her life in jail."

Vic shook his head, as if to show he was finding it all hard to believe while stating emphatically, "Of course I will help you in any way I can. Mark was my friend. No matter what happened, I know he wouldn't have wanted something like this to happen to Susan. So, I must help her! I'll do it both for her own sake and because he would've wanted me to do this for her. I'll tell you whatever I can remember now about Mark's life. Then, while I'm out working next week, I'll put my mind to trying to remember anything else which could also help.

"And I must talk to Susan as soon as I can! Perhaps I can help her find a way out of this mess. She may trust me more because she knew I was Mark's friend."

After this was said Vic began to reveal the many things he knew about Mark's life to them. The three of them remained sitting beside the pool, during the full heat of the afternoon, as Vic talked while Sandy and Alan wrote notes.

Vic began by telling them how he'd first met Mark out in the middle of the Tanami when his car had broken down and he'd walked for miles in the middle of summer to get help. "It was that bloody hot it would have killed anyone else," he said.

Then he told of working with Mark on many jobs and stations over the last ten years. He told them what a great marksman Mark was, how Mark was an all-around jack of all trades as well as a superb horseman, "he could have been a rodeo champion if he'd wanted. Some people even compared him to The Breaker," he said. He described Mark's vehicle and all the things he used to carry

VICTIM GRAHAM WILSON

around in it- particularly his rifles. According to Vic, his rifles were something Mark was a bit obsessed with.

Vic tried to think of any other people who were also Mark's friends or people who Vic had seen him with before. Vic was especially trying to think of anyone who might know an earlier Mark than he did. Really, on this subject, Vic knew little. He said, "Mark's past was like a closed book. It was something he wouldn't talk about with anyone. He knew a lot of station people. But I never heard him tell others of his past life. And most people only knew him as Mark B or MB."

Then, Vic added, "I remember Susan saying she really wanted to know about his past. She was head over heels in love with him- anyone could see it! Mark seemed to have a big crush on her, too. Mark even told me how he was going to collect some jewellery he had had made up for her when they went to Borroloola the next day. He said they were some special blue opals which matched her eyes perfectly.

"Before Susan, Mark never seemed to be able to keep any one of the girls around for long. They would come with him for a week, maybe two, and then just leave. But with her, it seemed different. Susan really seemed to want to know everything about him. Mark didn't want to tell her about his past, though. I can only guess the reason he wouldn't tell her was that he must have had some really bad secrets. Personally, I think he was abused as a child. His mother died when he was young, I believe. Mark never quite said it outright, but I picked up little bits here and there when he was telling me stories.

"Anyway, Susan really wanted to know all about him and Mark didn't want to tell her any of it. It seemed to be the only thing which spoiled how perfect it all seemed to be between them. But despite this minor disagreement between them, Mark appeared to be totally smitten with Susan. The jewellery almost sounded a bit like a marriage proposal- at least to me, it did. I reckon, knowing what Mark seemed to think of her, if he felt he could have proposed to her, he would have.

"Mark was a tough bastard and completely fearless. On the other hand, I never saw him do anything bad. He was gentle with animals. And he was always kind to the aborigines and old people. I never saw Mark hurt anyone- not even when throwing a punch in a bar fight. He would scrap, alright, but it was always in a good-natured way- as if it was all just a joke. Mostly, Mark would simply duck and step out of the way of the odd loose punch instead of throwing a one himself. Then, if it got too heated, he would send the other bloke, the one throwing his weight around, to the ground with a well-directed shove.

"Still, there were a couple of stories passed around about him and people who tried to bully or cheat him. The way he dealt with this, back then, sounded scary. Sometimes, he'd get a look in his eye with one of the pushy blokes. You know, the kind of look where you knew it would end badly for someone and it wasn't going to be him. Those times I saw it was definitely the other guy in the wrong. Fortunately, from the ones I remember, these people weren't so brave. They backed down when Mark called their bluff. Mind you- Mark could be mean enough if he thought someone was being an arsehole. The word of it got around, so most people knew better than to cross him."

After two hours straight of mostly Vic talking, Sandy and Alan knew all Vic could remember- or, at least, all he would tell them. It was funny- as the afternoon wore on, it seemed as if Vic was changing. His warmness towards Susan seemed to fade. At the same time, they glimpsed an edge of anger which came out when they tried to dig deeper into if Mark could have done something bad which caused Susan to kill him.

Despite this change in demeanour, Vic kept on telling Sandy and Alan what he knew about Mark. It was a lot more than they knew before- but also remarkably little considering how long and how well Vic claimed to have known him. Alan sensed there were still a couple of secrets Vic withheld from them.

In the end there were little hints towards possible explanations of the crime, yet the enigma remained as great as before they were able to identify the body. 'Mark B,' which is what Vic called him, was kind and gentle with most people. But there was a ruthless, dangerous side to him too. When the telling was done, despite all the information given by Vic, Mark's past was as hidden as ever.

As to Mark's real identity, Vic remained guarded. He repeated people called him 'Mark B' or MB and that was it. No one used his surname when talking to or about him. Mark signed everything as 'Mark B.' It was only on things like tax invoices that he ever used his surname. Vic said this was the only reason he knew it.

Vic said, "Of all the people who knew Mark, I reckon less than one in ten actually knew his surname." However, Vic did not say if he knew if this was Mark's real name or not. When they asked him directly, he merely dodged the question.

VICTIM   GRAHAM WILSON

Chapter 23 – Vickram Campbell

Vic was perplexed when the call came in asking him if he knew a 'Mark Bennet.' While his initial response was he did not know this person, his mind was working in parallel thinking about the strange request Mark made on the morning they last went flying. It was on this day he'd first known something was different about Susan, quite different to Mark's relationships with previous women.

Vic knew Mark had few real friends. He was as close to Mark as was anyone else in his life. From the time Mark and he had first worked together, around ten years ago, they'd struck an unlikely bond. He thought it was to do with them both having mixed ancestry and muddled identities. Both had also left pasts' behind as they'd forged their new careers working across the outback.

Mark was a city kid who'd grown up hard and tough to protect himself. Vic was a black kid who'd had to do much the same type of growing up. The real difference between the two of them was: Vic had a large, loving family which included a mother who always had time for him and a big tribe of sisters, brothers and cousins.

The Alice Springs town camp had not given him an ideal childhood environment. Drunkenness and violence were endemic and several of his relatives had been killed in drunken fights or from alcohol-related diseases such as, liver failure, kidney failure and diabetes. And half of his childhood friends sniffed glue or petrol, frying their brains, while stealing things to make a living.

Vic was the youngest of his siblings. This gave his mother a fierce determination to not let crime and delinquency happen to him, too. In part, Vic believed it was their mixed ancestry which made her want something better for him. She called herself an Arrente tribe woman- but this identification was only half of her lineage. Vic's mother had an Afghan grandfather on one side and a Scottish grandfather on the other side. So she had kept the Scottish Campbell name for herself while also continuing her grandfather's

Afghan name, Vickram, in her son. While most people only knew him as Vic, Mark was an exception.

Vic and Mark were not so different in their upbringings- except Vic had grown up with a mother and sister who had wanted better for him. His mother had watched helplessly as her other five children had run off the rails. Even though Vic still liked his brothers and sisters, only one other of his mother's children had amounted to anything. This was his closest to his age sister, Polly. Both of his older brothers had already spent several years in jail by the time Vic was born. One of his sisters became pregnant at fourteen. Currently, she had three children, all by different fathers and lived totally off social security. The second oldest sister married a man who was older, violent and was drunk frequently. He would regularly beat her.

His third sister, Polly, was only three years older than him. After a patchy start in which she had been one of a gang of kids who was into shoplifting and heading rapidly towards jail- she suddenly grew up. She seemed to have found religion and stability when she was seventeen. Polly left home after this occurred and got a job in Alice Springs and a place of her own. Now, she spent most of her time on church activities and trying to help other kids from their old neighbourhood.

Polly, as much as his mother, had been determined Vic would do better than his other siblings. He was both bright and a gifted athlete. They both thought it was he, in the family, who had inherited the best of their mixed ancestry. Vic had played Australian Rules football for a local team and was seriously looked at by some of Melbourne teams. He had the speed and agility to weave through any gap. An offer was made for him to go to Melbourne for a year and train for a big-name club. But it would have interrupted his last year at school.

Polly wanted better for Vic than him dropping out of school for sport. So she drove him to finish high school and get good marks. Once Polly realised Vic had his heart set on working on a cattle station, she looked for a better choice that he could do while working in the outback. The first time Vic saw a helicopter fly, he was hooked on these metal birds of the sky.

So, his sister encouraged Vic to pursue this interest.

Polly looked for work he could do at the airport and found an apprenticeship with a company there. This taught him an aircraft mechanic's trade and let him get affordable flying lessons as well.

Vic stayed with Polly while he got his mechanic's ticket. He saved money by doing other odd jobs anywhere he could. All his money went into his flying lessons. At the age of twenty-one, Vic got his fixed wing pilot's license. At the age of twenty-three, Vic got a helicopter license. Then, he worked for Helimuster and other firms for a few years while he built up his savings.

Finally, only three years ago, Vic had enough money to get his own machine. It was based in Borroloola and he mostly did work for miners and cattle stations. Vic didn't mind what type the work was, so long as he had his own helicopter. That was all that really mattered to him.

Mark was one of the few 'white fellas' Vic knew who his mum actually liked. He'd brought Mark home early on, just a couple of years after they'd first met. At that time they were doing a job together, far out northeast of Alice on the Sandover River. It was like his mum saw something good in Mark. At the same time she'd recognized Mark's unspoken need for a family. She'd immediately 'sort of' adopted Mark, no questions asked. Now, anytime Mark was in town, he nearly always went and saw Vic's mother- even when Vic was far away at the time.

Vic and Mark had stayed firm friends ever since they first met. A couple of times, over the years, they had little fallings out over girls. It wasn't the fact they both didn't have plenty each- but, now and then, they'd fancied the same one. Mark and Vic seemed to have very similar taste in women. It was a sort of blood brother thing. When they'd first met, they both scored the girls they saw as to which they wanted to hit on. They nearly always got the same score. It was supposed to be a game - but, sometimes, they had skirmishes about the game. At these times, Vic and Mark had done a bit of pushing and shoving at each other. It was never real, though. The girls would choose and, whichever won, the other was always a gracious loser. There were even times when they shared girls and their mateship continued unscathed.

As far as Vic knew, neither of them had found a girl they really wanted to settle down with for the rest of their lives. However, Vic suspected there had been a few women along the way- who Mark never actually spoke of- who had been more to him than just a good time. That was what Vic had thought, at least, until Susan had come along. The moment Mark rang Vic to ask him to find a day to take them flying in the Gulf, to a place along the Calvert and Robinson Rivers, which both Vic and Mark loved, Vic sensed there was something different with how Mark felt about Susan.

Mark told Vic there would be an English girl travelling with him. It was something in his voice which let Vic know she was different. Mark said he really wanted to show her a good time while explaining his love for this country to her.

From the moment Vic met Susan, he had understood why. There really was something different about her. She seemed to have a true affection for Mark- like they connected to each other at a different level than most people did. There was also genuine class about her. She was no prude, mind you, but there was an elegance and grace about her which was combined with a tomboy sort of 'devil-may-care' attitude. Vic would not have said she was a classic beauty. She was more of a pretty woman, but she had something indefinable within her which made her super attractive. Vic had flings with a lot of beautiful girls over the years. Flying a helicopter made it dead easy to attract the fairer sex- but he had only met a few like Susan.

There was something in Susan's eyes which drew you in. Also, when she talked to you, she made you feel as if there was no one in the room but you and her. However, she was his best friend's girl.

251

Vic knew he could not go there: even if she had shown interest in him- which she had not. Apart from a few friendly quips during the ride, Vic had not let himself think about Susan at all since the time he had spent with Mark and her. Despite this, her image was still very clear inside his mind.

Since Mark and Susan had gone on with their trip, Vic's feet had barely touched the ground. It was his busy time of year and work was absolutely booming. But, even with all his flights since, he still clearly remembered the day of flying he had spent with Susan and Mark. It stood out as one of life's magic moments.

Even more than the ride itself, Vic remembered what had come before it. Just before they took off, Mark had asked to talk to him in private for a minute.

Mark made out to Susan it was a private moment for planning the route or other business dealings. What Susan hadn't known was all the route planning had been done over the phone. The only thing left to take care of was an invoice, to be done at the end of the day, based on mate's rates. They'd already agreed on the price of the ride.

Instead, Mark was more frank than usual with Vic. He had pulled out a piece of paper and handed it over to Vic to read.

The words "Last Will and Testament of Vincent Marco Bassingham" were written on the top.

Mark said, as Vic was reading, "In case you're wondering: that's my real name. I want you to sign this. It's my will." Vic saw it named him as an executor of Mark's estate.

Mark continued, "We've been best friends for ten years. I know you and your family **BUT** I've told you very little about me. There's bad stuff I've done, I could tell you about it - but, I'd rather not. I've got a feeling that something bad- a payback, if you will- is going to happen to me real soon. It may all be in my imagination- but you never know. Sometimes, I think I can see these things coming. So I decided I want to make a will- just in case I'm right about this feeling.

"Since I met Susan, I'm completely crazy about her! Despite this, I can't tell her who I am. However, if anything should happen to me, I'm asking you to ensure that almost everything I have goes to her. My will names her as my main beneficiary. There is still a bit left which is to go to you and a few other friends. In the will, I also give instructions about how to access everything I own. It's worth a lot of money.

"If anything happens to me, I want you to handle things for Susan like you are my brother. I want you to help her and make sure she gets this. Will you do that for me?"

Vic had been tempted to ask more about what was really going on. However, Mark was so serious and earnest in his words to Vic, so all he did in response was nod, while saying, "Like a brother. Yeah- can do that. But I reckon you have the nine lives of a cat with eight still left. You'll outlive us all."

Mark had calmly replied, "I'm probably down to my last one now. I've had my share of good luck and can't ask for more. My Crocodile Spirits have been calling me- those blackfella totem ones from that Top End country where they gave me my skin name."

After Mark's statement, Vic had signed the will. Then, Mark put it in the car while giving him an enigmatic smile. Soon after this interaction, they'd gone flying along the pre-determined route. After the ride was done, Susan and Mark left. This had been the last he had seen or heard of either of them, until now.

Then today, the cops had rushed to Katherine to see him and tell him the story of finding Mark's body. That was it. And Mark's strange prophecy had been fulfilled.

Vic had mostly helped those cops. They had wanted his help to save Susan. A girl who they knew was guilty and, yet, believed was somehow not guilty. Or, at least, they believed she was somehow justified in what she'd done. They said they'd sought his help to discover the 'real Mark' in order to solve their mystery.

At first, he had helped them out fully, because he felt affection for the girl in her trouble. He remembered her fondly from the day they'd spent in the helicopter. But, as the afternoon wore on and he'd shared more of his knowledge, he began to see her in a different light.

Vic had not let himself think about Mark's loss and what it meant to him until now. *But- he really missed this man! He was the brother he'd have wanted if he could have chosen. He was not the crying type, but he felt sort of choked up thinking of that last day: the magic of the hunt and the fishing hole. Ten years of other magic times as well.*

Shit happens. Tomorrow, it could be his turn. The thread that holds one to life is so thin that one puff of wind can break it, he mused.

Vic could not put Susan in the same frame as Mark's death. But. at the same time, the cops were convincing in the story they'd told him, and evidence was evidence. Thinking of Susan killing Mark, no matter what Mark may have done before in his life, made Vic feel really angry towards Susan. Mark was his mate! The two of them had shared so much together and now, she had taken him away. He could feel his affection for her turning into something dark. Vic felt it becoming a desire for payback.

In contrast, Mark had made Vic promise to treat her like a sister. Mark had told him, though Vic barely read the will, what was contained inside it. The will stated that he, Vic, was the executor of his will and Susan its principal beneficiary. It was all completely whacky now.

Vic knew, despite everything, he must do what he'd promised. He also intended to find out the truth at the same time. As soon as Vic was finished this year of mustering, he would go and see Susan and get the real story. He would beat it out of her if he had to! As Vic had promised, he would look after her. While he was doing so, though, she would tell him the truth even if it killed him. Vic was not the type to be taken in by tears and silence. He had seen too much crazy stuff in his life to let anything so simple stop him from getting what he wanted.

When the cops had shown Vic her photo, he had started having warm thoughts about her- more like lust than warm, being honest. But now, when he thought about Susan killing Mark: the image of her in his mind was all changed.

Vic now saw her as an evil, dangerous and calculating bitch.

Perhaps Susan had really been charming his friend to get at his money. Then, she got rid of him when it had suited her. The cops had not talked about her as if they'd believed money was the reason for the murder, but it was unlikely they knew about his money.

Rather, they'd said she'd seemed to be totally infatuated with Mark and had remained so to this day.

Stuffed if he knew what to make of it all.

Vic decided he would find out- no matter what it took.

Chapter 24 – Crocodile Spirit Capture

Since Charlie had discovered the man's head in the billabong, he had a weird feeling most of the time. It was like there was almost always a thing inside his head trying to talk to him. It was not quite a voice- more like an alien presence, one which did not belong in there. It would send unexplained images into his head at times. These were things he was only partially aware of which kept bumping into his ordinary thoughts.

Charlie could be in the shed, working to make something out of wood, and he would become aware there was someone or something else with him, within his mind. This thing was watching with him from the inside while using Charlie's eyes to see the world outside. At other times, like when he was working with Elsie in the kitchen to stuff a chicken for dinner, he could feel this creature's hungry eyes looking out as well. At these times, it was more than watching. Charlie could feel it almost salivating with desire, wanting to have such a tasty morsel for itself.

He had half-talked about it with Alan, warning him about the dangerous crocodile spirit in the billabong. Charlie had also half-talked about it with Elsie. He found it hard to properly describe what he felt happening without seeming a bit mad. He did not think he was truly mad as the rest of him seemed as sane as ever, despite this thing being there inside his mind.

It seemed, to Charlie, like something got inside his head on that day when he had pulled up the man's head, in the tug of war he had with the crocodile spirit. Back then, when he fought with it, as it was trying to pull the head back into the water, Charlie thought he'd won. Charlie had believed that, once this horrible object was fully in his possession, the spirit had returned to the water.

Now, he was not so sure. It seemed like a part of this crocodile spirit had embedded itself into his mind and was now always hiding in there, somewhere out of sight- but never completely gone.

When Charlie's mind would relax, such as when he smoked or day-dreamed, the spirit would start to creep out. At night, Charlie felt the spirit come out much further. It was when his mind gave it free space to roam, as the rest of his mind shut itself down to rest. Then, he sensed it moving around inside his head, creating strange images and sensations.

At times, Charlie dreamt he was a crocodile. In these dreams, he knew the feeling of power when he seized his prey, felt it struggle to exhaustion and pulled it underwater to devour it. Each time his waking brain reasserted itself, this creature would slide away and disappear below the surface of his awareness again. In this way, it acted like its real reptile cousins: silently slipping back into a hidden position, where it waited, its existence known but unseen, until another opportune time came when it emerged again.

Charlie felt his mind could control it, for the most part, but was still unable to remove it. Sometimes, he wondered if this sense of control was just an illusion. The crocodile spirit could be just waiting, in a deep ambush, until the right time came to attack again. Charlie felt it was growing in power, too, by feeding on part of his spirit to draw more strength into itself. Each week which passed, he sensed a little more of it in his mind. It felt similar to the way a living creature grew as it fed.

Its' message seemed to be, "You have taken something which belongs to me. In return, I have taken a part of you."

The message gave Charlie a strange compulsion. It was to return to the place the man's head was found and talk to the ancient creature that had struggled with Charlie for possession of the man's head. He wondered what relationship existed between this thing, living inside his head, and the ancient crocodile spirit living in the billabong. Were they one and the same? Was the part within him part of the greater whole? Or was it the two spirits were like cousins? Or perhaps a whole tribe of spirit creatures lived in that billabong together, and each sought out human and animal souls to claim for themselves?

Charlie could not let himself give in to the compulsion to return to the billabong. He knew, if he went back there, he may be powerless to stop the ancient spirit from pulling him into the water and seizing his body in return for what he had taken from it. At times Charlie thought, if he went there with something to placate it, perhaps the carcass of a big pig, it may be enough to get the spirit leave him alone. But he was unsure if this trade would be accepted.

One night, as they were sitting down to a roast dinner, Charlie found himself staring at Elsie with eyes which did not feel like they were his own. These were hungry eyes and not only hungered for the meat but had a strange hunger for Elsie. This hunger was not like his usual desire for the woman he loved, but predatory.

Elsie looked at him, part-way through the meal, saying, "Why? Why do you keep looking at me with those hungry crocodile eyes?"

Charlie tried to explain it her in the best way he could, but all his words to describe it failed him.

During the night, Elise woke him up twice from crocodile dreams in which he and a huge crocodile were swimming together through the water, side by side, hunting for food. Each time Elsie woke Charlie by touching him, the crocodile located inside his mind slid away, leaving him alone. But, as soon as the sleep returned, it would slither back into the free space of his mind.

The next morning, Charlie woke up late to find Elsie had already packed up the car and had his steaming breakfast of bacon and eggs waiting to be eaten.

She announced, "Today, we go to my country- the stone country. We have an old medicine man who can talk to the spirits. I will ask him to tell this crocodile spirit to stop bothering you- to go away back to its own place and leave you in peace."

Charlie and Elsie drove east into the morning sun. They first crossed the Adelaide River and then the Mary River. Each time they passed over a large river, Charlie could hear, as if from far away, crocodiles in the river which passed below him, calling out to his own hidden crocodile. He could feel it was calling back to them each time, too. At the Mary River, this calling was much stronger than before- as if these were his true crocodile spirit's brothers and sisters. As Charlie and Elsie passed the road turning off to the billabong where Charlie had found the head, he had to force his arms to resist a compulsion to turn the car towards it. The spirit inside him was calling loudly for him to take it home to the billabong from whence it came.

Charlie felt his arms beginning to shake with tension as he kept driving east along the main highway. As they continued crossing additional rivers- the Wildman, West Alligator and, last, the mighty South Alligator with its huge brown tide flowing below them- the voices were still there but their power was weaker.

Charlie and Elsie continued to follow the main road, the Arnhem Highway, almost all the way to Jabiru. At an intersection before Jabiru, Elsie indicated to turn south. This change in direction meant they were now heading to Pine Creek. As they drove along, Charlie watched the silent ramparts of the stone country rise into view. The outlined cliffs and rocks, lifting into view before them, were softened by the heat haze of late morning light. The browns, yellows and oranges became subdued by the glare of the midday sun. Elsie sat watching beside him, smiling in delight as her own special country came into view.

Soon after crossing Nourlangie Creek, Elsie indicated to Charlie to pull over, saying, "From here I drive. My turn to bring you back to my own tribal country. It will please the Dreamtime Spirits for me to bring us back to show respect. I must talk to my ancestor spirits, those of the wallabies that live up in the big rocks, Nabarlek Dreaming Spirits."

Charlie nodded. He knew this was her sacred land in which her ancestor spirits still held power. He did not wish to offend them.

They followed a rough winding track for another half hour. It led them away from the main road, moving ever closer to the towering ramparts of the hills, looming above them. At a small spring within the trees, they came to an almost hidden bush camp.

Children rushed out to greet them, black bodies glistening in the midday sun. A crowd of people, young and old, gathered around them, all laughing and talking in their own language.

Charlie only partly understood what they were saying, as Elsie chattered freely. In the cooking fires, Charlie saw turtles, yams and a large flat damper. The damper's surface was encrusted with ash.

Clan members and the two visitors sat in a circle, passing around succulent portions of steaming turtle, yam and chunks of white floury damper, along with cups of sweet tea.

When the eating was finished, the clan shared with their visitors' many new stories of their families and of events which had taken place across all the tribes from near and far. In these stories, the people used kinship terms to place people into their separate clans. Then, they all stretched out under shady trees on the sand. They lay dreaming in the midday heat, as the sun slid slowly westward towards a smoky horizon.

Now, the hills above and beside them were glowing in iridescent light causing the colours to come alive. A chattering and thumping sound came to them from a nearby hill.

Elsie stood and stretched, indicating with her head for Charlie to walk behind her. As Charlie stood up, Elsie explained, "It's my ancestor, Nabarlek, calling out. Time we go and see our medicine man. He lives in the place where the Nabarlek drink."

Elsie led him along a sandy, scuffed path towards the high cliffs. He followed her as if they walked along. After a several minutes of walking, they came to the start of the hills. A ridge ran alongside but below the big cliffs above. Small wallabies, showing patches of red and dark fur, bounded away from them. Charlie knew these were the Nabarlek of Elsie's totem.

Charlie followed Elsie as she climbed the path up the ridge, looking back to a commanding view of the woodlands and floodplains which extended far to the west. Elsie pointed out the main features of her tribal land: Jim Jim Creek and where it met the South Alligator River in the place she called Woolwonga, it was the home of big crocodiles and buffalo. It was a place where she had camped as a girl, when her father worked for the buffalo shooters. He would skin big buffalo bulls they shot out on the plains while Elsie and her mother went gathering water lily bulbs, yams and turtles or caught catfish for their dinner. "Was a good time before they took me away," she said, lost in nostalgia.

At last they came to the base of a massive cliff which towered hundreds of feet above them. Its myriad colours were bright in the western sun as they stood in the shade far below. At its base was a crack in the cliff, in which there was a small clump of green trees which included fig trees and other trees with big leaves. As they came closer, they saw a pool of water below the cliff, with a white-haired man and woman sitting in the sand beside it. The man was painting patterns in red and brown ochre on a sheet of bark while the woman worked at weaving a yellow and orange string basket.

Elsie called out in their language and they looked up with their faces smiling in welcome.

Elsie explained to Charlie, "They are my tribal grandmother and grandfather. They are the medicine people of our tribe- those who can talk to the spirits." She led Charlie over to them and they sat in the sand opposite the elderly couple. Elsie spoke rapidly, in her own language, to them for a few minutes.

They nodded back, speaking only occasional words and questions, as the story was told to them. Then, the old man and woman stood up to stand beside Charlie. They each took a hand of his in theirs and placed their other hands on the top of his head.

As the medicine people did this, Charlie heard them searching for and then questioning the spirit which was within him. At first, it tried to stay hidden from them. Charlie heard them tell it clearly, that they could see it despite it trying to hide from them. It slowly slid out into full view. Soon, the questions to the spirit ceased and they turned to Elsie again and resumed speaking directly to her.

When they finished speaking, Elsie translated everything back to Charlie. "They say they have spoken to the crocodile spirit inside your head. He is not that big old spirit, the one of the ancestor crocodile dreaming, but another crocodile spirit- a young, cheeky one. One day, he came to the billabong of the big crocodile. The big crocodile caught him and ate him up. He was inside the big crocodile, along with many other spirits of the creatures the big one had eaten. He did not like it in there. He was always having to fight with other spirits for a place at the table. And, over time, the big crocodile kept capturing more and more spirits. They were all trapped in there. The big crocodile spirit watched them closely to make sure they did not escape when he ate.

"One day, when the big crocodile spirit was fighting with you to keep the man's head, because it was a big fight, he could no longer guard all the spirits inside him. So, it slid out and then, knowing it needed a new body- went inside you instead. He slipped inside you without you knowing because your own dreaming spirit, the catfish spirit, was busy fighting with the big crocodile sprit over the man's head. So, it's like it tricked its way in and now it doesn't want to leave. Our medicine man says we must try to trick it out and into another body- a real crocodile body- again. As this spirit inside you is not old and clever, they think they can trick it.

"Tomorrow, in the early morning when the fish and crocodiles are feeding, we will go to a billabong beside the big river. There we will find a new crocodile to take away the spirit from inside you."

As the sun was setting, they returned to the camp together. Over a dinner of roast kangaroo, a big one which had more than enough meat for the whole clan, the medicine man explained his plan to everyone. He needed the two best hunters of the tribe to help him with his plan. One was to catch a magpie goose and one to catch a crocodile in the first light of the early morning. He said this is the time when spirits can no longer roam freely using the darkness but must find a safe place to hide from the coming day.

Once the clan reached an agreement on who the hunters would be, they returned to their feast. Charlie watched bodies moving in the flickering firelight, dancing in a circle while tapping sticks. Soon he fell asleep on the sand and was covered by a blanket.

Elsie woke him when the stars were still shining brightly in the night sky. He could hear bird calls announcing that the coming of daylight was not far away. Four shadowed bodies stood in a semi-circle nearby. Soon all of them were driving towards the big billabong. They arrived as the first streams of light were touching the eastern sky and a noisy chorus of frogs were mixing calls with the faint honking of geese in the reed beds along the side. The billabong water was dark and still except for swirls created as hungry fish fed.

The medicine man sent a hunter to the reed beds, where the geese were still roosting, with instructions to catch a live goose and bring it back. The designated hunter walked off quietly, carrying a loop of string attached to a long pole. They watched as he came close to the reeds. He crouched down before sliding on his belly into them- soon vanishing from their sight. After a short time a chorus of honking and flapping wings erupted from the reed beds. The man returned, proudly holding a goose with its neck in a string noose. He trussed its wings and legs to prevent any possible escape.

They turned their attention to the dark water, squatting, watching intently. The second hunter signalled silently. He had seen his quarry surface a few meters out. Just two nostrils and eyes were visible. The first hunter carried the goose to the water's edge. It honked plaintively. The eyes and nostrils in the water drifted closer as it sensed the food. Charlie sensed his own crocodile spirit within him was sliding out to watch this with hungry eyes. It desired the goose as its meal instead.

Charlie watched the hunter raise a spear as the eyes drifted ever closer to the shore. Now, the eyes were barely a few feet away. A blur of movement was seen by Charlie as the spear shot forward, burying a harpoon head into the scales located a foot behind the eyes. The water became a thrashing and splashing place.

The two hunters held tight to a cord line which was attached to the spear lodged into this twisting and rolling creature. They slowly hauled it to the shore and dragged it from the water, its wet scales gleaming in the first light. They held fast to the spear to keep it in place. It was only about a big man's length, but its jaws were waving and snapping. One man kept holding onto the spear while the other man walked quietly behind it. He suddenly jumped forward to sit, legs astride, on the body of the crocodile- well away from the biting teeth.

The medicine man came close to the head while holding a big branch which was as thick as an arm. He waved this branch at the snapping head in order to bait it- encouraging it to bite. Each time it would attempt to grab the branch the medicine man would draw the branch away just as the teeth snapped shut. At last, just as the mouth opened extra wide for the next bite, he jammed the wood into its gaping maw. Now, the man sitting astride the body leapt forward even further to push his weight onto the head and force the jaws closed. The other hunter let go of the spear and added his weight to the man sitting astride the crocodile's head, too. This pinioned the jaws of the crocodile clamped on the stick. The medicine man took the cord from the end of the spear. He wrapped it around the jaws, which were still biting into the wood, to keep them closed.

The medicine man then slid his arm into the gullet of the crocodile, through the space between its teeth where its mouth was held open by the wooden gag. In a few seconds, he pulled out a dark shiny object which appeared to be a flat stone the size of a small fist. He brought this over to Charlie and told him to hold it. He told Charlie it contained a part of the spirit of this new crocodile. Next, he was told to bite on the goose as if he were going to eat it raw.

As Charlie bit down, he could sense he was now one with the spirit of the speared crocodile. In this unity, together they started consuming the goose. He could feel the hunger and jealousy of the

264

crocodile within him. It desired the same goose and did not want to let the crocodile of the stone take away this prize. This spirit creature within him rushed from his mouth and into the body of the goose, seeking to possess the goose for itself.

The medicine man knew the exact moment the spirit left Charlie. He immediately broke the neck of the goose and pulled it away from Charlie. The crocodile spirit which had been living in Charlie was now trapped inside the goose. Charlie sensed, in that last second, as the goose died, that this creature knew it had been tricked. It desperately tried to return to Charlie's mind. But the stronger spirit of the crocodile stone in his hand gave him the power to repel it.

The medicine man carried the dead goose to where the crocodile was still held on the ground by the hunter. He placed the goose body within the open jaws and pushed its head inside the crocodile's gullet. Then, he removed the harpoon from its shoulder, unwound the cord from its jaw and flicked the piece of wood aside. The jaws snapped shut, causing the crocodile to drive its teeth into the goose.

In unison, the hunters stood up and released their hold on the crocodile. As the crocodile became aware of its new-found freedom, it shook its head from side to the side and chomped its jaws, so as to gauge the new item in its mouth. Realising it was food, it opened its jaws wide taking the goose fully within its mouth and then swallowed it down. The crocodile looked at them with a baleful eye before it walked back to the water's edge and slid away. Elsie, the medicine man and the hunters were all grinning. Charlie was grinning the most.

The trick had worked! The alien spirit was gone from his body. He was back to being just Charlie- the man of the catfish dreaming and a catfish fisherman again. In his hand, Charlie felt the smooth dark stone. It was a thing imbued with the spirit of another crocodile and its power. The crocodile which once owned it would continue to live on with a second spirit inside it now- the spirit which had tried to live in Charlie.

In its place, Charlie knew a part of the spirit from the crocodile they had just captured would stay in the stone from now on. When he held this stone, he felt it connected him to the spirits of the other crocodiles without them being able to harm him. The stone served as a conduit between his spirit and the crocodiles' spirits without causing danger to him. He felt completely safe for now.

Charlie put the stone in his pocket. He decided he would keep it to help guard him against any future potential spirit possessions. He did not know why, but he had an overwhelming feeling telling him that this battle with this dreamtime creature was not yet finished. Before Charlie left this place, he would catch a big catfish as a fitting present from his spirit to the spirits of this crocodile clan who had helped him.

Chapter 25 – Susan Alone

Susan felt like she had been kept in a cage by herself for months. It seemed a lifetime ago since she had walked down a street on her own. Truly, it had only been about a month? But it was getting harder and harder for her to remember.

At first, when they'd put her in this cage, Susan had been so angry. The detectives had tried to trick a confession out of her. Gradually, a 'lost' feeling had come over her. Her life slowly descended into gloom; endless days spent staring at cell walls with no other people to talk to. There were no more happy days with friends and no more loving nights with men- except in her dreams.

Another problem was the dreams were turning bad now. There were still occasional tender moments with Mark involving loving embraces. But, despite Mark continuing to appear in her dreams, he was getting harder and harder to see clearly. At times he would appear with a snout, scales on his body, long pointed teeth and slit-like yellow crocodile eyes.

Whenever Susan woke up for a new day, she would be faced with hours and hours of nothing. She found herself unable to read because she would keep losing her place in the novels and be unable to make much sense of the words she was reading. She mostly just sat and stared at the walls now. She also found people's visits hard to bear. They reminded her of another life out there. A life which she could no longer experience. The visits were also difficult because people kept asking her to tell the truth.

What confused Susan was: they all knew the truth. The evidence did not lie. She had been traveling with Mark, she had killed him and then tried to hide what she had done. They were the ones who refused to accept what was right there in front of their eyes. They wanted her to be "Saint Susan." However, she was not a saint. She was someone who'd done a terrible thing. She must now pay for her crime. Why was it so hard for everyone to understand?

There had been only one day of sunshine since Susan had been told she would be extradited to Australia for her trial. Just one day in which the shadows had gone away for a while, the day on the aeroplane when she had been flying towards her new fate. It was a day of sunshine due to the kindness of her policeman escort, Alan, combined with a double connection to him through his girlfriend. The shared memories she had with Sandy also helped build the connection Susan felt with Alan.

Her words had come tumbling out. It was such a relief after the long self-imposed silence she had been keeping. Alan had talked a little, but she had talked much more. There was also a physical pleasure being in the company of an attractive man who touched her body and found her attractive, too. She had felt real again- if only for just one day.

What Susan most wanted was to feel a man's strong arms around her, again. She wanted to feel a real man loving her in the night, their bodies joined together- like the way she remembered feeling with all her lovers. Without doubt, Susan knew this act of making love to a man would push the darkness away. Even if the darkness was only held away for an hour, she would still accept it gratefully. Instead of this fantasy coming true, her life was filled with endless hours of darkness. In her mind she knew that even one hour of escape would be wonderful.

Susan particularly remembered Alan's male arousal when she put his hand on her lower belly. Then, after she knew he could sense the life in her, she had moved his hand down even lower. She had felt his touch so clearly and they both knew what was being done. She had pressed down over his fingers with her other hand while trying to bring her body up to meet his fingers. He had moved his fingers over the area to stroke and caress her there. His fingers touched her there with such exquisite sensitivity. Part of her had wanted to cover them both with a blanket to give them more privacy. Then, he could have lifted her skirt up and touched her more. In this imagined privacy, what would have followed would have been inevitable.

Eventually, even though it had only lasted a minute in actuality, Susan had taken his hand and moved it back up again. She had then explained to him how they could not be lovers since they were bound to others. Neither of them truly believed it, but it was a convenient fiction to help them stay separate from one another.

It was not because Alan would choose her over Sandy or, in turn, Susan would pick Alan over Mark or David. The reason she sought this touch was because she greatly needed physical intimacy and affection in her place of emptiness. For a short time after, she had felt comforted by the remembrance of experiencing this man's touch. For the rest of the plane trip, Susan had cuddled into him in the same way one would cuddle a lover after sharing such pleasure together. For the remainder of the plane trip, she had a beautiful sleep in a place where no horrors dwelt.

Then, Susan's short period of peace had ended when the flight was over. They led her away to her jail cell while Alan went home to his real lover. She felt a sharp pang of jealousy for what she knew they would be sharing now. Sometimes, now, Susan would touch herself to bring the memory back of his touch. This action would momentarily give her something real, within her caged life- but, as more days passed, even this memory was slowly fading.

Since the plane ride ended, darkness had fully enfolded her. All her days were dark, nights were even more dark than the days. She could not remember how many days passed at this point. Dreams of Mark had become infrequent now and mostly contained other reptilian monsters who entered her body and shared in the dreams.

When her friends and family came to visit her now, she could barely hear them speak. It was like she was hearing them speak while living underwater. Each time, without fail, they asked her to explain about that distant day and tell the truth about what exactly happened. What Susan's friends and family refused to understand was: there was nothing to explain. What remained within Susan was only a loud silence which sought to muffle the screams in her soul. Her family and friends barely came to see her anymore now. Susan thought, *Perhaps the underwater talking is hard for them, too.*

The only thing Susan knew with absolute certainty was that she wanted it all to be over. She did not know exactly what over was, precisely, but there must be a different place to this. She tried to imagine an outside place, a place where she could walk in sunshine while talking to animals and, maybe, people. Perhaps someone would give her a puppy to play with. Such a thing would be nice. Then, Susan could skip and dance again like a little girl.

One day, Susan did not know which one exactly, she realised the warden was trying to talk to her, in order to tell her something. Finally, some of the underwater sounds reached her brain. It was the words, "You have a visitor."

Susan asked, "What day is it?"

The warden answered, "It's two days before Christmas."

The visitor was a man who had dark skin- sort of a yellow brown. He was old and not very tall. He had grey hair and wrinkled skin on his forehead. He told Susan his name was Charlie.

Charlie walked with her to a visitor's room. The warden left them alone. Charlie sat directly opposite her. Susan looked at him intently. She had an unexplained feeling that, for some reason, she should know him. Finally, a realisation came of where she knew him from- he was a cousin to the "Chink" who was remembered in Mark's diary as being the person who had cooked the pig at Seven Emus. She did not know how she knew the two men were cousins, but he did seem to look like him, at least a little bit.

It was the only thought which seemed clear in her muddled brain. At least the clarity in her mind about this connection was a good thing. Susan had liked the man who had roasted the pig and still remembered the delicious taste of his food. Perhaps the two of them could make pork dumplings together while they were here in this room. They could use the stove which she could see in the corner. When Charlie had walked into the room, she had seen a bare wall where the stove was now located. He must have carried it in with him- even if she could not remember him doing so.

Charlie was trying to get her to look at him. Susan realised he was pointing to her and talking. She tried to hear what he was saying, but it sounded garbled. Charlie gestured he wanted her to hold out her hand, lay it palm up on the table. Susan complied with his request. He took her hand in his.

Suddenly, the fog cleared from her brain. She could see and hear clearly for the first time in days. Involuntarily, Susan went to pull back her hand, feeling suddenly confused by all the brightness and noise surrounding her. Charlie held onto her hand firmly.

Susan looked down at the table. Both his hands were laid on the table side-by-side. One of his hands was firmly wrapped around her own hand while the other one was holding something flat and round. She looked at the object he held in puzzlement. Next, Charlie took the hand he was holding of hers and turned it palm upward. He placed the round object into her hand. It felt as cool and smooth as a flat river stone. As her fingers closed around it, he let her hand go.

Charlie sat completely still and looked at her with an appraising expression. Her mind remained clear despite the fact Charlie was no longer touching her. She could feel something passing from her and going into the stone. It felt to Susan like the stone was drawing the darkness out of her mind. She asked him, "What is this?"

He answered, immediately, "It is a crocodile spirit stone. It is very powerful medicine."

Charlie could see she did not understand this statement. He tried to explain further. Susan nodded along, even though she could not really understand what he was saying. At the same time, it did seem to make a strange sort of sense.

Charlie continued explaining, "Last week, a man and lady (a bit old, but not so old as me) they come to see me. They say they your mother and father. They say they very worried because you sit in this room, say nothing, talk to no one, like you cannot hear. They say that Sergeant Richard, that policemen from billabong, tell them, maybe they should come and talk to me. They is trying to understand this bad thing.

"I know you, you the one they say kill the man in the billabong- out longa Mary River. I find that head, man who belong to crocodile. Find it when I was fishing for catfish. I see the bad spirit try to take him back. He fight with me, when I find that head, he try to pull it back, I already caught two big catfish for Elsie to make fish curry. Then, I try to catch one more fish, but instead I catch a head. When I catch the head, that crocodile spirit pull back, try to take it away from me.

"But that man, him belong to the head, him not want to go back with crocodile spirit. He want to come and see you. He want you to touch him, even if dead. But that bad crocodile spirit, him really want to keep head, too. I'm in middle of tug-of-war. First I pull the head one way, then crocodile spirit pull the other way. But finally- I win. Now crocodile spirit very angry and very sad.

"I think, maybe, if crocodile spirit can't have man, it try have you instead. Man love you, you love man but you kill him because you frightened. Now man comes in dreams, and you love man, but crocodile spirit it comes too. Gets inside your head, makes it a dark very bad place. Rest of the world goes dark. You cannot hear, you cannot see or think proper.

"When your mother and father tell me this, I say I will try help.

I have been to see medicine man and now I have this crocodile stone. It helped me, too. It take away bad crocodile spirit from me.

"In my country, we hunt and kill crocodile, we eat the meat of crocodile. Sometimes, we find stone inside crocodile belly and we call it crocodile spirit stone. When crocodile eat fish or kangaroo, everything goes away, all taken and used up by crocodile. The spirit of other animals goes into crocodile and makes it stronger. But this stone is left behind. Crocodile cannot take it- is even stronger spirit than your crocodile. It holds the spirit of many creatures, some crocodile, some fish, some of lots of things. All leaves a part of their spirit within it.

"When you hold it, it stop other bad crocodile spirit coming from outside. Where stone is- other bad crocodile spirit not come.

"We call it a crocodile spirit stone. Is very valuable stone- very hard to get. But medicine man help.. He put hand inside crocodile belly and take it out. He give stone to me to keep me safe from bad crocodile. In return for stone, Elsie make him special catfish curry.

"Now- you must keep stone, keep stone in hand or pocket at all times, have stone next to you when you sleep. While stone is close, bad crocodile spirit cannot come inside you. In one week, maybe in two weeks- crocodile spirit get tired and go away.

"Now I go away, but come visit you next week or some other time again. I bring Elsie's curry. It help make you strong, too."

Susan kept the stone touching her skin all night. It was the first night in months in which her dreams were clear. The next morning, she woke able to think clearly for the first time in months. She even knew what day it was and where she currently was. It did nothing to take her troubles away or even make her happy- but at least she could see and hear the world clearly again.

Around lunchtime, she heard the sound of visitors arriving. It didn't sound like one or two visitors but several. It was her mother and father, Tim, Anne and David. They set up a little Christmas tree on a table complete with presents around it. A Christmas cake and various treats finished the full ensemble. For two hours they sat around the Christmas tree table, laughing, talking and listening to Christmas carols. They said they could not visit tomorrow, on the actual Christmas Day, but this was the next best thing.

Susan felt grateful for another ray of sunshine in her current bleakness. As soon as they were gone, though, she was sad again. She settled into the late afternoon with renewed determination. Time to read a book and escape from here, since her mind was clear today. *Maybe,* she thought, *she could even read again tomorrow so she did not feel so lonely.*

Suddenly there was a banging sound on the door. It was past visiting time so it could not be another visitor for her. She heard a man's loud voice having a serious discussion, but he did not sound angry to Susan. Then the warden came to her cell.

"You have another visitor. I know it's past time for visits, but he is persuasive. I've told him he can see you for half an hour."

Chapter 26 – Knowing the Truth?

Susan wondered who else could have possibly come to see her today. She was also curious how he was able to talk his way into see her when visiting hours had been over for a while. *Hopefully,* she thought to herself, *it's not the police coming to present her with a new revelation in the case or, God forbid, another delaying tactic!* Susan sat down in a chair facing the table and waited. She felt very anxious.

Susan could hear a man's voice saying, "Please, I need you to leave us alone and undisturbed for ten minutes. I promise I won't try to hurt her or to smuggle something in to her. You can search me if you like."

Susan heard some more muttering voices before the door finally opened. In front of her stood a mid-sized, wiry man. He had dark hair and features. Susan sensed she should know who he was-but having been out of practice with general thinking, her mind seemed to be moving very slowly. The man walked towards her in an emotionless, business-like manner.

He said, "Hello, Susan. Do you remember me?"

Finally, recognition dawned. It was Vic! If her memory was right, his full name was Vickram. He was the helicopter pilot from the day she spent with Mark in the Gulf. It seemed a century ago.

Susan remembered his past mischievous, twinkling eyes, along with a trademark grin set in a smiling face. There was no sign of these traits now. His face had a hard, angry set to it.

Susan remembered Vic had been her friend. She had first met him because he was Mark's friend. All of them had spent a wonderful day together. Susan could not remember him without feeling deep-seated pleasure and affection.

A spontaneous and involuntary smile came to her face as she said, "Vic, it's hard to believe you are here. It all seems so long ago now. Can it really be you?"

Susan instantly stopped her babbling when she noticed his facial expression had not shifted. She tried to change her mannerisms and tone to be more business-like, too. "Thank you for coming to see me. Can I help you in some way?"

Susan could visibly see Vic calming himself. He was most definitely angry. He replied, through gritted teeth, "Last Sunday, the police came to see me. A Sergeant Richards to be exact. I had not heard the news for several months at the time. Honestly, I had not heard it at all since the last time I saw you. Sergeant Richards told me that, at the end of September, the body of my best friend, Mark, had been found in a billabong. The policeman said he had been murdered and the murderer was you."

Susan could hear Vic speaking words which sounded completely unreal- almost like a news report about someone else. Susan found it hard to believe he was talking about her as a killer. She thought emphatically, *It has to be someone else*!

Vic continued on, "At first, I couldn't believe it- that you'd done it. So, he took me through all the evidence. In the end, I agreed. It seemed crystal clear. But it didn't make sense. So, I've come to see you to ask you to your face: Did you murder my friend, Mark? And if so, why?"

Susan felt utterly shocked when she heard him say those words. There was no courtroom courtesy or police politeness in the way he asked the question. He spat it out in barely suppressed anger. He was angry with her- very angry. She could not quite understand the reason for his anger. She muttered something to herself. She did not seem to know how to reply to his questions. She turned her head to the side to seek additional time to think.

In a flash, Vic had come round the table and pulled her from her chair, hauling her to her feet to face him. Their faces were only inches away from each other. He asked her again. This time he spoke slowly and clearly, enunciating each syllable, "Did you kill my friend, Mark?"

Susan tried to look away from the ferocious eyes boring into hers. His hand flashed towards her face. He hit her cheek with an open-handed slap. She turned her face away from the blow. He slapped the other side of her face with his opposite hand.

This violence from Vic broke down the wall of silent denial she had built within her mind. She could no longer avoid his eyes. They bored into her with a determination to know the truth. Part of her felt like crying. Another part of her felt an exultant joy knowing this man cared and grieved for his friend- her Mark.

She faced him squarely and looked back into his eyes. "Yes," she said, clearly, "Yes- I killed Mark. That's what everyone says. It's true. I stabbed him with a knife. Then, I hit his head with a piece of wood. As he lay on the ground, not moving, I dragged his body to the water so the crocodiles could take him and finish him off."

Vic looked stunned. Susan thought, *he must have expected more silence or denials from me- not this*. He turned his face away from her. She saw his shoulders were shaking and realised he was crying.

A minute passed before he looked at her, composed once again. "Why? Did you really have to kill him? I thought you loved him. I know he loved you. Whatever happened? Surely, you could've worked it out if you had a fight? Why did you kill him?"

Susan realised she could not run away from answering him. For others, they asked her simply because it was a legal formality. They did not know the man she had killed. They did not really care. This man compelled her to answer. Vic knew Mark and truly cared about the fact he was dead. Susan must tell him the truth- at least as far as she could without adding another betrayal to Mark.

Susan responded, "I killed him because I was frightened. I thought he was going to kill me. I know now I was wrong. And I must live with that terrible thing I did for the rest of my life."

With her answer, it seemed like the anger and fight went from Vic. He looked completely deflated. He sat now with his body slumped into his chair. Susan sat down again to face him from across the table. She waited silently. It was his turn to speak.

Vic sat silently for a minute while looking completely uncertain. Then, he said quietly, "Please tell me why you were frightened of him. What did he do?"

Susan shook her head while answering, "Please believe me- I would tell you if I could. But I cannot. I must face the consequences of what I did. When this is over, I expect I'll be in jail for a very long time for my actions and that's entirely fair. Until I saw you today, I was going to remain silent in the trial. I wasn't going to enter a plea of any kind. But, that would be wrong. It would keep the truth from people, like you, those who knew Mark and care about why he is no longer in this world. I see it clearly now: I will plead guilty. I'll say, 'Yes I killed him,' as I said to you. The court must determine my punishment for murder. Reasons behind the act aren't relevant and I will not be saying them."

Vic said, "I'm sorry I hit you, but I needed to know."

Susan replied, "I'm glad that you did. It showed me how much you cared about Mark. Until today, I had not met anyone who cared about what happened to Mark. So, I don't want you to apologize for the slap. It told me a really important thing: Mark mattered to someone else, like he still does to me."

Vic looked at her, perplexed, and asked "But what about you? Don't you care what will happen to you if you protect a secret?"

Susan responded, "Some secrets are worth protecting. One must be willing to pay the price that kind of loyalty requires. I don't look forward to a life in prison. But, if that's my only choice, in order to keep a secret, then I'll do it- as best I can."

There was something unnaturally calm in Susan's demeanour. Vic knew it was a sign of trouble to come. She pretended to be strong, but was not strong enough for this. He said, "That is too much, even for one as loyal as you. There must be a way out of this choice, some alternative we can find."

She retorted, "There's one thing I must tell you. I'm carrying his child. In part, my choice is to protect our child and its legacy. I think it's enough for this child to bear having a killer for a mother-any more would be too big a load for any child to bear."

Vic replied, "There's something I must also tell you. On that day I met you, before the helicopter trip, Mark asked me to witness his will which named you as his beneficiary. I don't know what's become of it. Mark also told me, in the event of his death, that he was relying on me to protect you, in the way a brother would do. I promised I would try. So, it seems I have two obligations to fulfil. I'm not doing very well in meeting either one right now.

"In addition, there's one more thing I want to ask you and it's only a request. In the years when Mark and I worked together, he'd often go off by himself early in the morning to write in his diary. At times I would ask him what he wrote and why. He would say, 'It's both to release my demons and tell of my joy. The paper on which I write is a window into which my soul speaks. It tells of all, both the good and bad.'

"One time, he read me a story he wrote in it about my helicopter written from the view of a bird flying outside it. It was very funny. The bird told of my strange looks, antics and how clumsy I was compared to its skill in the air. I asked him if I could read it for myself.

Mark said, 'No, it's private- for my eyes only while I live. But, if anything happens to me, it will be yours to read. Then, you'll know of the real me. You will know the good and the bad- particularly the bad. After that, you may tell the world my story if you chose to do so- even the bad parts.'

"I've never seen Mark's bad side. I know only of his friendship. But I wish to hold him to that promise: to know who he was and what has been lost to this world. As you were the last person to see him, I ask if you know what became of his diary. It was kept in his briefcase which was stored behind his seat. When the car was found, everything was gone. I ask you, on account of his promise to me, can you tell me what became of this book? That which told the story of his life- his diary?"

Susan sat quiet and still for a long time. It was as if she had not heard what he had said. Mark had entrusted the diary to her, but he had also promised it to Vic. The promise to Vic had been made long before the promise to her. Did Mark's promise to her, invalidate this same promise to Vic?

It was Mark's ultimate sign of trust to allow another to see his inner-most soul- including all its secrets. He had given to them both an unconditional right to do so. In giving it to her, he had not taken it away from his friend. Therefore, she must honour this promise to Vic.

Knowing some of what Vic would read made her mind tremble at the consequences. Despite this, trust was trust and promises must be respected. Even her unborn child could not stand in front of this.

Without a word, Susan sat down and took off her left shoe. It was a plain black sandal with a leather instep. With her fingernails, she pried its leather edge loose in the centre. Underneath this exact spot lay a small plastic square. She removed this plastic-coated object which was a memory card wrapped in sticky tape. It was barely a centimetre by a centimetre and a millimetre thick.

Susan placed this tiny object into Vic's hand. "He entrusted this to me for me to give to you. It's yours to use as you see fit. The memory of the man it holds is very precious to me, so I ask you use it with great care."

Vic closed his fingers over it and nodded, stating "I will- that's my promise to you."

After Vic had gone, she sat quietly holding the stone in her hand. This stone was from the belly of a crocodile and imbued with the presence of so many things. It was just a plain, black stone which was flattened and rounded. It was not unlike many she had skipped on ponds as a child except it was larger and heavier.

It was a good thing it let her think clearly. It allowed her to clearly remember Vic and his serious, solemn eyes as he gave her his promise: to treat Mark's story with care. Those eyes gave her a sliver of hope. Maybe there was a way out of this place for her.

However, the presence of the stone did more for her. She let her mind sink into its depths. At its centre, under all the other layers of existence, sat an incredibly ancient being. In part, this being was the monster of her dreams. At the same time, it was so much more. It held part of the core of every crocodile which had every walked or swum across this land: the Dreamtime ancestor spirit of all. It had the power to both protect her and harm her. The scary part was she did not know which it would ultimately be.

In this instant, Susan came to a realisation: while she had lost something when she killed Mark, she had also gained something. Part of her was now intricately joined to this spirit creature of an ancient dreaming. It was part of her soul and, in turn, she was part of its. She wondered if this joining could ever be undone. Would it consume her and incorporate her spirit within its own- as it had done to her lover?

Part of her knew a desire for freedom. Another part ached to be forever in its thrall- alongside and joined to the man she loved.

GRAHAM WILSON

About the Author

Graham Wilson lives in Sydney Australia. He's written 13 books which include 12 novels and a family memoir as follows:

 1. The Old Balmain House Series – 3 novels
 2. Crocodile Dreaming Series – 5 novels and a 2 book prequel

He has also written two stand-alone novels, *Risk Free* and *Mysteries*.

The *Old Balmain House Series* starts with the novel, *Little Lost Girl*, which was previously titled, *The Old Balmain House*. Its setting is an old weatherboard cottage, in Sydney, where the author lived for seven years. Here a photo was discovered of a small girl who lived and died about 100 years ago. The book imagines the story of her life and family, based in the real Balmain, an early inner Sydney suburb, with its locations and historical events providing part of the story background. The second novel in this series, *Lizzie's Tale*, builds on the Balmain house setting. It is the story of a working class teenage girl who lives in this same house in the 1950s and 1960s. It tells of how, when pregnant, she is determined not to surrender her baby for adoption, and of her struggle to survive in this unforgiving society. The third novel in this series, *Devil's Choice*, follows the next generation of the family in *Lizzie's Tale*. Lizzie's daughter is faced with the awful choice of whether to seek the help of one of her mother's rapists' in trying to save the life of her own daughter who is inflicted with an incurable disease.

The *Crocodile Dreaming Series* is based in Outback Australia. It starts with the first novel, *Visitor,* which tells the story of an English backpacker, Susan, who visits the Northern Territory and becomes captivated and in great danger from a man who loves crocodiles. This second book in the series, *Victim*, follows the consequences of the first book based around the discovery of this man's remains and diary with Susan being placed on trial for murder. The third book, *Void*, is about Susan's struggle to retain her sanity in jail while her family and friends desperately try to find out what really happened on that fateful day before it is too late. In Book 4, *Vanished,* Susan disappears too. It tells the story of the search for her and four other lost women, whose passports were found in the possession of the man she killed. The final book in the series, *Invisible,* is the story of a woman who appears in a remote aboriginal community in North Queensland, without any memory except for a name. It tells how she rebuilds her life from an empty shell and how, as past fragments return, with them come dark shadows that threaten to overwhelm her.

The two books in the Prequel, collectively titled Vengeance, are the story of Mark, the boy becoming a man, at first seeking to walk in the footsteps of his childhood hero, Breaker Morant, but who, over time, becomes a monster and is ultimately destroyed, as the vengeance he seeks turns upon himself.

The books in the Crocodile Dreaming Series were previously published as ebooks in an earlier edition. They have now been extensively revised and edited, with reader input. The improved versions are being released in print format, over the next 2 years.

Risk Free is a tale of corporate greed and corruption in Sydney. *Mysteries* is a story set in Sydney about a mother and child who disappeared without trace 30 years ago and an old house with hidden secrets.

The book *Arnhem's Kaleidoscope Children* is the story of the author's life in the Northern Territory: his childhood in an aboriginal community in remote Arnhem Land, in Australia's Northern Territory, of the people, danger and beauty of this place, and of its transformation over the last half century with the coming of aboriginal rights and the discovery of uranium. It also tells of him surviving an attack by a large crocodile and of his work over two decades in the outback of the NT.

In writing these books Graham has drawn extensively on his experiences growing up in an aboriginal community, with many childhood aboriginal friends, and his identity as part of the aboriginal community of Oenpelli (now Gunbalanya). He proudly acknowledges his aboriginal skin name. His everyday name of Ngaginka (crocodile leg) reflects his own crocodile scar. It is widely used by others in the community as they talk to him.

As an adult working in the NT, he had many close aboriginal friends spread across the NT, from whom aspects of book characters are drawn. While he has not sought specific approval for parts of this story that reference aboriginal customs, particularly having regard to several of these people now being deceased, he is satisfied he has told this story in a way that fits with cultural ideas of those people he knows who have given him these insights.

He is also in the early stages of planning a memoir about his family's connections with Ireland called *Memories Only Remain* and is seeking ideas for books about the early NT cattle industry, its people and history. He is also compiling stories of people who worked for the NSW National Parks and Wildlife Service.

Graham writes for the creative pleasure it brings him. He is particularly gratified each time an unknown person chooses to download and read something he has written and write a review, good or bad, as this gives him an insight into what readers enjoy and helps him make ongoing improvements to his writing.

In his other life Graham is a veterinarian working in wildlife conservation and for rural landholders. He has lived a large part of his life in the Northern Territory. His books reflect this experience and give an authentic background to many stories.

More information about Graham and his books and writing is available from the following sites:

Graham Wilson – Australian Author on Facebook
Graham Wilson's Webpage:
http://grahamwilsonbooks.com

If you want to contact Graham about his writing please use the email grahamwilsonbooks@gmail.com

VICTIM   GRAHAM WILSON

VICTIM   GRAHAM WILSON

www.ingramcontent.com/pod-product-compliance
Lightning Source LLC
Chambersburg PA
CBHW020910130726
47904CB00006BA/1806